An Introduction
to Womanist Biblical Interpretation

An Introduction
to Womanist Biblical Interpretation

NYASHA JUNIOR

WJK WESTMINSTER
JOHN KNOX PRESS
LOUISVILLE · KENTUCKY

© 2015 Nyasha Junior

First edition
Published by Westminster John Knox Press
Louisville, Kentucky

15 16 17 18 19 20 21 22 23 24—10 9 8 7 6 5 4 3 2 1

Book design by Sharon Adams
Cover design by Lisa Buckley Design
Cover art: Afro-Girl (Aqua) © Kim Wilson

Library of Congress Cataloging-in-Publication Data

Junior, Nyasha.
  An introduction to womanist biblical interpretation / Nyasha Junior. -- First edition.
     pages cm
  Includes bibliographical references and index.
  ISBN 978-0-664-25987-7 (alk. paper)
1. Bible--Black interpretations. 2. Womanist theology. 3. Bible--Feminist criticism. I. Title.
  BS521.2.J86 2015
  220.6082--dc23

                                                                    2015014669

Most Westminster John Knox Press books are available at special quantity discounts when purchased in bulk by corporations, organizations, and special-interest groups. For more information, please e-mail SpecialSales@wjkbooks.com.

This book is dedicated to my first teacher,
my mother,
Abbie Gale Junior

Contents

Contents

Preface

In *In Search of Our Mothers' Gardens*, Alice Walker explains, "I write all the things I should have been able to read."[1] I am an African American woman, a Hebrew Bible scholar, and teacher, and I wish that I had been able to read an introduction to womanist biblical interpretation when I was in graduate school. While I drew on womanist discourse for my dissertation in Old Testament at Princeton Theological Seminary, I had never taken a course in feminist or womanist biblical interpretation, and I found few resources on womanist approaches in biblical studies. As a professor, I find that there are still relatively few resources on womanist biblical studies that I can use with my students. I am writing this book for anyone who is interested in womanist biblical interpretation but especially for the graduate student who is scouring the library and searching for some introductory material on this subject. I have kept the footnotes and jargon to a minimum, but I have provided enough breadcrumbs for students and others to pursue their own research related to this topic.[2]

Some of my colleagues have questioned why I chose to write an introductory-level book. I am a teacher first and foremost, and I wanted to write something that would be useful to my students and to others. I was influenced in part by Vincent Wimbush, an African American New Testament scholar. Wimbush is the first person of color to be president of the Society of Biblical Literature (SBL), the major professional association for biblical scholars. In his 2010 presidential address, Wimbush explains that while SBL was founded in 1880, African Americans became active within SBL in noticeable numbers a century later in the 1980s. Wimbush contends that while African Americans and others in the

---

1. Alice Walker, "Saving the Life That Is Your Own: The Importance of Models in the Artist's Life," in *In Search of Our Mothers' Gardens: Womanist Prose* (Orlando, FL: Harcourt, Inc., 1983), 14.
2. If you waited until the last minute to begin your research paper, see the bibliography at Layli Phillips, "A Womanist Bibliography (including Internet Resources)," in *The Womanist Reader* (New York: Routledge, 2006), 405–13.

church and in the public square are interested in the Bible, they will remain uninterested in the work of biblical scholars unless biblical scholars are "talkin' 'bout something.'"[3] Those trained in the field have the tools of their discipline at their disposal, but engagement with biblical texts is not the sole domain of those in the field. It is my hope that this volume is "talkin' 'bout somethin'" that will be useful for those within and outside of the field of biblical studies.

I am grateful for financial support from the Wabash Center for Teaching and Learning Summer Research Fellowship, the Howard University Summer Faculty Research Fellowship, the Howard University Advanced Faculty Research Fellowship, and the Association of Theological Schools/Lilly Faculty Fellowship.

I appreciate the support of my Howard University School of Divinity community and the feedback from the students in my Feminist and Womanist Biblical Interpretation course.

My loyal friends and colleagues are too numerous to mention, but among them, I would like to thank James Logan, Joe Scrivner, G. Brooke Lester, Amy Erickson, Kenneth Ngwa, Deborah Mumford, Africa Hands, Rhon Manigault-Bryant, Lisa M. Allen-McLaurin, Jamal Hopkins, Roger Sneed, Aisha Brooks-Lytle, Teddy Burgh, Dennis Wiley, Cecilia Moore, Marva Gray, Barbara Glenn, Joni Russ, Cheryl Hicks, and Misty Lawson. Bridgett Green gets a double shout-out as a loyal friend and a patient editor. Also, I would like to thank my many Twitter colleagues who kept me company virtually while I wrote this book.

None of my work in biblical studies would have been possible without the foundational lessons taught to me by my extended family and my church family at Greater Bethlehem A.M.E. Church.

Jeremy Schipper has been unwavering in his devotion to me and his belief in this project. He is my biggest supporter, my loudest cheerleader, my kindest reader, and my best friend. For me, as a bookworm, there is no greater commitment than to commingle one's books. I am happy that Jeremy and I now share our library and our lives as husband and wife.

3. Vincent L. Wimbush, "Interpreters—Enslaved/Enslaving/Runagate," *Journal of Biblical Literature* 130, no. 1 (2011): 24.

Introduction

Womanist biblical interpretation is relatively new in the development of academic biblical studies, but African American women are not newcomers to biblical interpretation. The purpose of this book is to provide a brief introduction to womanist biblical interpretation with relevant background on feminist biblical interpretation, feminism, and womanism. It sketches the history of womanist biblical interpretation and analyzes critical issues related to its development and future. The volume links various reading strategies employed in contemporary womanist biblical interpretation with African American women's engagement with biblical texts starting in the nineteenth century. It argues that womanist biblical interpretation is not merely an offshoot of feminist biblical interpretation but part of a distinctive tradition of African American women's engagement with biblical texts. This introduction defines key terms and provides an overview for the book.

DEFINITIONS

Development of the Term *Womanist*

What is a womanist? If you saw a womanist on the street, would you be able to pick her out? The term *womanist* is often used to refer to an African American woman. Some treat the two as synonymous, but there is a lot of confusion about the term *womanist*. The nineteenth-century term *womanism* referred to "advocacy of or enthusiasm for the rights, achievements etc. of women," while *womanist* referred to a "womanizer."[1] Alice Walker uses *womanist* in a short story in 1980, but her 1983 definition of the term popularized it. Walker is an African

---

1. *Oxford English Dictionary*, 2nd ed. (Oxford: Oxford University Press, 1989).

American activist and writer who was awarded the Pulitzer Prize for Fiction in 1983 for her novel *The Color Purple*.[2]

Walker's first use of *womanist* was in "Coming Apart," a short story that served as an introduction to an edited volume on pornography.[3] The story explores the conflict between a black husband and wife regarding his use of pornography. Prior to book publication, the story was published in *Ms. Magazine* as "When Women Confront Porn at Home."[4] Also, it was included in Walker's volume of short stories *You Can't Keep a Good Woman Down* (1981).[5] In the story, although the husband "attacks her as a 'women's liber,'" the narrator of the story explains, "The wife has never considered herself a feminist—though she is, of course, a womanist. A 'womanist' is a feminist, only more common."[6] In a footnote in the short story, Walker explains her preference for this term:

> "Womanist" encompasses "feminist" as it is defined in Webster's, but also means *instinctively* pro-woman. It is not in the dictionary at all. Nonetheless, it has a strong root in Black women's culture. It comes (to me) from the word "womanish," a word our mothers used to describe, and attempt to inhibit, strong, outrageous or outspoken behavior when we were children: "You're acting *womanish*!" A labeling that failed, for the most part, to keep us from acting "womanish" whenever we could, that is to say, like our mothers themselves, and like other women we admired.
>
> An advantage of using "womanist" is that, because it is from my own culture, I needn't preface it with the word "Black" (an awkward necessity and a problem I have with the word 'feminist'), since Blackness is implicit in the term; just as for white women there is apparently no felt need to preface "feminist" with the word "white," since the word "feminist" is accepted as coming out of white women's culture.[7]

Walker's 1980 definition is not often cited. Another not-well-known description of the term *womanist* appears in Walker's 1981 review of Rebecca Cox Jackson's *Gifts of Power: The Writings of Rebecca Jackson*. Jackson was a nineteenth-century African American minister who founded a Shaker community in Philadelphia.

2. The novel was adapted into a film in 1985 and into a Broadway musical in 2005. While Walker is most well-known for *The Color Purple*, she is a prolific writer of fiction and nonfiction works, such as *The Third Life of Grange Copeland; Anything We Love Can Be Saved: A Writer's Activism;* and *The Cushion in the Road: Meditation and Wandering as the Whole World Awakens to Being in Harm's Way*.

3. Alice Walker, "Coming Apart," in *Take Back the Night: Women on Pornography*, ed. Laura Lederer (New York: W. Morrow, 1980), 95–104.

4. Alice Walker, "When Women Confront Porn at Home," *Ms Magazine*, 1980, 67, 69–70, 75–76. In the magazine's table of contents, the same short story is titled "Confronting Pornography at Home—A Fable."

5. Alice Walker, "Coming Apart: By Way of Introduction to Lorde, Teish and Gardner," in *You Can't Keep a Good Woman Down* (Orlando, FL: Harcourt, 1981), 41–53. In *You Can't Keep a Good Woman Down*, Walker mentions being invited by Laura Lederer to write an introduction for Lederer's edited volume in 1979. Walker refers to the introduction prior to book publication as "A Fable," although it is also called "Coming Apart."

6. Walker, "Coming Apart," 100.

7. Ibid.

In discussing the relationship between Jackson and Jackson's woman companion, Walker takes issue with the editor's speculation regarding a possible lesbian relationship. Walker writes,

> The word "lesbian" may not, in any case, be suitable (or comfortable) for black women, who surely would have begun their woman-bonding earlier than Sappho's residency on the Isle of Lesbos. Indeed, I can imagine black women who love women (sexually or not) hardly thinking of what Greeks were doing; but, instead, referring to themselves as "whole" women, from "wholly" or "holy." Or as "round" women—women who love other women, yes, but women who also have concern, in a culture that oppresses all black people (and this would go back very far), for their fathers, brothers, and sons, no matter how they feel about them as males. My own term for such women would be "womanist."[8]

In 1983 Walker provides what became the seminal definition of the term *womanist*. It appeared in the front matter of a collection of essays, *In Search of Our Mothers' Gardens: Womanist Prose* (1983). She writes,

> 1. From *womanish*. (Opp. of "girlish," i.e., frivolous, irresponsible, not serious.) A black feminist or feminist of color. From the black folk expression of mothers to female children, "You acting womanish," i.e., like a woman. Usually referring to outrageous, audacious, courageous or *willful* behavior. Wanting to know more and in greater depth than is considered "good" for one. Interested in grown-up doings. Acting grown up. Being grown up. Interchangeable with another black folk expression: "You trying to be grown." Responsible. In charge. *Serious.* 2. Also: A woman who loves other women, sexually and/or nonsexually. Appreciates and prefers women's culture, women's emotional flexibility (values tears as a natural counterbalance of laughter), and women's strength. Sometimes loves individual men, sexually and/or nonsexually. Committed to survival and wholeness of entire people, male *and* female. Not a separatist, except periodically, for health. Traditionally universalist, as in "Mama, why are we brown, pink, and yellow, and our cousins are white, beige, and black?" Ans.: "Well, you know the colored race is just like a flower garden, with every color flower represented." Traditionally capable, as in: "Mama, I'm walking to Canada and I'm taking you and a bunch of other slaves with me." Reply: "It wouldn't be the first time." 3. Loves music. Loves dance. Loves the moon. *Loves* the Spirit. Loves love and food and roundness. Loves struggle. *Loves* the Folk. Loves herself. *Regardless.* 4. Womanist is to feminist as purple to lavender.[9]

Walker does not offer a definition of *feminist*, although sections 1 and 4 of her definition elaborate on the relationship between *feminist* and *womanist*. For

---

8. Alice Walker, "Gifts of Power: The Writings of Rebecca Jackson," in *In Search of Our Mothers' Gardens: Womanist Prose* (Orlando, FL: Harcourt, Inc., 1983), 81.

9. Alice Walker, *In Search of Our Mothers' Gardens: Womanist Prose* (Orlando, FL: Harcourt, Inc., 1983), xi–xii.

reasons that will become clear, I will return to this definition at several points later in this book.

Feminism

In a basic sense, feminism involves support for and action directed toward the elimination of women's subordination and the equality of men and women. Historically, women's rights advocates and women activists have used various terms for self- and group identification. Although activists may be in support of what others may regard as feminist aims, these activists may not identify themselves as feminist for numerous personal, political, or historical reasons. One should not confuse a label with a commitment.

Some African American women and others choose not to identify themselves as feminists because they regard the term *feminism* as implying a type of white feminism. Other African American women who identify as feminists express the opposition that they faced by identifying as such. For example, African American writer Michelle Wallace describes her development and identification as a black feminist in a 1975 article that was originally published in the *Village Voice*, a New York City weekly paper. She explains, "When I first became a feminist, my Black friends used to cast pitying eyes upon me and say, 'That's whitey's thing.'"[10] While race was a source of contention within feminism, class divisions were also present as white women were sometimes perceived as wealthy elites with petty complaints. For example, in 1970 Linda Larue, an African American woman, writes of the alleged "common oppression" of African Americans and white women. She explains:

> "Common oppression" is fine for rhetoric, but it does not reflect the actual distance between the oppression of the black man and woman who are unemployed, and the "oppression" of the American white woman who is "sick and tired" of *Playboy* fold-outs, or Christian Dior lowering hemlines or adding ruffles, or of Miss Clairol telling her that blondes have more fun. Is there any logical comparison between the oppression of the black woman on welfare who has difficulty feeding her children and the discontent of the suburban mother who has the luxury to protest the washing of the dishes on which her family's full meal was consumed?[11]

LaRue minimizes the complaints of white women, but her observations reflect the concerns of some African American women who felt that white women did not experience the same harsh conditions faced by African American women.

Some women regard mainstream feminism as a wealthy, heterosexual, white woman's enterprise that focuses on issues of gender to the exclusion of race,

10. Michelle Wallace, "A Black Feminist's Search for Sisterhood," in *All the Women Are White, All the Blacks Are Men, but Some of Us Are Brave: Black Women's Studies*, ed. Gloria T. Hull, Patricia Bell Scott, and Barbara Smith (Old Westbury, NY: Feminist Press, 1982), 10.

11. Linda LaRue, "The Black Movement and Women's Liberation," in *Words of Fire: An Anthology of African-American Feminist Thought*, ed. Beverly Guy-Sheftall (New York: New Press, 1995), 164. Reprinted from "The Black Movement and Women's Liberation," *Black Scholar* 1 (May 1970): 36–42.

ethnicity, class, and other factors. Others, despite sharing the critiques of mainstream feminism, choose to identify as feminist but add modifiers to highlight their unique experiences. For example, some feminists identify as black feminists, Marxist feminists, lesbian feminists, Jewish feminists, Latina feminists, postcolonial feminists, and hip-hop feminists. Also, some add geographic descriptors and identify as African feminists, Caribbean feminists, third-world feminists, and a host of other terms.[12] For these feminists, it is important to acknowledge the importance of not gender alone but gender, race, and ethnicity alongside other factors.

While the term *feminist* can be used as a label to identify oneself, it can be used also to define one's perspective or approach to scholarship. Within the academy, *feminism* is used in a variety of ways. Some scholars may or may not identify themselves as feminists personally but may use feminist approaches in their scholarly work. Scholars have developed feminist approaches in diverse fields, such as literary theory, architecture, cinema, and bioethics. Yet even scholars within the same field may use feminist approaches differently. A feminist approach may involve focusing on women's experiences, exposing and critiquing patriarchy, and/or recovering the neglected work of previous generations of women. There are no agreed-on methodologies or guidelines regarding what constitutes a feminist approach. Given such diversity, the definition and distinctiveness of feminist approaches remain hotly debated.

Although these issues of terminology have been part of academic discourse, one's choice to self-identify as feminist has become a more mainstream issue for many U.S. women. The percentage of U.S. adults who identify themselves as feminists varies dramatically in survey data in part due to the phrasing of the question and the definition of the term, if offered.[13] Still, the issue of self-identification is part of a national conversation, especially as women who are public figures, including celebrities, politicians, and other women in leadership, are now routinely questioned and critiqued regarding their choice whether to identify themselves as feminists.

Womanism

Given the importance of race and gender for African American women and the racial divisions that are part of the historical development of feminism, some African American women embraced the term *womanist* following the 1983 publication of *In Search of Our Mothers' Gardens*. It offered an explicit inclusion of

12. Some men who support feminism refer to themselves as "pro-feminist" in order to express their solidarity with feminists. These men prefer not to use the term *feminist*, which some men and women regard as referring to women only. Other men are comfortable identifying themselves as feminists. For a pro-feminist example, see Gary L. Lemons, *Black Male Outsider: Teaching as a Pro-Feminist Man: A Memoir* (Albany: State University of New York Press, 2008).

13. Leonie Huddy, Francis K. Neely, and Marilyn R. Lafay, "Support for the Women's Movement," *The Public Opinion Quarterly* 64, no. 3 (2000): 309–50; and Janice McCabe, "What's In a Label? The Relationship between Feminist Self-Identification and 'Feminist' Attitudes among U.S. Women and Men," *Gender and Society* 19, no. 4 (2005): 480–505.

race and provided distance from the term *feminist*, which was perceived at times as a designation for white women's feminism. The most basic undersanding of *womanist* comes from the first part of the first segment of Walker's 1983 definition, which defines a *womanist* as "a black feminist or feminist of color."[14] While some women identify themselves as womanists, others describe their perspective or their artistic and scholarly work as womanist. Although Walker's definition has become more popularly well-known than have the essays within *In Search of Our Mothers' Gardens*, the definition was part of the front matter of her collection of essays. The definition was not part of an extensive essay or article on feminism itself and does not present a fully developed treatise on feminism or womanism. Still, her definition has taken on a life of its own.

Walker's definition includes the understanding of a womanist as "a black feminist or feminist of color,"[15] but to interpret womanism as simply a racial designation is to misconstrue Walker's understanding of the concept. In a 1984 interview, Walker explains why she wanted to keep "womanist" in the title of *In Search of Our Mothers' Gardens*. She states, "I just like to have words to explain things *correctly*. Now to me 'black feminist' does not do that. I need a word that is organic, that really comes out of the culture, that really expressed the spirit that we see in black women. And it's just . . . *womanish*." Walker continues, "You know, the posture with the hand on the hip, 'Honey, don't you get in my way.'"[16] For Walker, womanism is a multilayered philosophy, perspective, and expression that is distinct from white feminism and white culture.

In the same interview Walker shares her concerns regarding feminism. She says, "You see, one of the problems with white feminism is that it is not a tradition that teaches white women that they are capable. Whereas my tradition *assumes* I'm capable."[17] Here, Walker contrasts African American and white perceptions of women within their respective communities. This contrast is evident in part 2 of her definition of *womanist*. She defines a *womanist* as "traditionally capable, as in: 'Mama, I'm walking to Canada, and I'm taking you and a bunch of other slaves with me.' Reply: 'It wouldn't be the first time.'"[18] A daughter's plan for a group escape from slavery is met not with surprise but with an unimpressed acceptance by her mother. For Walker, womanism does not simply distinguish women by race; it emphasizes differences in the expectations of those women. Thus, the African American mother does not bat an eyelash when confronted with her daughter's audacious plan because the mother expects such bravery and competence.

Of course, Walker's definition is not universally accepted by African American women. Some of these women regard *womanist* and *black feminist* as

---

14. Walker, *In Search of Our Mothers' Gardens*, xi.
15. Ibid.
16. David Bradley, "Novelist Alice Walker: Telling the Black Woman's Story," *The New York Times*, January 8, 1984, http://www.nytimes.com/books/98/10/04/specials/walker-story.html.
17. Ibid.
18. Walker, *In Search of Our Mothers' Gardens*, xi

synonymous given that Walker includes the idea of black feminism within her definition of a womanist. Others reject black feminism because they understand it as inextricably linked to feminism, which they regard as by and for white women. Instead, they embrace womanism as distinctive in its focus on African American women. Due to this focus, some question whether only African American women can identify themselves as womanists. Psychologist Layli Phillips (Maparyan) offers space for inclusivity with some caution. She states, "You're a womanist if you say you're a womanist, but others can contest you or ask you what womanism means for you."[19] Others have questioned the presumption that African American women should identify as womanists. Writer bell hooks explains her concerns:

> I hear black women academics laying claim to the term "womanist" while rejecting "feminist." I do not think Alice Walker intended this term to deflect from feminist commitment, yet this is often how it is evoked. Walker defines womanist as black feminist or feminist of color. When I hear black women using the term womanist, it is in opposition to the term feminist; it is viewed as constituting something separate from feminist politics shaped by white women. For me, the term womanist is not sufficiently linked to a tradition of radical political commitment to struggle and change.[20]

For hooks, *womanism* connotes a negativity that pits black women against white women. While acknowledging the racism of some white women, hooks contends that the feminist struggle can help to bring about positive change for blacks and whites. She recommends, "I believe that women should think less in terms of feminism as an identity and more in terms of 'advocating feminism.'"[21] For hooks, feminism is not a personal label that describes oneself but rather an idea toward which one devotes one's time and energy. Given the variety of understandings of these terms, even if someone self-identifies using a particular term, one cannot make assumptions about what that particular term means to that person and why she chooses that term over another.

Other Womanisms

Chikwenye Okonjo Ogunyemi and Clenora Hudson-Weems have constructed forms of womanism that differ from Walker's. Ogunyemi, a Nigerian writer, claims that she developed the term *womanism* independently of Walker.[22] In contrast to feminism and African American womanism, Ogunyemi views her "African womanism" as less individualistic, more familial, and more focused on

19. Layli Phillips, "Womanism: On its Own," in *The Womanist Reader* (New York: Routledge, 2006), xxxvi.

20. bell hooks, *Talking Back: Thinking Feminist, Thinking Black* (Boston: South End Press, 1989), 181–82.

21. Ibid.

22. Chikwenye Okonjo Ogunyemi, "Womanism: The Dynamics of the Contemporary Black Female Novel in English," *Signs* 11, no. 1 (1985): 63–85.

the distinctiveness of African struggles within a global community.[23] Clenora
Hudson-Weems has developed the concept of "Africana womanism," which she
distinguishes from feminism, womanism, and African womanism.[24] Instead of
using the terms *African American*, *black*, or *African*, Hudson-Weems uses the
more inclusive term *Africana*, which refers to continental Africans as well as to
those who are part of the African diaspora. She does not use the term *womanism* as defined by Walker. Instead, she links womanism with the term *woman*
and with the struggles of Africana women such as nineteenth-century former
slave and abolitionist Sojourner Truth, who challenged traditional notions of
womanhood. For Hudson-Weems, Africana womanism focuses on community
and on the collective work of Africana men and women. The terms as developed by Ogunyemi and Hudson-Weems are not as well-known outside of the
academy.[25]

Womanist Approaches

Both *womanist* and *black feminist* can be used as a personal identifiers as well as
descriptions of one's approach to scholarship. Like feminist approaches, womanist and black feminist approaches are diverse. There is no single agreed-on
womanist or black feminist approach or unifying womanist or black feminist
theory. In addition, scholars differ as to whether womanist and black feminist
scholarship constitute the same type of inquiry. For some, they are synonymous,
while others regard womanism as a different type of enterprise.[26] Furthermore,
due to its focus on African American women, some question whether only
African American women can use womanist approaches. Sociologist Patricia
Hill Collins outlines six distinguishing features of black feminist thought. She
stakes out the basic consensus position by claiming, "Living life as an African-
American woman is a necessary prerequisite for producing Black feminist
thought."[27] Regardless of the prerequisites or particular elements, scholarship that is explicitly labeled as womanist or black feminist is produced almost
entirely by African American women and other women of African descent.[28]

23. Chikwenye Okonjo Ogunyemi, *African Wo/Man Palava: The Nigerian Novel by Women*
(Chicago: University of Chicago, 1996).
24. Clenora Hudson-Weems, *Africana Womanism: Reclaiming Ourselves* (Troy, MI: Bedford,
1993).
25. For a discussion of these three writers, see Layli Maparyan, "Womanist Origins: Reading
Alice Walker, Chikwenye Okonjo Ogunyemi, and Clenora Hudson-Weems," in *The Womanist Idea*
(New York: Routledge, 2012), 15–32.
26. Patricia Hill Collins, "What's in a Name? Womanist, Black Feminism, and Beyond," *The
Black Scholar* 26, no. 1 (1996): 9–17.
27. Patricia Hill Collins, "The Social Construction of Black Feminist Thought," *Signs* 14, no.
4 (Summer, 1989): 770.
28. For helpful resources on black feminist and womanist thought, see Gloria T. Hull, Patricia
Bell Scott, and Barbara Smith, eds., *All the Women Are White, All the Blacks Are Men, but Some of Us
Are Brave: Black Women's Studies* (Old Westbury, NY: Feminist Press, 1982); Barbara Smith, ed.,
Home Girls: A Black Feminist Anthology (New York: Kitchen Table: Women of Color Press, 1983);
Stanlie M. James and Abena P. A. Busia, *Theorizing Black Feminisms: The Visionary Pragmatism of
Black Women* (New York: Routledge, 1993); Guy-Sheftall, ed., *Words of Fire* ; Layli Phillips, ed.,

Scholars may use black feminist and womanist approaches in many different ways, but, in general, these approaches may share some basic characteristics.[29] First, they critique what is perceived as white feminism's focus on gender to the exclusion of other factors such as race and class and its preoccupation with the particular concerns of white women. Second, they address the simultaneity of multiple and overlapping oppressions, such as racism, classism, and sexism. Third, they foreground the experiences of African American women.

Multiple jeopardy and intersectionality are two important concepts that have become associated with womanist and black feminist thought, although they do not appear in Walker's definition. Developed by legal scholar Kimberlé Williams Crenshaw, intersectionality refers to the ways in which various oppressions intersect and overlap.[30] Intersectional analysis interrogates race, class, gender, and other issues not as separate and distinct but as interlocking elements. Linked to intersectionality is the concept of "matrix of domination." According to Collins while intersectionality analyzes simultaneous forms of oppression, the matrix of domination "refers to how these intersecting oppressions are actually organized."[31] Another key concept is Deborah King's notion of "multiple jeopardy," which stresses the importance of treating forms of oppression not as additive but as multiplicative.[32] It emphasizes the ways in which African American women face racism, sexism, and classism at the same time and in ways that compound one another.

Despite the importance of these concepts and Walker's definition of *womanism*, black feminist and womanist thought and the experiences that help to shape these concepts precede these particular labels. For example, Crenshaw's development of the concept of intersectionality was predated by the Combahee River Collective's 1977 "A Black Feminist Statement," which became an important

---

The Womanist Reader (New York: Routledge, 2006); and Layli Maparyan, *The Womanist Idea* (New York: Routledge, 2012). On African American men's perspectives on race and gender, see Michael Awkward, *Negotiating Difference: Race, Gender, and the Politics of Positionality* (Chicago: University of Chicago, 1995); and Rudolph P. Byrd and Beverly Guy-Sheftall, eds., *Traps: African American Men on Gender and Sexuality* (Bloomington: Indiana University Press, 2001).

29. Patricia Hill Collins identifies six characteristics of black feminist thought: 1) connecting experience and consciousness, 2) linking experience and ideas, 3) coming from the standpoint of U.S. black women's experiences, 4) including theory and action, 5) operating as dynamic, and 6) involving social justice. See Patricia Hill Collins, "Distinguishing Features of Black Feminist Thought," in *Black Feminist Thought: Knowledge, Consciousness, and the Politics of Empowerment*, 2nd ed. (New York: Routledge, 2000), 21–43.

30. Kimberlé W. Crenshaw, "Demarginalizing the Intersection of Race and Sex: A Black Feminist Critique of Antidiscrimination Doctrine, Feminist Theory and Antiracist Politics," *University of Chicago Legal Forum* (1989), 139–67; and Kimberlé W. Crenshaw, "Mapping the Margins: Intersectionality, Identity Politics, and Violence Against Women of Color," *Stanford Law Review* 43, no. 6 (1991): 1241–99.

31. Patricia Hill Collins, *Black Feminist Thought: Knowledge, Consciousness, and the Politics of Empowerment* (New York: Routledge, 2000), 18.

32. Deborah King, "Multiple Jeopardy: The Context of a Black Feminist Ideology," in *Feminist Frameworks: Alternative Theoretical Accounts of the Relations between Women and Men*, ed. Alison M. Jaggar and Paula S. Rothenberg (New York: McGraw-Hill, 1993), 220–36.

early treatise on black feminist thought and activism. The statement includes the following:

> We are actively committed to struggling against racial, sexual, heterosexual, and class oppression and see as our particular task the development of integrated analysis and practice based upon the fact that the major systems of oppression are interlocking. The synthesis of these oppressions creates the conditions of our lives. As Black women we see Black feminism as the logical political movement to combat the manifold and simultaneous oppressions that all women of color face. [33]

Also, King's work on "multiple jeopardy" was preceded by the work of Frances Beale, an African American journalist and activist who addressed the importance of both racism and sexism for African American women in her 1970 essay "Double Jeopardy: To Be Black and Female."[34] Beale's work follows the path of a 1925 essay by Elise Johnson McDougald, "The Double Task: The Struggle of Negro Women for Sex and Race Emancipation."[35] Still earlier, Maria W. Stewart provides a nineteenth-century antecedent to this emphasis on race and gender through her political activism and emphasis on the experiences of African American women.[36] Likewise, the actions and writings of African American women such as Sojourner Truth, Anna Julia Cooper, and others illustrate the ways in which African American women's lives as women and as African Americans have affected their perspectives on the world, their research, and their activism. [37] Despite the development of new terminology in the twentieth century, African American women have been conscious of and endeavored to address issues of race, gender, and other factors prior to the development of this terminology. That is, African American women's personal experiences have informed their action in support of improving the lives of other African American women and African American communities before the popular usage of the terms *feminist* or *womanist*. Furthermore, such action does not require using these terms. One can engage in what some might call feminist or womanist work without identifying oneself or one's work in those same terms. The work predates the naming of the work.

33. Combahee River Collective, "A Black Feminist Statement," in *All the Women Are White, All the Blacks are Men, but Some of Us Are Brave: Black Women's Studies*, ed. Gloria T. Hull, Patricia B. Scott, and Barbara Smith (Old Westbury, NY: Feminist Press, 1982), 13.

34. Frances Beale, "Double Jeopardy: To Be Black and Female," in Guy-Sheftall, ed., *Words of Fire* 146–55.

35. Elise Johnson McDougald, "The Double Task: The Struggle of Negro Women for Sex and Race Emancipation," in Guy-Sheftall, ed., *Words of Fire*, 80–83. Reprinted from "The Double Task: The Struggle of Negro Women for Sex and Race Emancipation," *Survey Graphic* 53 (October 1924–March 1925): 689–91.

36. R. Dianne Bartlow, " 'No Throw-Away Woman': Maria W. Stewart as a Forerunner of Black Feminist Thought," in *Black Women's Intellectual Traditions: Speaking their Minds*, ed. Kristin Waters and Carol B. Conaway (Lebanon, NH: University Press of New England, 2007), 72–88.

37. See Bert James Loewenberg and Ruth Bogin, *Black Women in Nineteenth-Century American Life: Their Words, Their Thoughts, Their Feelings* (University Park: Pennsylvania State University Press, 1976) and Waters and Conaway, *Black Women's Intellectual Traditions*.

I do not identify myself as a feminist or as a womanist. I do not find these terms to be useful for my personal identification, especially since they are burdened by so many conflicting assumptions. If I say that I am a womanist, by itself that label tells you nothing about me, my research agenda, or my political allegiances. Instead of a one-word litmus test, I prefer that someone ask me directly about my contributions to scholarship, teaching, or service to the academy and other communities. Who I am as a biblical scholar and as an African American woman informs what I teach and what I research, but neither can be reduced to a single descriptor. As to whether this book qualifies as a womanist work, you will have to determine that after reading it.

BIBLICAL STUDIES

Biblical scholars are not the only ones who interpret biblical texts. Scholars in disciplines outside of biblical studies and those outside of academia also interpret biblical texts. Nonetheless, it is important to understand biblical studies as its own distinct academic discipline. This discipline involves the study of biblical texts and related materials and includes two major areas: Hebrew Bible/ Old Testament and New Testament/Christian origins.[38] This distinction is central to understanding the development of womanist biblical interpretation within biblical studies as an academic discipline. As I will discuss later in this book, although womanist work is often linked together across fields, much of the womanist work that engages biblical texts comes from fields outside of biblical studies.

Biblical interpretation includes an array of ways that one could interpret biblical texts while biblical studies involves applying critical methods to biblical interpretation. That is, it is critical in the sense that it involves rational, critical arguments. Biblical scholarship refers primarily to the scholarly production of professionally trained biblical scholars or other scholars whose primary training is in other fields but whose cross-disciplinary work has been influential in biblical studies, such as that of cultural theorist Mieke Bal.[39] Usually, biblical scholars hold doctoral degrees in Old Testament/Hebrew Bible and New Testament/Christian origins, and they use biblical texts, comparative literature, and ancient material culture as their main source material. These scholars present and publish critical scholarship that is in conversation with the work of other

38. The name "Hebrew Bible" is used by some scholars to refer to the books of the Old Testament in a more religiously neutral way in order to avoid using the explicitly Christian name, Old Testament, or the more explicitly Jewish Tanakh.

39. For examples, see Mieke Bal, *Lethal Love: Feminist Literary Readings of Biblical Love Stories* (Bloomington: Indiana University Press, 1987); *Death & Dissymmetry: The Politics of Coherence in the Book of Judges* (Chicago: University of Chicago Press, 1988); *Murder and Difference: Gender, Genre, and Scholarship on Sisera's Death* (Bloomington: Indiana University Press, 1988); and *Anti-Covenant: Counter-Reading Women's Lives in the Hebrew Bible*, vol. 81 (Sheffield, England: Almond Press, 1989).

biblical scholars. Scholars in related fields, such as Near Eastern languages and civilizations, Assyriology, Egyptology, and classics may conduct scholarship that overlaps with that of biblical scholars although they may choose not to refer to themselves as biblical scholars since biblical texts may not be their primary academic focus.

When I tell people that I teach biblical studies, usually they think that I am a theologian. They do not expect religion professors to have areas of specialization, or they may have never heard of biblical studies as an academic discipline. Yet we expect medical professionals to have different specialties. We understand that cardiologists, pediatricians, and obstetricians are different types of doctors who treat different types of patients. While we may assume that cardiologists and pediatricians have some knowledge of the reproductive system and even some experience of delivering infants at some point in their training, we expect to see an obstetrician in the maternity ward.

While there are significant connections and intersections among academic disciplines, in many ways these disciplines are separate and distinct. Academics are trained by others in their discipline, and they have particular approaches to their research. For example, we understand that an economist, a historian, and an ethnographer would have distinctly different perspectives on the 2012 presidential election. The economist might use quantitative data from the Bureau of Labor Statistics or the U.S. Census. The historian might mine library archives for speeches by presidential candidates. The ethnographer might conduct a participant-observation study in one candidate's hometown campaign office. They will present their findings at different academic conferences, publish their results in different academic journals, and engage with other scholars in their respective fields. Each scholar uses different sources and asks different questions even when conducting research on the same subject.

Similarly, biblical scholars, theologians, and ethicists are all trained differently. Given the importance of the Tanakh and the Christian Bible in Jewish and Christian communities and in the Western world, many of these scholars may use biblical texts in their research. Nevertheless, they do so from the vantage point of their respective disciplines. For example, a doctoral student in homiletics (preaching) may have some basic facility with Hebrew and Greek due to the centrality of the Bible in her field. Yet a doctoral student in New Testament would have substantially more language training in order to offer her own translations of biblical and extrabiblical texts. The homiletics student might study liturgics and communications theory while the biblical studies student might study linguistics and archaeology. A homiletical analysis of Rev. C. L. Franklin's classic sermon "The Eagle Stirreth Her Nest" (Deuteronomy 32:11) may be suitable for a homiletics seminar research paper whereas an analysis of honor and shame in 1 Corinthians 11:2–16 in light of its Greco-Roman context may be more appropriate for a biblical studies research assignment. Although both students engage the Bible in their work, they do so in very different ways.

While womanist scholarship in religious studies and in biblical studies is often grouped together, discipline differences are important in order to appreciate the specific impact that such scholarship has had within the field of biblical studies. Within the academy, the division between biblical studies and religious studies is clearly illustrated in two different organizations. The American Academy of Religion (AAR) is an organization dedicated to the academic study of religion whereas the Society of Biblical Literature (SBL) is an organization devoted to academic biblical studies. Biblical scholars are typically the types of scholars who would be members of the Society of Biblical Literature. The annual meetings of AAR and SBL are held separately but in the same location (except 2008–2010). Some scholars attend both meetings and use interdisciplinary approaches that cross these boundaries. Other scholarly organizations, such as the American Academy of Homiletics or the Society of Christian Ethics, focus more narrowly on their respective subspecialties, but in general the scholars who produce biblical scholarship are likely to be SBL members.

Feminist Biblical Interpretation and Womanist Biblical Interpretation

Feminist biblical interpretation refers to the use of a feminist approach within the academic discipline of biblical studies. At a basic level, it addresses gender and power relations. The standard narrative of feminist biblical interpretation includes the development of womanist biblical interpretation as an offshoot of feminist biblical interpretation. According to this narrative, some nineteenth-century women's rights supporters offered new interpretations of biblical texts in order to challenge notions of women's subordination. These interpreters were the forerunners of twentieth-century feminist biblical interpretation. Contemporary feminist biblical interpretation began in the 1970s as some scholars began to develop feminist approaches to biblical studies. Just as feminism faced critiques for its focus primarily on gender, feminist biblical interpretation faced similar criticism. Some scholars began to develop alternatives to feminist biblical interpretation, including womanist biblical interpretation. Thus womanist biblical interpretation began with the publication of Renita J. Weems's *Just a Sister Away: A Womanist Vision of Women's Relationships in the Bible* (1988).

While 1988 would seem to be the appropriate year in which to begin an investigation of womanist biblical interpretation, we are not going to begin our inquiry with biblical scholars. Womanist biblical interpretation is usually understood as a late-twentieth-century derivative element of feminist biblical interpretation. Yet in order to understand why and how it developed, we cannot treat womanist biblical interpretation as merely a racialized corrective to or an African American version of feminist biblical interpretation. This book disrupts the standard narrative regarding the development of womanist biblical interpretation by tracing its roots from multiple sources, including U.S. women's activism, womanist scholarship in religion-related fields, and feminist biblical scholarship. By including the reading strategies employed by nonprofessional readers, scholars outside of biblical studies, and biblical scholars, this book offers a richer, fuller history of African American women's engagement with biblical texts. It considers the particular ways in which African American women have interpreted biblical texts in light of their personal experiences and how those approaches have led to the development of womanist biblical interpretation within biblical studies.

OVERVIEW

In this introductory book, I am not attempting to construct a history of African American women, nor do I try to bridge the so-called divide between the academy and the church. Rather, I am seeking to write an accessible, introductory text that illustrates how womanist biblical interpretation is related to feminist biblical interpretation and also how it is deeply rooted in the work of previous generations of African American women scholars and interpreters of the Bible. This project reframes womanist biblical interpretation to include a long-range historical view of the tradition of African American women's engagement with biblical texts that includes nonprofessionally trained writers and activists as well as scholars outside of biblical studies. Such reframing contributes to African American women's intellectual history by including the voices of African American women as biblical interpreters.

Part 1 focuses on historical issues. Chapter 1 addresses some of the popular misconceptions regarding feminism and womanism and provides background on the so-called "waves" of feminism and the importance of race and gender in women's rights discourse and action. Chapter 2 discusses the early efforts of women's rights supporters to use biblical texts to combat women's subordination. This early activism provides the groundwork for the later development of twentieth-century feminist biblical interpretation by biblical scholars. In chapter 3, I discuss the unique ways in which African American women activists used biblical interpretation in addressing issues of both race and gender. This chapter serves to link these often neglected early interpretations with developments in later womanist scholarship in religious studies and in biblical studies.

Part 2 focuses on contemporary issues. Chapter 4 describes womanist work in religious-studies-related academic fields, including its engagement with biblical texts. Although this work does not constitute biblical scholarship by biblical scholars, it is important to understand the contributions of womanist work outside of biblical studies to the development of womanist biblical studies. Chapter 5 provides background on feminist biblical interpretation within biblical studies in order to contrast its growth and development with that of womanist biblical interpretation. In chapter 6, I discuss the history and current status of womanist biblical interpretation within biblical studies and link its development to womanist religious-studies-related fields, African American biblical scholarship, feminist biblical interpretation, as well as the work of previous generations of African American women interpreters of biblical texts. In the conclusion, I offer my thoughts on the future of womanist biblical interpretation.

Since this historical background may be more than what you bargained for when you picked up this book, its organization breaks up material into manageable sections. If you want to focus on historical issues, see part 1; if not, start with contemporary scholarship in part 2. If you want to concentrate on the discussion of womanist biblical interpretation within biblical studies, jump to chapter 6. Of course, I recommend that you read from beginning to end in order to appreciate the constellation of factors affecting the growth and development of womanist biblical interpretation. Also, you will have a greater understanding of the historical and ongoing importance of race and gender for African American women's activism and scholarship. If you stick with me, it will be worth it.

RESOURCE LIST

Collins, Patricia Hill. *Black Feminist Thought: Knowledge, Consciousness, and the Politics of Empowerment*. New York: Routledge, 2000. This book explores some of the origins and features of black feminist thought.

Guy-Sheftall, Beverly, ed. *Words of Fire: An Anthology of African-American Feminist Thought*. New York: New Press, 1995. This important anthology provides a sample of African American feminist thought, including nineteenth- and twentieth-century works by African American women.

Hull, Gloria T., Patricia Bell Scott, and Barbara Smith, eds. *All the Women Are White, All the Blacks Are Men, but Some of Us Are Brave: Black Women's Studies*. Old Westbury, NY: Feminist Press, 1982. This anthology is an early collection on black feminism. It includes the Combahee River Collective's "A Black Feminist Statement."

Phillips, Layli, ed. *The Womanist Reader*. New York: Routledge, 2006. This helpful anthology provides essays on womanist thought from scholars in a variety of disciplines.

Walker, Alice. *In Search of Our Mothers' Gardens: Womanist Prose*. Orlando, FL: Harcourt, Inc., 1983. This classic work is a must-read for its definition of *womanist* and for examples of Walker's earlier work.

PART I
HISTORICAL
BACKGROUND

Chapter 1

Three "Waves" of Feminism

"Feminism is only for white women." "Alice Walker is the founder of womanism." These are just some of the popular misconceptions regarding feminism and womanism that I encounter when I teach classes and when I read popular media. Although this book focuses on womanist biblical interpretation, some context regarding the factors that led to the development of black feminism and womanism is necessary. To locate the beginning of African American women's consciousness of race and gender in 1983 with Alice Walker's definition of *womanism* is to fundamentally misunderstand African American women's history and agency. The issues raised by the term *womanist* began long before Walker offered her definition. African American women's concerns regarding race and gender did not appear in the late twentieth century as a second- or third-wave corrective to the largely gender-focused efforts of white women activists. African American women have addressed issues of race and gender continually within their activism and scholarship. Facing racism and sexism, they have fought to incorporate issues of race within gender-focused efforts as well as issues of gender within race-based efforts. Yet the specific gender focus of much of the women's rights activism and discourse is taken to refer to white women, and the framing of women's concerns largely extends only to the concerns of relatively affluent

3

white women. African American women are generally racialized but not gendered. That is, African American women are regarded as African Americans, while white women are treated as representative of all women. Furthermore, African American men are treated as representative of all African Americans.

This chapter reviews the basic narrative of the three so-called "waves" of feminism. It then disrupts that narrative by addressing some of the problems with the waves narrative. Without attempting a lengthy treatment of U.S. women's history, it discusses some of the issues related to African American women's activism and the interaction of race and gender as historical background for later chapters. This chapter is not an exhaustive review of U.S. women's history or African American women's history. Instead, this chapter shows that efforts for the advancement of women were not restricted only to white women, and it illustrates the importance of both race and gender in women's activism as background for the more focused discussion of biblical interpretation in later chapters.

FEMINISM

As discussed in the introduction, while *feminism* is difficult to define, in general a feminist approach involves support for the equality of men and women and action directed toward the elimination of women's subordination. Feminism in the United States is often described as having three waves or major time periods. These periods are called first-, second-, and third-wave feminism, and they extend roughly from the mid-nineteenth century to the early twentieth century, the 1960s to the 1980s, and the 1980s into the twenty-first century, respectively. As we will discuss, the notion of waves is problematic, but it is important to be familiar with this terminology due to its frequent and continued use.

First-Wave Feminism

First-wave feminism is usually identified as the period from 1848 to 1920. In 1848, activists Elizabeth Cady Stanton and Lucretia Mott assembled a convention at Seneca Falls, New York, to discuss women's rights. The Seneca Falls Convention is often considered to be the start of the U.S. women's rights movement.[1] The period of first-wave feminism is generally regarded as ending with the ratification of the Nineteenth Amendment to the U.S. Constitution in 1920, which gave U.S. women the right to vote.

Second-Wave Feminism

A particular starting date for second-wave feminism is difficult to determine. One possible start date is 1963 due to the publication of Betty Friedan's

---

1. Lisa Tetrault, *The Myth of Seneca Falls: Memory and the Women's Suffrage Movement, 1848–1898* (Chapel Hill: University of North Carolina Press, 2014).

Feminine Mystique. While describing society's encouragement of women to seek fulfillment as wives and mothers, Friedan claims that American women faced a profound dissatisfaction with their lives, which she calls "the problem that has no name."[2] Her research included a sample of women who were Smith College graduates, so her findings were not generalizable to the entire population of U.S. women. Yet this book was one of many developments that brought attention to the particular issues and concerns of women during this period.

Another starting point could be the founding of the National Organization for Women (NOW) in 1966. Its purpose was "to take action to bring women into full participation in the mainstream of American society now, exercising all the privileges and responsibilities thereof in truly equal partnership with men."[3] Despite these potential starting dates, it was not until 1968 that Marsha Lear coined the phrase "the second feminist wave" in a *New York Times Magazine* article.[4] No single organization had responsibility for advocating a specific second-wave feminist agenda. During this period, the term *feminist* was used as a personal identifier and as a descriptor of efforts by various groups, coalitions, and individuals to secure greater rights and protections for women.

Significant victories for U.S. women were achieved during this period. For example, women's rights advocates secured the Equal Pay Act of 1963, which prohibited sex discrimination in payment of wages and worked to ensure the inclusion of sex discrimination in Title VII of the Civil Rights Act of 1964. Although the Fourteenth Amendment provided for "equal protection," the Civil Rights Act of 1964 forbade employment discrimination on the basis of race, color, religion, sex, or national origin. Thus employers may not discriminate against job applicants or employees in hiring, firing, and promotion. Title VII also created the Equal Employment Opportunity Commission that serves to enforce federal nondiscrimination laws.

Women's rights advocates also lobbied to obtain the passage of Title IX of the Education Amendment of 1972. Title IX mandated nondiscrimination in academic programs receiving federal funds. While it is commonly perceived as providing greater opportunities for women in high school and college athletic programs, Title IX addressed inequality related to a variety of elements in education, including student services, academic programs, recruitment, employment, and other areas. Overall, these efforts increased awareness of the many limitations placed on women due to gender as well as marital or familial status.

Feminist efforts continue through our contemporary period, but some regard second-wave feminism as coming to an end with the failure to ratify the Equal Rights Amendment (ERA) in 1982. Suffragist Alice Paul drafted the first proposed amendment for equal rights in 1923 for the 75th anniversary of the 1848 Seneca Falls Convention. It specified that both men and women were entitled

2. Betty Friedan, *The Feminine Mystique* (New York: W.W. Norton, 1997), 15.
3. National Organization for Women, "National Organization for Women's 1966 Statement of Purpose," http://www.now.org/history/purpos66.html.
4. Marsha Lear, "The Second Feminist Wave," *The New York Times Magazine*, March 10, 1968, 24–25.

to equal rights under the U.S. Constitution. In 1972, the ERA was passed by Congress, but in 1982, even after a ratification deadline extension, the amendment died without the required ratifications from three-fifths or thirty-eight of the state legislatures. Some supporters continue to push for its ratification today. They contend that the U.S. Constitution does not provide adequately for the rights of both men and women and argue that the ERA is necessary to state explicitly a guarantee of equal constitutional rights. An end point of 1982 is of course artificial. Some would argue that despite these gains second-wave feminism has not ended because the struggle for women's rights continues.

Third-Wave Feminism

Third-wave feminism is a term used for a wide range of feminist activism that seeks to distinguish itself from second-wave feminism. The term *third wave* became popular after the publication of a 1992 essay titled "Becoming the Third Wave" by writer Rebecca Walker, who is the daughter of Alice Walker.[5] Rebecca Walker's essay provided her response to the divisive U.S. Senate confirmation hearings for then–U. S. Supreme Court nominee Clarence Thomas. Following the retirement of Justice Thurgood Marshall in 1991, President George H. W. Bush nominated Clarence Thomas as an associate justice. Following the leak of FBI interviews, Anita Hill, a law professor at the University of Oklahoma, was called to testify before the Senate Judiciary Committee. She claimed that Thomas had engaged in inappropriate behavior of a sexual nature toward her when they worked together from 1981 to 1983. The Senate voted 52 to 48 in favor of Thomas's confirmation, but the televised hearings in which Thomas and Hill, both African Americans, were questioned by a committee of white men, created a national dialogue on issues of race, gender, and sexual harassment.[6]

For Rebecca Walker the confirmation hearings were not about determining if Thomas was guilty of sexual harassment but about "checking and redefining the extent of women's credibility and power."[7] In speaking with her "peers," she cautions, "Let Thomas's confirmation serve to remind you, as it did me, that the fight is far from over."[8] Walker concludes the essay by declaring, "I am not a postfeminism feminist. I am the Third Wave."[9] Walker distances herself from previous generations of feminism and from postfeminism, which often implies a rejection of traditional feminist concerns.[10]

5. Rebecca Walker, "Becoming the Third Wave," *Ms. Magazine* (1992): 39.
6. See Hill's discussion of her ordeal in Anita Hill, *Speaking Truth to Power* (New York: Doubleday, 1997).
7. Walker, "Becoming the Third Wave," 39.
8. Ibid.
9. Ibid.
10. *Postfeminism* is often used as an ill-defined umbrella term to describe the general position that feminism has run its course and is no longer necessary given the gains that women have made in U.S. society. Other feminists counter that postfeminism downplays the continued damaging effects of sexism and takes for granted the significant strides made by previous generations of feminists.

Third-wave feminism does not focus on any single issue related to women. It claims to embrace diversity and to address gender in conjunction with various factors such as race, gender, class, and sexuality. Furthermore, it includes diverse issues such as ecofeminism and sex positivity, which affirms sexuality as a healthy, positive element of adult relationships. There is no distinctive end to third-wave feminism as some would argue that it continues in our contemporary period.

COUNTER TO THE WAVE NARRATIVE

First Wave?

Despite its commonplace usage to periodize women's rights activism, the term *first-wave feminism* is anachronistic. The term *feminist* does not appear in English until 1894 and was not widely used at that time.[11] Although early women are sometimes regarded as first-wave feminists, these activists did not refer to themselves as feminists. Nor did they use a single particular term or share a collective identity or aim. The nineteenth- and early-twentieth-century efforts to improve the condition of women is known as first-wave feminism because women in later periods label it as such. Just as the film *Rocky* was not referred to as *Rocky I* until its sequel *Rocky II* existed, there was no notion of a first wave until the term *second wave* became popular. This retrospective labeling is the result of contemporary women grouping together early women reformers and identifying them as feminists or "proto-feminists" in order to link contemporary activism with that of earlier generations and create a broader history of feminism that extends from the nineteenth century through the present. Yet equating women's activity in these different time periods with feminism may create the false impression that these women share significant similarities regarding their strategies and aims.

For many people today, notions of equal rights involve equal pay or antidiscrimination employment legislation. While contemporary efforts for women's rights tend to focus on the de facto (not officially sanctioned) discrimination faced by women, in the past efforts focused largely on de jure (by law) inequities facing women. For example, in earlier periods, women were not granted the right to vote and were prevented from holding political office. Laws varied from state to state, but due to the common-law doctrine of coverture, once a woman married, her legal rights were subsumed under those of her husband. Thus a woman lost control of any property that she owned and any wages or income that she acquired. Also, she could not enter into contracts or initiate a lawsuit. Divorce was quite uncommon during this period, and women who wished to divorce faced significant difficulties in obtaining one. Although many

11. Oxford English Dictionary, 2nd ed. (Oxford: Oxford University Press, 1989).

men, including those in poverty, immigrants, Native Americans, and African Americans, were not granted the same legal, political, and economic rights as educated white men, there were particular restrictions for women, especially for affluent white women. While contemporary women continue to fight gender discrimination, they are not engaged in the same type of struggle against the widespread, legalized gender discrimination that existed in previous eras.

First-Wave Suffrage?

Another misconception regarding first-wave feminism is the notion that early women's activism focused on voting rights for women. Although nineteenth-century women's activism is often thought of as relating primarily to suffrage, it was not the primary focus of women's activism in this period. Before Seneca Falls and after the ratification of the Nineteenth Amendment, women activists, including African Americans, advocated for women's rights, for greater racial equality, and for diverse social causes affecting women, men, and children. These activists did not use a single term in referring to themselves collectively. They were abolitionists, temperance workers, club women, suffragists, and women who were fulfilling what they perceived as their religious or civic duties. Many women worked to secure not only suffrage but also other political, economic, legal, and social rights for women and men.

The mistaken impression that the purpose of early women's activism was to achieve the goal of voting rights for women may be due to the setting of first-wave feminism's end date at 1920 due to the ratification of the Nineteenth Amendment. Also, it may result from the view of the Seneca Falls Convention as a suffrage effort. The Seneca Falls Convention was a watershed in the quest for women's rights due to its focus on women and the subsequent publicity storm that it generated. Yet even its organizers were not solely "suffragists." Prior to organizing the 1848 Seneca Falls Convention, both Elizabeth Cady Stanton and Lucretia Mott were abolitionists. They and other women faced opposition from some male abolitionists who disapproved of women's public participation in the abolitionist movement. According to Stanton, she and Mott conceived of a women's rights convention following their rejection as delegates to the World Anti-Slavery Convention in London in 1840. Regarding this experience, Stanton wrote, "The movement for woman's suffrage, both in England and America, may be dated from the World's Anti-Slavery Convention."[12] While Stanton overstates the direct relationship between abolition and woman's suffrage, working toward suffrage was not an isolated advocacy position.

Although Seneca Falls has become nearly synonymous with the quest for women's right to vote, it provides an excellent example of the diversity of issues with which activists grappled. This convention was held July 19–20, 1848, with

12. Elizabeth Cady Stanton, Susan B. Anthony, and Matilda Joslyn Gage, *History of Woman Suffrage*, vol. 1 (1881; repr., New York: Arno Press, 1969), 62.

approximately three hundred male and female delegates. The gathering's stated purpose was "to discuss the social, civil, and religious condition and rights of women."[13] The convention addressed numerous women's rights issues, including legal rights, education, and gender roles. Voting rights for women was the most controversial issue discussed, and of the resolutions on which the attendees voted, the suffrage resolution was the only resolution not to pass unanimously.

At the conclusion of the Seneca Falls Convention, some of the delegates signed a Declaration of Sentiments, which was modeled on the U. S. Declaration of Independence. It included the following statement: "We hold these truths to be self-evident: that all men and women are created equal; that they are endowed by their Creator with certain inalienable rights; that among these are life, liberty, and the pursuit of happiness."[14] The gender inclusiveness of this statement illustrates the importance of women's equality for the conference delegates. Still, their concern for greater equality was not limited to voting rights. Furthermore, although the Seneca Falls Convention was called in order to discuss the rights of women, the concerns addressed by the delegates were primarily the concerns of middle- and upper-class women with some access to property and wealth. Working-class, poor, and enslaved women were facing more basic struggles.

Third Wave?

Some question whether a third wave of feminism exists. As exemplified in the title of the 2006 edited volume *We Don't Need Another Wave: Dispatches from the Next Generation of Feminists*, some women feel no need to identify themselves with a wave or a particular group or a particular term, especially if the term seems too old-fashioned, confining, or ill-defined. This is also the case for some women of color who have had a stormy relationship to the term *feminist*. The perceived lack of focus within contemporary feminism may make it appear to be less of a movement and more of a splintered catch-all grouping that does not require its own "wave." Yet first- and second-wave feminism also had a variety of goals directed toward improving women's rights, and both lacked a clearly unified agenda, although the wave narrative suggests otherwise. Thus, third-wave feminism, if one chooses to recognize it, is not remarkably different from its predecessors. Furthermore, third-wave feminists would contend that the more diverse and disparate elements of third-wave feminism are not negatives but important elements of this new movement. For example, self-identified third-wave feminists Jennifer Baumgardner and Amy Richards write, "The fact that feminism is no longer limited to arenas where we expect to see it—NOW, *Ms.*, women's studies, and red-suited Congresswomen—perhaps means that young

13. Ibid.
14. Stanton, Anthony, and Gage, *History of Woman Suffrage*, 1:70.

women today have really reaped what feminism has sown.[15] Baumgardner and Richards explain, "The presence of feminism in our lives is taken for granted. For our generation, feminism is like fluoride. We scarcely notice we have it—it's simply in the water."[16] The diverse concerns of contemporary or third-wave feminism and its efforts to distinguish itself from previous generations may reflect the growth and development of feminism over time. Whether they identify themselves as feminists, contemporary activists take on issues and problems facing women of previous generations as well as the women of a new generation.

RACE AND GENDER

First-Wave Suffragists

The combination of race and gender has always been a complicating factor within women's activism, but it is often thought of as a twentieth-century issue that begins with the post–Civil Rights era. Yet as early white women activists sought to expand rights for white women, they drew parallels between their condition as women and the condition of enslaved men and women. For example, the 1848 Seneca Falls Convention discussion of resolutions, as recorded in *History of Woman Suffrage*, notes, "At this time, the condition of married women under the Common Law was nearly as degraded as that of the slave on the Southern plantation."[17] Despite comparing themselves to enslaved persons, some white women distanced themselves from African Americans, and the nineteenth-century break between those who supported woman suffrage exposed the fault lines of race and gender in this early period of activism.[18]

While some suffragists were also abolitionists, the Fourteenth and Fifteenth Amendments created a split among women's rights advocates who disagreed regarding the priorities of their political activism. The Thirteenth, Fourteenth, and Fifteenth Amendments are considered Reconstruction amendments as they focus on the legal and political status of African Americans in the period immediately following the Civil War. In 1865, the Thirteenth Amendment abolished slavery in the United States. In 1868, the Fourteenth Amendment specified the rights and privileges of those born in the United States, including citizenship, due process, and equal protection, and in 1870, the Fifteenth Amendment ensured that voting rights could not be limited due to "race, color, or previous condition of servitude."[19] Suffrage activism waned during the Civil War as activists focused on the war effort, but it reemerged in the years following the war.

15. Jennifer Baumgardner and Amy Richards, *Manifesta: Young Women, Feminism, and the Future* (New York: Farrar, Straus & Giroux, 2000), 130.
16. Ibid.
17. Stanton, Anthony, and Gage, *History of Woman Suffrage*, 1:73.
18. On African American women's suffrage activities, see Rosalyn Terborg-Penn, *African American Women in the Struggle for the Vote, 1850–1920* (Bloomington: Indiana University Press, 1998).
19. The Constitution of the United States, Amendment XV, sect. 1.

The American Equal Rights Association (AERA) was created in 1866 to advocate for the rights of women and African Americans. It focused its efforts on universal suffrage, which permitted voting for all adult U.S. citizens, including men and women. Article 2 of the AERA constitution stated, "The object of this Association shall be to secure Equal Rights to all American citizens, especially the right of suffrage, irrespective of race, color or sex."[20] AERA members and other women's rights advocates argued over supporting the Fourteenth Amendment in part because section 2 of the amendment included the word "male" in specifying the voting rights of "male" citizens. The modifier "male" had never been used previously in the U.S. Constitution. Some members opposed the Fifteenth Amendment because it did not include gender as a nondiscrimination factor. Together, the Fourteenth and Fifteenth Amendments provided for universal male suffrage instead of universal suffrage. Other women's rights advocates, including the AERA, supported the Fourteenth and Fifteenth Amendments as compromise measures that at least provided for incremental change for one previously disenfranchised group, African American men.

Some suffragists opposed the ratification of the Fourteenth and Fifteenth Amendments because these amendments permitted universal male suffrage but did not guarantee the rights of women. Nevertheless, some bias against African American men and immigrant men played a significant role in opposition to these amendments. For instance, in her address to the National Woman Suffrage Convention in Washington, D.C. in 1869, Elizabeth Cady Stanton asked, "Shall American statesmen, claiming to be liberal, so amend their constitutions as to make their wives and mothers the political inferiors of unlettered and unwashed ditch-diggers, boot-blacks, butchers, and barbers, fresh from the slave plantations of the South, and the effete civilizations of the Old World?"[21] Stanton did not support the extension of rights to additional groups of men before the granting of rights to white women.

Related to this focus on white woman suffrage was the notion of "educated suffrage," which meant that those who could read and write and who were thus regarded as educated deserved to be allowed to vote. Educated suffrage excluded those who were uneducated, which included a large number of immigrants, many African Americans, and the poor. At the 1903 National American Woman Suffrage Association (NAWSA) Convention, speaker Belle Kearney explained more clearly the notion of educated suffrage and racist and nativist sentiments. She stated, "The enfranchisement of women would insure immediate and durable white supremacy, honestly attained, for upon unquestioned authority it is stated that in every southern state but one there are more educated women than

20. American Equal Rights Association et al., *Proceedings of the First Anniversary of the American Equal Rights Association*, held at the Church of the Puritans, New York, May 9 and 10, 1867. Phonographic report by H. M. Parkhurst (New York: R. J. Johnston, printer, 1867), 80.

21. Stanton, Anthony, and Gage, *History of Woman Suffrage*, 2:354.

all the illiterate voters, white and black, native and foreign, combined."[22] Kearney linked the political and social goal of white supremacy with women's suffrage. Not all suffragists were in favor of white supremacy, but some suffragists supported the enfranchisement of white women as part of an overall solution to what some perceived as the growing threat of immigrant and African American male voters. In their quest for white women's suffrage, they argued that educated white women were better qualified to be voters than men who are uneducated.

First-Wave African American Women on Race and Gender

While African American women were consistently in favor of abolition, some African American women were active in both abolition and women's suffrage efforts. In general, the plight of African American women was not directly addressed by suffragists. Nevertheless, African American women continued to remind white women of the differences in their relative situations. For example, at the 1866 National Women's Rights Convention, Frances Ellen Watkins Harper distinguished the plight of African American women. She explained, "I do not believe that giving the woman the ballot is immediately going to cure all the ills of life. I do not believe that white women are dew-drops just exhaled from the skies." She told the audience how she was not permitted to ride the street car in Philadelphia due to her race and explained, "You white women speak here of rights, I speak of wrongs."[23] As an African American woman, Harper faced both gender and racial discrimination, which were not addressed by delegates focusing on voting rights.

African American women asserted the importance of both race and gender concerns. For example, Sojourner Truth (Isabella Baumfree) highlighted the false dichotomy of race versus gender that was present in the struggle for rights. At the AERA meeting in New York City in 1867, she exclaimed, "There is a great stir about colored men getting their rights, but not a word about the colored women; and if colored men get their rights, and not colored women theirs, you see the colored men will be masters over the women, and it will be just as bad as it was before."[24] Truth's words forecast the debate among suffragists regarding setting priorities.

22. Ida Husted Harper, ed. *History of Woman Suffrage*, vol. 5 (1922; repr., New York: Arno Press, 1969), 82–83.

23. Frances Ellen Watkins Harper and Frances Smith Foster, *A Brighter Coming Day: A Frances Ellen Watkins Harper Reader* (New York: Feminist Press at the City University of New York, 1990), 218.

24. Stanton, Anthony, and Gage, *History of Woman Suffrage*, 2:193. Gage's account of Truth's speech changed significantly over time. On the controversy, see Olive Gilbert, Sojourner Truth, and Nell Irvin Painter, *Narrative of Sojourner Truth: A Bondswoman of Olden Time, with a History of Her Labors and Correspondence Drawn from Her Book of Life; also, A Memorial Chapter* (1884; repr., New York: Penguin Books, 1998), 264; Nell Irvin Painter, *Sojourner Truth: A Life, a Symbol* (New York: W.W. Norton, 1996); and Roseann M. Mandziuk and Suzanne Pullon Fitch, "The Rhetorical Construction of Sojourner Truth," *Southern Communication Journal* 66, no. 2 (2001): 120–38.

Due to differences regarding the Fourteenth Amendment and continued controversy regarding the Fifteenth Amendment, the AERA disbanded in 1869. After the AERA disbanded, two separate organizations were created, the American Woman Suffrage Association (AWSA) and the National Woman Suffrage Association (NWSA). With the leadership of Lucy Stone and Julia Ward Howe, the AWSA continued to work for both racial and gender equality and supported the ratification of the Fifteenth Amendment despite its exclusion of women. The more radical NWSA focused on voting rights for women with the support of women such as Susan B. Anthony and Elizabeth Cady Stanton. The AWSA and NWSA also disagreed over the direction of the suffrage movement regarding strategy as the AWSA advocated a state-by-state strategy while the NWSA pushed for a constitutional amendment.

In 1890, the AWSA and the NWSA merged to create NAWSA with Elizabeth Cady Stanton as its first president. Despite the earlier efforts of the AWSA to work for the rights of women and African Americans, the NAWSA was more conservative in its approach. It focused on the enfranchisement of white women, and certain NAWSA chapters excluded African American women from membership.

African American men also downplayed the significance of both race and gender for African American women. At the 1869 AERA Convention in New York, Frederick Douglass argued for extending suffrage to African American men. Douglass, an African American former slave and abolitionist, attended the Seneca Falls Conference and signed the Declaration of Sentiments. His commitment to the expansion of rights to all races and genders is exemplified by the gender-specific but still inclusive motto of his influential newspaper *The North Star*. The motto reads, "Right is of no sex; truth is of no color; God is the Father of us all, and we are all brethren." Yet Douglass cast suffrage as a struggle between white women and African American men. He argued, "I must say that I do not see how anyone can pretend that there is the same urgency in giving the ballot to woman as to the negro."[25] Thus, Douglass equates "negro" with "men" and does not include "negro" women within his notion of "negro." In doing so, he marginalizes African American women by removing them from consideration within the debate.

Also, after Douglass describes the horrific conditions facing black men, someone in the audience asked, "Is that not all true of black women?" Douglass responded, "Yes, yes, yes, it is true of the black woman but not because she is a woman but because she is black."[26] Thus, again Douglass classifies African American women primarily as "black" and not as women. Such regard for African American women as primarily racialized but not gendered illustrated ongoing conflicts for African American women.

25. Stanton, Anthony, and Gage, *History of Woman Suffrage*, 2:382.
26. Ibid.

These conflicts were highlighted by African American educator and speaker Anna Julia Cooper, who addressed the particular struggles of African American women. In "The Status of Woman in America" (1892), she explained, "The colored woman of today occupies, one may say, a unique position in this country. In a period of itself transitional and unsettled, her status seems one of the least ascertainable and definitive of all the forces which make for our civilization. She is confronted by both a woman question and a race problem, and is as yet an unknown or an unacknowledged factor in both."[27] Cooper highlights the importance of both gender and race for African American women.

First-Wave African American Women's Activism

One issue that comes up repeatedly in conversations regarding second-wave feminism is the mistaken idea that African American women only became activists in the mid- to late-twentieth century. African American women have been activists for women's rights as well as other political, economic, and civil rights since the colonial era. Yet their contributions have often been erased from the traditional wave narrative that focuses primarily on large-scale white women's activism.[28] African American women participated in interracial coalitions and created their own spaces and organizations in order to address the particular and multiple concerns of African American women and their communities.

Since the colonial period, mutual aid societies as well as religious groups, fraternal organizations, benevolent groups, trade guilds, and unions have provided food, clothing, medical care, insurance, and other assistance to their members and to others in need. These groups formed along religious, ethnic, racial, class, and occupational divisions and provided vital social services before the development of national government assistance programs. While some were women's auxiliaries of all-male societies, others were founded, led, and controlled by women. For instance, the Female Hebrew Benevolent Society was organized by Jewish women in 1819 in Philadelphia and is still in existence today.[29] African American women created their own organizations, such as the African Female Benevolent Association in Newport, Rhode Island, which was founded in 1809. Also, women's abolitionist groups formed, such as the Female Anti-Slavery Society, which was founded by African American women in Salem, Massachusetts, in 1832.

During the nineteenth century, some middle- and upper-class women began to create other types of all-female gatherings, including literary societies and self-improvement groups. Some women's groups developed plans of study that

27. Charles Lemert and Esme Bhan, eds., *The Voice of Anna Julia Cooper, including A Voice from the South and Other Important Essays, Papers, and Letters* (Lanham, MD: Rowan & Littlefield Publishers, Inc., 1998), 112.

28. See Paula Giddings, *When and Where I Enter: The Impact of Black Women on Race and Sex in America*, 2nd Quill ed. (New York: W. Morrow, 2001) and Deborah G. White, *Too Heavy a Load: Black Women in Defense of Themselves, 1894–1994* (New York: W.W. Norton, 1999).

29. On the Female Hebrew Benevolent Society, see http://www.fhbs.org/.

focused on art, music, and literature and held private gatherings in one another's homes. Again, African American women were also part of this trend. For example, the Female Literary Association of Philadelphia was founded by free African American women in 1831. While this group and other groups worked for self-improvement, they fostered community improvement by helping to better women's lives. The notion of social groups for women with leisure time may sound frivolous, but they provided important opportunities for women to learn, share ideas, and collaborate. Given that women's educational opportunities were quite limited during this period, these groups performed important social and educational functions.

During the Civil War, there was less public activism, specifically for women's rights, but women played an important role in the war effort. Hundreds of women concealed their identities in order to enlist and serve in the war as male soldiers for both the Confederacy and the Union.[30] African American women were among those who served officially as undercover operatives, guides, nurses, cooks, and laundresses. For example, Harriet Tubman was one famous Union scout. Other women volunteered by fund-raising, cooking, and sewing for the troops.

The proliferation of women's organizations or clubs, particularly in the post–Civil War era, became what is called the Women's Club Movement. These women were called "club women," and their clubs supported self-improvement and volunteer service to communities for health care, sanitation, education, gardens, and libraries.[31] African American women created their own clubs, but like the clubs organized by white women, their activities were not focused solely on women's issues. For instance, formed from African American women's clubs, the National Association of Colored Women (NACW) was created in 1896 with the leadership of women such as Mary Church Terrell and Ida B. Wells-Barnett.[32] The NACW and individual African American women's clubs worked to obtain civil and political rights for both African American men and women, particularly in the post-Reconstruction era in which lynchings and other attacks against African Americans increased, African American men were disenfranchised, and Jim Crow laws required segregation of public areas such as restrooms, schools, and public transportation.

Second-Wave African American Women on Race and Gender

African American women's activism is often not regarded as women's activism because it is not focused solely on so-called "women's" issues. While first-wave feminism sought to extend basic rights to women, second-wave feminism attempted to combat gender discrimination and to push for equal access to

30. Bonnie Tsui, *She Went to the Field: Women Soldiers of the Civil War* (Guilford, CT: TwoDot, 2003).
31. See the General Federation of Women's Clubs at http://www.gfwc.org/.
32. Renamed as National Association of Colored Women's Clubs in 1957. See http://www.nacwc.org/index.html.

social, economic, legal, and political opportunities. Second-wave feminism was a continuation of previous efforts to expand women's rights. Still, many of the gains for women in the twentieth century owe a significant debt to the civil rights movement, which began in the 1950s. While African Americans and other racial and ethnic minorities continued to work to secure legal protections that provided basic rights in the period following the Civil War, the civil rights movement was a continuation of efforts designed to overcome the de facto discrimination that had persisted unabated since Reconstruction. The social protests and other political actions used to combat segregation and other forms of racial discrimination helped to create conditions that supported efforts toward the extension and protection of civil rights to women.

The efforts of women activists like Fannie Lou Hamer and Ella Baker in support of civil rights are not as well-known as the work of prominent men such as Martin Luther King Jr. Even Rosa Parks, the well-known icon of the Montgomery bus boycott, is less well known for her work as an antirape activist. Civil rights concerns were not typically addressed by white women activists and are not usually regarded as women's activism. Although African American women, including Shirley Chisholm, Pauli Murray, and Aileen Hernandez, were instrumental in the establishment of NOW, they are not held up as women's rights activists but rather African American women activists.

While second-wave feminism was successful in expanding opportunities and limiting discrimination against women, often it continued to marginalize issues of race just as had been the case with first-wave feminism. Within women's activism, issues of race and gender were often treated as separate matters such that African American women were asked to prioritize either race or gender over the other. For instance, in 1969, Shirley Chisholm, an African American Congresswoman, gave a speech in the U.S. House of Representatives in support of the ratification of the ERA. She stated, "As a black person, I am no stranger to race prejudice. But the truth is that in the political world I have been far oftener discriminated against because I am a woman than because I am black."[33] Chisholm stresses her gender over her race in order to press her point in support of the ERA.

During this time of social protest in the 1960s and 1970s, African American women continued to be caught between opposing factions. Often, women's rights was regarded as a gender issue with primary concern for white women, while civil rights was treated as a race issue with primary concern for African American males. Furthermore, the civil rights movement as well as the more militant Black Power movement tended to relegate women to support roles and did not often include substantial public leadership roles for women. The difficult position in which African American women found themselves is encapsulated by the 1982 book titled *All of the Blacks Are Men, All of the Women Are Whites,*

33. Shirley Chisholm, "Equal Rights for Women," Duke University Special Collections Library Digital Scriptorium, http://scriptorium.lib.duke.edu/wlm/equal/.

But Some of Us Are Brave.[34] This edited volume collected materials related to the experiences of African American women and advocated for the growth and development of black women's studies in the academy.

Some African Americans were part of predominantly white groups that worked to advance the rights of women. Other African American women were concerned that feminism and feminist organizations focused too narrowly on the issues and concerns of white women. Some African American women developed separate organizations that highlighted their particular concerns as women of color. For example, the National Black Feminist Organization was founded in 1973. These and other African American women's groups highlighted their unique situation as both women and as African Americans. In 1977, the Combahee River Collective, a group of black feminists in Boston, wrote "A Black Feminist Statement," which stated, "As Black women we see Black feminism as the logical political movement to combat the manifold and simultaneous oppressions that all women of color face."[35] They expressed their desire to create a separate space for themselves. They wrote, "It was our experience and disillusionment within these liberation movements, as well as experience on the periphery of the white male left, that led to the need to develop a politics that was antiracist, unlike those of white women, and antisexist, unlike those of Black and white men."[36]

CONCLUSION

These historical developments are often described chronologically as first, second, or third waves. This notion of waves is problematic in that it suggests that feminism has evolved in an orderly, linear fashion. The notion of waves does not fully capture the extent of women's activism and diversity of causes supported by women's groups and organizations. In particular, it does address adequately the post–World War I efforts in support of women's rights. Furthermore, this standard wave narrative marginalizes the activity of many African American women and women who were engaged in smaller-scale, community activism by focusing on the more-institutionalized activity of middle- and upper-class white women. The various actions by U.S. women toward gender equality have been circuitous and fragmented. Furthermore, the notion of waves tends to focus on mainstream white women's activism and does not acknowledge fully the importance of race, which has shaped women's activism and discourse regarding women's rights since its beginnings.

34. Gloria T. Hull, Patricia Bell Scott, and Barbara Smith, eds. *All the Women Are White, All the Blacks Are Men, but Some of Us Are Brave: Black Women's Studies* (Old Westbury, NY: Feminist Press, 1982).
    35. Combahee River Collective, "A Black Feminist Statement," in ibid., 13.
    36. Ibid.

Much of women's activism is lost to recorded history. A Methodist women's sewing circle that raised money for community health care or an Atlanta women's group that taught reading and public speaking skills were unlikely to produce or keep documents that survive. Also, secretive activity such as serving as a spy or assisting as a "conductor" on the Underground Railroad, a network for assisting those who had escaped from slavery, is generally not recorded. Identifying early women's activism with a narrow view of women's rights and particularly with suffrage focuses attention on larger, better-funded, institutionalized action, but it obscures the many ways in which women were active in bringing about change in their communities in different ways.

RESOURCE LIST

Andolsen, Barbara Hilkert. "*Daughters of Jefferson, Daughters of Bootblacks*": *Racism and American Feminism*. Macon, GA: Mercer University Press, 1986. Highlights the importance of racial divisions in the development of U.S. feminism.

Breines, Wini. *The Trouble between Us: An Uneasy History of White and Black Women in the Feminist Movement*. New York: Oxford University Press, 2006. Discusses the divergent paths of white and African American women in their approach to feminism.

Collier-Thomas, Bettye. *Jesus, Jobs, and Justice: African American Women and Religion*. Philadelphia: Temple University Press, 2014. Using the slogan of African American educator Nannie Helen Burroughs, Collier-Thomas highlights the intersections of religious faith and political and social activism among African American women.

McGuire, Danielle L. *At the Dark End of the Street: Black Women, Rape, and Resistance—A New History of the Civil Rights Movement from Rosa Parks to the Rise of Black Power*. New York: Alfred A. Knopf, 2010. Offers a stunning reappraisal of civil rights icon Rosa Parks and the role of African American women in protesting sexual assault.

Morgan, Joan. *When Chickenheads Come Home to Roost: My Life as a Hip-Hop Feminist*. New York: Simon & Schuster, 1999. This collection of essays discusses race, gender, and pop culture.

Ross, Rosetta E. *Witnessing and Testifying: Black Women, Religion, and Civil Rights*. Minneapolis: Fortress Press, 2003. Provides a detailed account of African American women's activism, including civil rights work.

Chapter 2

Feminist Biblical Interpretation: Forerunners

"You shouldn't cut your hair," he proclaimed as he leered over his *Oakland Tribune*. It was too late; my stylist had already shaved a thick row of my chemically straightened hair down to its naturally curly roots, so I ignored him. With his Newport Menthols–inflected voice he ranted, "Hair—a woman's hair—that's a woman's glory!" The response was the buzzing of the clippers and the crinkle-crackle of my hair pulling through the blades. He shook his head in disapproval and snapped back to his newspaper.

This gentleman did not quote a specific biblical text, but the sentiment that he was expressing is based on a particular interpretation of 1 Corinthians 11:14–15. In this text, Paul addresses the church at Corinth regarding head coverings and specifically the wearing of head coverings for prayer. Paul writes, "Does not nature itself teach you that if a man wears long hair, it is degrading to him, but if a woman has long hair, it is her glory? For her hair is given to her for a covering." Although the gentleman may not have been aware that he was mangling a biblical text, he was offering an interpretation of the text as prescribing long hair for women as justification for his effort to police my gender expression. This salon incident shows that even when biblical texts are not cited explicitly, they remain influential in efforts to maintain and perpetuate patriarchy.

Illustrating the important linkage between biblical interpretation and nineteenth- and early-twentieth-century women's activism, this chapter demonstrates the explicit and implicit use of biblical texts both to support women's subordination and to advocate for greater women's equality. It provides historical context regarding the links between gender and biblical interpretation and analyzes selected examples of biblical interpretation by white women activists of this period. While the subordination of women did not require significant justification because it was regarded as "natural," arguments for women's equality had to be constructed, and some of those arguments included appeals to biblical texts. These early biblical interpretations were foundational for the development of feminist biblical scholarship in the twentieth century. As we will see, the neglect of the intersection of race and gender by white women activists contrasts with biblical engagement of African American women activists of this same period. This key difference contributes to the later development of womanist biblical interpretation.

HISTORICAL CONTEXT

Use of Biblical Texts

Despite the popular view of the United States as promoting religious tolerance, most European colonizers understood themselves as building a Christian and even "biblical" nation. They legitimized the subjugation of the land and the native peoples as well as the enslavement of Africans by treating it as the will of God.[1] In the nineteenth century, the Bible had a central role in American life and politics. Although the United States was founded in part on principles of religious freedom and tolerance, the Christian Bible and particular interpretations of it played an important role in American culture and the construction of social norms. The Bible was authoritative in that it was regarded as important and significant for U.S. culture. Also, it was normative in that it was presumed to provide guidance regarding standards and norms for behavior. Thus, understandings of the Bible as authoritative and normative shaped gender expectations, although these notions of appropriate roles and behaviors for women applied predominantly to white, affluent women. African American women as well as enslaved women, Native women, immigrant women, poor women, and others were outside of the purview of the dominant white society.

Biblical studies as an academic discipline developed in the United States in the late nineteenth century as separate and distinct from other disciplines,

---

1. For overviews, see Nathan O. Hatch and Mark A. Noll, *The Bible in America: Essays in Cultural History* (New York: Oxford University Press, 1982); James P. Byrd, *Sacred Scripture, Sacred War: The Bible and the American Revolution* (New York: Oxford University Press, 2013); and Stephen R. Haynes, *Noah's Curse: The Biblical Justification of American Slavery* (New York: Oxford University Press, 2002).

including theology and history, but such scholarship was not engaged by the public. In popular discourse, the Bible was important, but in most instances biblical texts were not cited by chapter and verse explicitly. Instead, public debates often involved natural-law arguments which held that there are universal God-given laws that are knowable through reason and by which society should be governed. In particular, in arguments regarding the role of women in society and understandings of gender and gender roles were intertwined with biblical and theological notions regarding the "natural" order that was presumed to be what was intended by God.

The direct citation of biblical texts to support foundational beliefs about men and women was not generally necessary as these beliefs as well as laws, policies, and practices based on these beliefs were pervasive and often unchallenged. Men and women were thought to be biologically, physically, emotionally, and cognitively different, and these differences were considered to be "natural." Moreover, those who publicly expressed such opinions were able to do so without needing to cite scientific evidence. Thus men were regarded as naturally stronger and more intelligent while women were thought of as naturally weaker, emotional, frail, and less intelligent, although more pious and morally superior. Yet what were regarded conventionally as normative spaces, roles, behaviors, and attributes were in fact socially constructed notions of gender. That is, while there are some biological differences between men and women, ideas about the proper role of men and women in society are socially determined.

For opponents of improved rights and conditions for women, policing what they regarded as the "natural" boundaries between men and women remained important. The separation of men and women into their separate spheres was considered necessary for the maintenance of peace and domestic tranquility. The opponents of women's equality argued that greater rights for women would blur what are regarded as the rigid and distinct lines between men and women in their supposedly natural order ordained by God. They generated arguments regarding what was "natural" in their efforts to keep women from gaining greater equality with men. Undergirding these arguments regarding what was "natural" were implicit appeals to particular biblical interpretations and theological understandings. To go against nature was to go against God and God's intended plan for creation. The separate-spheres ideology and its related cult of true womanhood provide examples of the ingrained understandings about women and their roles and the ways in which these ideas were interlocked with ideas about the "natural" order. Only when these views were challenged do we see biblical proofs stated more explicitly and more forcefully.

The Ideology of Separate Spheres

Nineteenth-century U.S. women's rights advocates were attempting to change opinions about women that were deeply entrenched in U.S. society. During this period, many middle- and upper-class women and men held to an ideology that regarded women and men as having separate spheres—that is, men should be active and engaged in public life while women should focus their attention on home and family. Women's public activism and public speaking was considered to be inappropriate and unladylike, and even women's desire for greater equality with men was perceived as unseemly.

"The Pastoral Letter of the General Association of Massachusetts, June 28, 1837" provides a separate-spheres argument against women's public activism.[2] Written by the Congregational Union of Massachusetts, a group of Congregational ministers, this statement provides a clear rebuke of women engaged in public speaking. It does not name Sarah Moore Grimké and Angelina Grimké (later Grimké Weld), two prominent women abolitionists who were popular public speakers, but the statement was interpreted as a public censure of the Grimkés and women like them.

In the statement, the clergymen praise women who serve in more traditional roles within the domestic sphere and warn their congregants of the dangers of women's public activism. They write,

> The power of woman is in her dependence, flowing from the consciousness of that weakness which God has given her for her protection and which keeps her in those departments of life that form the character of individuals and of the nation. . . . But when she assumes the place and tone of a man as a public reformer, our care and protection of her seem unnecessary, we put ourselves in self defence [sic] against her, she yields the power which God has given her for protection, and her character becomes unnatural. . . . We cannot, therefore, but regret the mistaken conduct of those who encourage females to bear an obtrusive and ostentatious part in measures of reform, and countenance any of that sex who so far forget themselves as to itinerate in the character of public lecturers and teachers.[3]

The writers base their claims on their authority as ministers and as biblical interpreters. For example, they cite Hebrews 13:17: "Obey them that have the rule over you and submit yourselves; for they watch for your souls as they that must give account" (KJV). In this passage from this first-century-CE letter, the unknown author (although attributed to Paul) offers advice on how to be a good Christian. Believers are exhorted to offer mutual love, service to others, and obedience to one's leaders. These ministers use this text to remind their audience of the importance of a "natural" hierarchy in which Christians should be dutiful and obey their leaders. The ministers extend this argument to admonish especially women who do not submit to the teachings of their leaders. For these clergymen, women are unlike men due to their dependency, and when they step

2. *Minutes of the General Association of Massachusetts, 1831–1840* (Boston: Crocker & Brewster, 1831), http://www.archive.org/details/minutesofgeneral3140gene.

3. "Minutes of the General Association of Massachusetts, at their Meeting at North Brookfield, June 28, 1837," in *Minutes of the General Association of Massachusetts, 1831–1840*, 21, https://archive.org/stream/minutesofgeneral3140gene#page/n317/mode/2up.

outside of that dependency into the public sphere, they are going against what God intends for women.

Unlike the Congregationalist ministers who do not name names, Catherine Beecher "calls out" Angelina Grimké for her public role as an abolitionist. Beecher was also an abolitionist, but she argues against public action by women abolitionists. In *An Essay on Slavery and Abolitionism with Reference to the Duty of American Females* (1837), Beecher writes, "In this arrangement of the duties of life, Heaven has appointed to one sex the superior, and to the other the subordinate station. . . . But while woman holds a subordinate relation in society to the other sex, it is not because it was designed that her duties or her influence should be any the less important, or all-pervading. But it was designed that the mode of gaining influence and of exercising power should be altogether different and peculiar."[4] For Beecher, although they are subordinate to men, women have an important private role to play in society, but this role should not involve the acquisition of public power and influence. She does not cite biblical texts but relies on the literary device of metonymy by using "Heaven" to refer to God and to support what she believes is God-ordained gender hierarchy.

According to Beecher, women can be persuasive and influential. Nevertheless, she thinks that women's powers should be limited to the domestic sphere, while men should engage in public debate. She continues, "A man may act on society by the collision of intellect, in public debate. . . . Woman is to win everything by peace and love; by making herself so much respected, esteemed and loved, that to yield to her opinions and to gratify her wishes, will be the free-will offering of the heart. But this is to be all accomplished in the domestic and social circle."[5] Both Beecher and Angelina Grimké support women's activism, but they differ in their understandings of what is appropriate for women.[6]

A newspaper statement from the *Public Ledger and Daily Transcript* titled "The Women of Philadelphia" (1848) provides an example of the entrenched gendered notions related to the separate-spheres ideology. It contrasts the women of different cities and highlights the particular virtues of Philadelphia women. It claims,

> Our Philadelphia ladies not only possess beauty, but they are celebrated for discretion, modesty, and unfeigned diffidence, as well as wit, vivacity, and good nature. . . . The Boston ladies contend for the rights of women. The New York girls aspire to mount the rostrum, to do all the voting, and we

4. Catharine Esther Beecher, *An Essay on Slavery and Abolitionism with Reference to the Duty of American Females* (Philadelphia: Henry Perkins, 1837). Project Gutenberg 2008, ebook #26123, http://www.gutenberg.org/ebooks/26123.

5. Ibid.

6. Grimké got the last word with a rebuttal in the form of thirteen letters. Angelina Emily Grimké, *Letters to Catherine E. Beecher, in Reply to An Essay on Slavery and Abolitionism, Addressed to A. E. Grimke* (Boston: Isaac Knapp, 1838;, rev. by the author, reprt. New York: Arno Press, 1969).

suppose, all the fighting too. . . . Our Philadelphia girls object to fighting and holding office.[7]

Contrasting the Philadelphia women with those of other cities, the statement highlights particular desirable feminine qualities of Philadelphia women. The writer claims that they do not share other women's desire for greater equality. Furthermore, the statement continues,

> Women have enough influence over human affairs without being politicians. Is not everything managed by female influence? Mothers, grandmothers, aunts, and sweethearts manage everything. . . . A woman is nobody. A wife is everything. A pretty girl is equal to ten thousand men, and a mother is, next to God, all powerful. . . . The ladies of Philadelphia, therefore, under the influence of most serious "sober second thoughts," are resolved to maintain their rights as Wives, Belles, Virgins, and Mothers, and not as Women."[8]

The statement positions women as having influence over domestic matters, but it argues that women are important only due to their family and relationship status, not as individual adult women. The statement contends that unlike women activists, Philadelphia women are content with their power and influence in private arenas rather than the public square. It compares a woman's power as a mother to that of God, but in doing so, it reduces her to a role. These are not adult "women," because "woman" as an identity category does not exist apart from its connection with particular gendered relationships. These women exist only in relationship to others. This view served to invalidate women's activity that was outside of what was regarded as women's separate, private sphere.

Those who oppose women's activism also oppose women's suffrage based on the notion of separate spheres. For example, in 1897, writer Helen Kendrick Johnson published an anti-suffrage treatise *Woman and the Republic*. She claims, "The home is not a natural institution unless it is maintained by natural means, and woman suffrage and the home are incompatible."[9] For Johnson, the public and private spheres are naturally distinct, and the distinction should be maintained.

In 1903, Lyman Abbott, a professor and Congregationalist pastor, details reasons why women do not want to vote. In "Why Women Do Not Wish the Suffrage" Abbott writes,

---

7. "The Women of Philadelphia," *Public Ledger and Daily Transcript*, ca. 1848. Reprint, Stanton, Anthony, and Gage, eds. *History of Woman Suffrage*, 1:804.

8. Stanton, Anthony, and Gage, eds. *History of Woman Suffrage*, 1:804.

9. Helen Kendrick Johnson, *Woman and the Republic: A Survey of the Woman-Suffrage Movement in the United States and a Discussion of the Claims and Arguments of its Foremost Advocates* (New York: D. Appleton & Co., 1897). Project Gutenberg April 9, 2003, ebook #7300, http://www.gutenberg.org/ebooks/7300.

Man is not an inferior woman. Woman is not an inferior man. They are different in nature, in temperament, in function. We cannot destroy this difference if we would; we would not if we could. In preserving it lies the joy of the family; the peace, prosperity, and well-being of society. If man attempts woman's function, he will prove himself but an inferior woman. If woman attempts man's function, she will prove herself but an inferior man. Some masculine women there are; some feminine men there are. These are the monstrosities of Nature.[10]

Abbott contends that gender differences are "natural" biological differences that must be preserved. Any deviation from these "natural" roles he regards as unnatural and monstrous.

Also advocating a separate-spheres ideology, the following statement from the New York State Association Opposed to Woman Suffrage argues that granting women the right to vote could undermine women's domestic activity. Its *Thirteenth Annual Report* (1908) states,

> The seekers after the suffrage cannot separate from the privilege they desire to acquire, the duties which are inseparable from it—jury duty, office holding, the attendance at Primaries, and Conventions where policies are determined, and men are chosen for office, matters which may be confirmed, but are not arranged, at the polls. These affairs, when participated in by women, must surely be disruptive of everything pertaining to home life. Those who oppose their attempt, whether actively or passively, form an enormous body of American women, who believe in American Institutions, American Ideals and American Homes.[11]

The report makes a slippery slope argument. If women gain the right to vote, other public roles and responsibilities will be available to them, and they could disrupt what are regarded as "traditional" American institutions and social organization. For those opposed to suffrage, this opportunity for women would create problems for the division of the sexes in society and destroy supposed ideals for American home life. For those opposed to women's public activism in general, women's efforts to gain greater equality were a threat to the American way of life. They argue that men and women have separate functions and that women should remain confined to their domestic, private sphere.

This ideology of separate spheres does not rely directly on biblical texts. Instead, it depends on notions of "natural," "normal," or "traditional." Thus, gender norms and behavior are strictly policed as they are understood to be ordained by God. Understanding this kind of implicit religious argument clarifies the ways in which the cult of true womanhood and its supporters argue

10. Lyman Abbott, "Why Women Do Not Wish the Suffrage," *The Atlantic* 92, no. 551 (September 1903): 289–96, http://www.theatlantic.com/past/docs/issues/03sep/0309suffrage.htm.

11. New York State Association Opposed to Woman Suffrage, *New York State Association Opposed to Woman Suffrage Thirteenth Annual Report*, 1908, Library of Congress, http://hdl.loc.gov/loc.rbc/rbcmil.scrp5011203.

for their views of an ideal woman based on religious notions as well as biblical proof-texts.

Cult of True Womanhood

Related to the separate-spheres ideology was the cult of true womanhood, which was also called the cult of domesticity. Among middle- and upper-class U.S. society, the cult of true womanhood provided an idealized notion of a woman with particular virtues of piety, purity, submissiveness, and domesticity.[12] The ideal woman was religious and served as moral guardian for her family and society. She remained a virgin until she surrendered to her husband on her wedding night. Also, she was dependent, passive, and subordinate to her husband. She focused her energies entirely on her home, husband, and children. Women's public activism was entirely at odds with this view of gender roles.

George Washington Burnap, a Unitarian minister, provides instruction on the ideal woman in *The Sphere and Duties of Women: A Course in Lectures* (1848). This book was one of many popular advice books on being a proper Christian wife with a happy home. Burnap argues that the Bible supports the notion of separate spheres. Invoking Genesis 2:18, which describes Eve as a "help meet" (KJV) for Adam, he writes, "She was made to be the helpmate, the delight, and the comforter of man."[13] Burnap identifies the ideal characteristics and occupations of a woman. He explains, "To woman [is given] the care of home, the preparation of food, the making of clothing, the nursing and education of children. To her is given in larger measure sensibility, tenderness, patience."[14] Burnap admits that women may have been created equal to men, but in their ideal setting, men and women are distinct. He argues,

> But whatever may be the original equality of the sexes in intellect and capacity, it is evident that it was intended by God that they should move in different spheres, and of course that their powers should be developed in different directions. They are created not to be alike but different. The Bible with a noble simplicity expresses in a few words all that can be said upon this subject. 'God created man in his own image, in the image of God he created him, male and female he created them' [KJV].[15]

Burnap interprets Genesis 1:27 as not the creation of equals who were both created in the image of God but as distinct creations. Thus he invokes the ideology of separate spheres. Given that male and female humans are so dissimilar, they should operate in separate spheres, as God must have intended. For Burnap, the

12. Barbara Welter, "The Cult of True Womanhood: 1820–1860," *American Quarterly* 18, no. 2, pt. 1 (Summer, 1966): 151–74.
13. George Washington Burnap, *The Sphere and Duties of Woman: A Course of Lectures* (Baltimore: J. Murphy, 1848), 52, https://archive.org/details/spheredutiesofwo00burn.
14. Ibid., 46
15. Ibid., 45.

ideal woman understands her proper place as in the home, which is the only appropriate place for her.

This view of women is encapsulated in the famous narrative poem *The Angel in the House*, by English poet Coventry Patmore. It does not engage biblical texts but still offers a representation of an idealized woman based on notions of separate spheres and the cult of true womanhood:

> Man must be pleased; but him to please
> Is woman's pleasure; down the gulf
> Of his condoled necessities
> She casts her best, she flings herself.[16]

According to the poem, a woman's role is to please a man, and she is delighted to have this function. Contrasting women and men, Patmore writes,

> Be man's hard virtues highly wrought,
> But let my gentle Mistress be,
> In every look, word, deed, and thought,
> Nothing but sweet and womanly!
> Her virtues please my virtuous mood,
> But what at all times I admire Is,
> not that she is wise or good,
> But just the thing which I desire.
> With versatility to sing
> The theme of love to any strain,
> If oft'nest she is anything,
> Be it careless, talkative, and vain.
> That seems in her supremest grace
> Which, virtue or not, apprises me
> That my familiar thoughts embrace
> Unfathomable mystery.[17]

In this poem, men have "hard virtues" that differ from those of women. Women are fundamentally different and mysterious, but what matters is that a woman has the admiration of a man. This "angel in the house" metaphor is a prime example of the ideology of separate spheres and the particular ideals espoused within the cult of true womanhood that were assumed to be "natural."

The Bible and Women's Rights

Deeply entrenched institutions and beliefs that supported women's subordination did not require significant justification. For politicians, ministers, and others in leadership, citing biblical texts to support women's subordination was not required as these beliefs regarding men and women were "understood," but as

16. Coventry Patmore, *The Angel in the House*, 5th ed. (London: George Bell and Sons, [n.d.]). Published originally in 1854 and 1856 and later revised in 1862.
17. Ibid., "The Koh-I-Noor," *The Koh-i-noor*, pp. 219–20, canto 8, lines 1–16.

some women began to advocate for women's rights, they did increasingly empha-size traditional biblical interpretations that supported such subordination. Yet those attempting to counter the status quo had to construct arguments against it. Women's rights supporters argued against normative patriarchy—that is, against the understanding that women were "naturally" inferior and subordinate to men. Borrowing strategies from the abolitionists, some of whom were also in favor of women's rights, women's rights advocates offered new interpretations of biblical texts in order to challenge the notion that women's subordination was ordained by God and thus part of the natural order of the world.

Feminist biblical interpretation is generally understood to begin in the 1970s, but many feminist biblical scholars consider their work to be a second wave of feminist biblical interpretation. Like feminism in general, feminist bibli-cal interpretation in the United States is described as having three major time periods or waves from the nineteenth century to the present. The so-called first-wave of feminist biblical interpretation refers to the interpretation of biblical texts by women in the nineteenth and early twentieth centuries. These women offered new interpretations of biblical texts in support of improved legal, politi-cal, economic, and social rights and conditions for women. They and their work are often retroactively labeled as the first wave by later generations. Like the first-wave feminists or "proto-feminists," these early female interpreters would not have identified themselves as feminists. Even so, their revolutionary work illustrates the close relationship between the Bible and women's early activism and forms the foundation for the twentieth-century development of feminist and womanist biblical scholarship.

This section analyzes four key documents that illustrate the importance of the Bible in women's early activism in support of greater women's equality: Harriet Livermore's *Scriptural Evidence in Favor of Female Testimony*, Sarah Moore Grim-ké's *Letters on the Equality of the Sexes and the Condition of Women*, the Seneca Falls "Declaration of Rights and Sentiments," and *The Woman's Bible*. These documents are not representative examples of nineteenth-century women's biblical interpreta-tion, especially since some women engaged biblical texts in support of traditional patriarchal views. Instead, these documents provide a range of examples of early approaches to biblical interpretation in support of greater women's equality and demonstrate the foundational importance of nineteenth-century biblical engage-ment to the development of twentieth-century feminist biblical interpretation.

Scriptural Evidence in Favor of Female Testimony

Scriptural Evidence in Favor of Female Testimony (1824) was written by Har-riet Livermore, a popular nineteenth-century preacher, singer, and writer.[18] She was the daughter of a U.S. Congressman, and on four different occasions she

---

18. Harriet Livermore, *Scriptural Evidence in Favor of Female Testimony in Meetings for Christian Worship in Letters to a Friend* (Portsmouth, NH: R. Foster, 1825). Internet Archive: http://archive.org/details/scripturaleviden00live.

preached in the U.S. Hall of Representatives. *Scriptural Evidence* was her first of several published books. In the form of letters written to a friend, she offers biblical arguments for expanding women's roles in religious leadership. Her work provides an important early example of a woman's justification for women's public speaking and teaching.

Although Livermore is not affiliated with a particular Christian denomination, she stands within Protestant Christian tradition by upholding the authority of Scripture and cites 2 Timothy 3:15–16 (KJV): ". . . able to make thee wise unto salvation through faith which is in Christ Jesus. All scripture is given by Almighty inspiration; and is profitable for doctrine, for reproof, for correction, for instruction in righteousness." Also, to support her claim, she cites Romans 15:4 (KJV): "For whatsoever things were written aforetime were written for our learning, that we through patience and comfort of the scriptures might have hope." As an organizing principle for her work, she uses Jeremiah 4:3 (KJV): "Break up your fallow ground, and sow not among thorns." By this, she means that she will elucidate these texts that have been misunderstood. She begins by addressing the writings of Paul, which have been used to deny women's public roles in churches. Livermore highlights 1 Corinthians 11:4–13 and argues that this text supports allowing women to speak but not with their heads uncovered. She notes that 1 Corinthians 12 describes spiritual gifts, which Livermore claims are available to both men and women. Also, she points out that equality between various groups, including men and women, is supported by Galatians 3:28 (KJV): "There is neither Jew nor Greek, there is neither bond nor free, there is neither male nor female: for ye are all one in Christ Jesus."

Livermore supports her argument for women's leadership by focusing on 1 Corinthians 14:34 (KJV): "Let your women keep silence in the churches: for it is not permitted unto them to speak; but they are commanded to be under obedience, as also saith the law." Yet she emphasizes "as also saith the law." Livermore claims that "the law" here refers to the state of humanity after what she calls Eve's "rebellion" in Genesis 3:16. Thus her inquiry begins with the Old Testament to determine if other biblical texts outside of 1 Corinthians 14 forbids women's public address. Seeking examples of women's leadership, she identifies key female biblical characters, such as Eve, the unnamed women on Noah's ark, Miriam, Deborah, Jael, and Esther. She points out their actions and their significance within biblical texts. Also, she invokes the words of the prophet Joel as permitting women to speak: "And it shall come to pass afterward, that I will pour out my spirit upon all flesh; and your sons and your daughters shall prophesy, your old men shall dream dreams, your young men shall see visions. And also upon the servants and upon the handmaids in those days will I pour out my spirit" (Joel 2:28–29 KJV).

After working through the Old Testament, Livermore turns to New Testament female characters such as Elizabeth, Mary, and Anna as additional examples of key women in leadership. She notes that some religious denominations and groups permit women to preach, including the society of Friends (Quakers), Methodists, Free-Will Baptists, and the Christian Connection. Finally, she contends that the biblical restrictions against women's leadership are time-bound instructions that are not applicable to contemporary women.

Despite her vigorous defense of women's "testimony" as public speakers and preachers, Livermore does not advocate equality between men and women. For example, in letter 3, she claims that men should retain "rule and authority which he can justly claim over households, churches and nations and desire every female to say amen."[19] Also, in letter 12, despite her lengthy argument in favor of women's public religious roles, Livermore admits that she does not believe that women should speak from the pulpit as laypersons or be ordained. Nonetheless, she advocates for women to be able to speak in other public settings. Livermore's work illustrates some of the diversity of women's biblical engagement in the nineteenth century as it upholds scriptural authority and male authority while promoting greater women's rights.

Letters on the Equality of the Sexes and the Condition of Women

Sarah Moore Grimké and Angelina Grimké (later Grimké Weld) were sisters and advocates for the abolition of slavery and for women's rights. Both sisters used biblical texts in their arguments, but Sarah Grimké's *Letters on the Equality of the Sexes and the Condition of Women* (1837) provides an example of how early women's biblical interpretation combats women's subordination.[20] The Grimkés were among the first female public speakers in the United States. In 1835, Angelina Grimké wrote a personal letter to William Lloyd Garrison that encouraged his antislavery efforts. Garrison, a journalist and abolitionist, published the letter in his newspaper *The Liberator* without her permission, and this event catapulted the public speaking careers of both sisters. Born into a slaveholding family in Charleston, South Carolina, the sisters shared their personal experiences regarding slavery, which made them popular speakers. Their abolitionist views generated additional controversy because they were women who spoke in front of what was called a "promiscuous assembly," meaning a mixed audience of men and women.

In a series of letters addressed to Mary S. Parker, the president of the Boston Female Anti-Slavery Society, S. Grimké offers new biblical arguments to support women's legal, economic, and social equality. The letters were published serially in *The Liberator* and later as a collection. According to S. Grimké, her primary purpose in writing these letters is to counter what she understands as the mistranslation and misinterpretation of the Bible in matters relating to women. Grimké engages both Old and New Testament texts in addressing women's equality. She regards the "original" biblical texts as inspired by God, but she does not regard the work of the King James Version translators as inspired by

---

19. Ibid.
20. Sarah Moore Grimké, *Letters on the Equality of the Sexes and the Condition of Women*, addressed to Mary S. Parker (New Haven, CT: Yale University Press, 1988).

God (cf. 2 Tim. 3:16–17) Nevertheless, she looks forward to the innovative translations and interpretations that she believes women will offer once they are permitted to study Greek and Hebrew. | WOW ♡

Grimké uses texts that have traditionally been used to support women's subordination in order to argue for equality between men and women. "Letter I: The Original Equality of Woman" provides Grimké's commentary on the creation accounts in Genesis. Although Grimké does not discuss the Hebrew terminology, she argues that the creation of "man" in Genesis 1:26–27 uses a generic term for man and woman. She regards man and woman as equals who share dominion over creation but not each other. Regarding the second account of creation, Grimké notes that the animals created could have provided company for the man but that woman was created to be a companion who was his equal. She identifies the serpent in the garden as Satan and contends that both Eve and Adam sinned and "fell" from their state of innocence but not from equality. Although Genesis 3:16 specifies that the woman is subject to her husband, Grimké considers this so-called "curse" to be a "simple prophecy." That is, God anticipates that Eve will be subject to Adam in the sense of a prediction but not a command. Grimké reinterprets texts that have traditionally been used to support women's subordination and argues that those texts support the notion of equality between men and women.

At the end of "Letter I," Grimké presses her argument for women's equality by revising English poet John Milton's classic *Paradise Lost*. This highly influential seventeenth-century poem offers a reinterpretation of Adam and Eve's creation and expulsion from the Garden of Eden. Book 12 of Milton's poem reads:

> Authority usurpt, from God not giv'n:
> He gave us only over Beast, Fish, Fowl
> Dominion absolute; that right we hold
> By his donation; but Man over men
> He made not Lord; such title to himself
> Reserving, human left from human free.[21]

Milton depicts God as permitting humanity to have dominion over creation, but he holds that all men are created equal and are subject only to God. Grimké revises Milton and writes,

> Authority usurped from God, not given,
> He gave him only over beast, flesh, fowl,
> Dominion absolute: that right he holds
> By God's donation: but man o'er woman
> He made not Lord such title to himself
> Reserving, human left from human free.[22]

21. John Milton, *Paradise Lost: A Poem in Twelve Books,* a new edition edited by Merritt Y. Hughes (Indianapolis: Hackett Publishing Company, Inc., 2003), 292, lines 66–71.
22. Grimké, *Letters on the Equality of the Sexes,* 34.

Milton's verse reads "man over man," but Grimké substitutes "but man o'er woman." Although Milton stresses the equality of men, Grimké rewrites Milton to argue that men and women have dominion over creation but that both men and women are created equal. Men and women are subject not to each other but only to God. As a biblical interpreter, Grimké engages Milton's classic biblical interpretation by making the equality of humanity explicitly the equality of men and women.

In her "Letter III: The Pastoral Letter of the General Association of Congregational Ministers of Massachusetts," Grimké provides a response to "The Pastoral Letter of the General Association of Massachusetts, June 28, 1837," which condemns women's public speaking. In arguing for women's public activism, she highlights that texts do not specify gender in prescribing behavior for Christians. For example, she quotes from the Sermon on the Mount: "Let your light so shine before men, that they may see your good works, and glorify your Father which is in Heaven" (Matt. 5:16 KJV). She notes that Jesus does not specify gender in requiring service to humanity. Also, she argues that the fruits of the spirit (Gal. 5), which identify the traits of Christian believers, are not specified for men or for women but for all followers of Jesus. Although the pastoral letter requires the "unostentatious prayers and efforts of women," Grimké upholds the prophet Anna (Luke 2) as a woman in public leadership. While the pastoral letter permits women to lead "religious inquirers to the pastor for instruction," Grimké counters that men and women are to "lead souls to Christ, and not to Pastors for instruction."[23] Again, Grimké does not find fault with biblical texts but with the particular interpretations that support inequality. She contends that the distinction of masculine and feminine virtues is part of the "anti-christian 'traditions of men'" not the "commandments of God," and fundamentally, she regards the pastoral letter as "unscriptural."[24] For Grimké, the Scriptures provide a higher authority than the Congregationalist ministers who, in her view, have misinterpreted these biblical texts.

In "Letter XIII: Relation of Husband and Wife" Grimké addresses the New Testament household codes (e.g., Eph. 5:22; Col. 3:18; 1 Pet. 3:2) that are often used to support women's subordination. Her anti-Judaism is exposed as she blames Judaism for the epistles' limitations on women. Commenting on Paul's writings, she states, "I believe his mind was under the influence of Jewish prejudices respecting women."[25] She compares the household codes and notes that these instructions to wives also include a set of instructions to husbands. She argues that the sense of woman as a "weaker vessel" (1 Pet. 3:7) refers only to physical strength. In "Letter XIV: Ministry of Women," she focuses on supporting women in religious leadership. Like Livermore, she claims that the restrictions on women's speaking do not apply to contemporary women. She notes

23. Ibid., 40.
24. Ibid., 38.
25. Ibid., 81.

that on the day of Pentecost (Acts 2) both men and women were present and filled with the Holy Spirit. In addition, she mentions Anna, Miriam, Deborah, Huldah, Priscilla, and other female biblical characters as examples of women in public leadership and ministry.

Grimké's biblical argumentation is a radical departure from the traditional interpretation of texts regarding women during her time. Yet she remains firmly ensconced within Protestant Christian theology. She believes in God and maintains the authority of the Bible and the concept of the fall. Her quarrel is with what she perceives as mistranslation and misinterpretation. Using novel interpretations, she argues for the equality of men and women, including in religious leadership.

Seneca Falls Declaration of Sentiments and Resolutions

The 1848 Seneca Falls Convention was a seminal moment in the struggle for women's rights, and the Declaration of Sentiments and Resolutions provided a public statement of the delegates' concerns regarding women's rights.[26] Modeled on the U.S. Declaration of Independence, the Declaration of Sentiments lists a series of grievances against men for their subjection of women. Instead of throwing off the tyranny of King George and the British, the delegates demand a change of government that provides equality for men and women. The declaration's resolutions offer the delegates' key arguments regarding the condition of women and the necessity of greater equality between men and women. The Declaration of Sentiments and Resolutions does not cite any biblical texts explicitly, but it provides theological and religious arguments based on biblical texts. Furthermore, it offers a direct link to the feminist approaches that develop in critical biblical scholarship in the twentieth century.

The declaration argues for improved women's rights, including religious rights. Also, it claims that both men and women are equals and that they are entitled to basic rights by God. The declaration contends that women have the same abilities as men and should not be limited to the private sphere. Arguing against the ideology of separate spheres, the declaration claims, "He [referring to men] has usurped the prerogative of Jehovah himself, claiming it as his right to assign for her a sphere of action, when that belongs to her conscience and to her God."[27] It continues by pointing out that men are putting themselves in the place of God unjustifiably by circumscribing women's behavior. In arguing against the "disenfranchisement" of women, the declaration also decries the "social and religious degradation" of women. It notes that women are not allowed the same educational or economic opportunities and that "as a teacher of theology, medicine, or law, [woman] is not known."[28] It illustrates

---

26. Stanton, Anthony, and Gage, eds., *History of Woman Suffrage*, 1:70–73.
27. Ibid., 1:71.
28. Ibid.

the importance of theology and religious concerns among other professional roles and social institutions in the struggle for women's rights.

Also, the Declaration of Sentiments and Resolutions decries women's limited roles in Christian churches. It reads, "He [referring to men] allows her in Church, as well as State, but a subordinate position, claiming Apostolic authority for her exclusion from the ministry, and with some exceptions, from any public participation in the affairs of the Church."[29] The "Apostolic authority" mentioned here refers to the view that the power of the church rests in a lineage that extends from Jesus through Peter to contemporary leadership. No biblical text is cited, but the notion of apostolic succession rests on a particular biblical interpretation that only men are authorized church leaders due to the New Testament's portrayal of Jesus' selection of male disciples. Despite the important role of women in ministry in the New Testament and in the early church, some church authorities treat the Bible as providing a normative example of male-only leadership, but the Declaration argues against this narrow interpretation.

In supporting the twelve resolutions, the delegates construct a natural-law argument that there are universal, "divinely implanted" laws, knowable through reason, by which society should be governed. Laws that support the subjugation of women are thus not in keeping with the laws of nature. The resolutions argue that a woman is equal to a man and "was intended to be so by the Creator" and that women have been limited by "corrupt customs and a perverted application of the Scriptures." Furthermore, rejecting a separate-spheres ideology, they claim that women "should move in the enlarged sphere which her great Creator has assigned her."[30] Like Grimké's letters, the resolutions contend that the misinterpretation of biblical texts has limited women's opportunities. The delegates hold to belief in God and the authority of the Bible, but they argue that God does not support women's subordination and that traditional interpretations of the Bible are contrary to the will of God.

Although arguing for equality, the resolutions use the then-current notion that women are naturally morally superior while men are intellectually superior. They claim that since women are morally superior, women should be allowed to speak at religious gatherings. Claiming equality as well as moral superiority, the resolutions support women's private action and public activism, including in religious communities and religious leadership. The eleventh resolution claims that both men and women should be allowed to speak on behalf of moral and religious causes in public and in private.

Related to religious leadership, the final, twelfth resolution states, "The speedy success of our cause depends upon the zealous and untiring efforts of both men and women, for the overthrow of the monopoly of the pulpit and for the securing to woman an equal participation with men in the various trades,

29. Ibid.
30. Ibid., 72.

professions and commerce."[31] As the declarations had noted women's limited educational and employment opportunities, the resolutions stress religious leadership as a key element of women's participation in public life. Like Grimké in her letters, the delegates are willing to submit to the authority of God but not to that of another human being. The Declaration of Sentiments and Resolutions does not offer the same type of detailed commentary on particular biblical texts that Grimké's letters do, yet both documents illustrate the early perspective of women's rights advocates in stating that traditional biblical interpretation has perverted the will of God. They contend that if these texts were properly interpreted, these same texts would allow for equality between men and women. The Bible thus remains a central authority.

In addition, the Declaration of Sentiments and Resolutions illustrates the importance of theological education, which provides access to religious leadership. In turn, this religious leadership provides the opportunity for public teaching and preaching, which gives women opportunities to offer their own interpretations of biblical texts. The publication of the Declaration of Sentiments and Resolutions generated a great deal of publicity, much of which was negative. This publicity pushed some of those who had signed the document to ask to have their names removed in order not to be associated with it. Although widely regarded as a suffrage document, the Declaration of Sentiments and Resolutions addresses religious issues and illustrates the importance of biblical interpretation in efforts to increase women's rights.

The Woman's Bible

Although other nineteenth-century women offered new interpretations of biblical texts in support of women's rights, *The Woman's Bible* is a classic work that is the usual starting point for understanding first-wave feminist biblical interpretation.[32] Headed by abolitionist and suffragist Elizabeth Cady Stanton, this commentary project discusses key texts concerning women in the Old and New Testaments. Part 1 covers Genesis, Exodus, Leviticus, Numbers, and Deuteronomy, while part 2 covers Joshua through Revelation. Although written with a committee, Stanton wrote most of the entries. Not as well-known as *The Woman's Bible* is the pamphlet written by Stanton titled "The Bible and Church Degrade Women," which was included in the 1898 publication of *The Woman's Bible*. Stanton and her committee did not have formal training in academic biblical studies, and the few women who did have facility with Greek and Hebrew chose not to participate in the project. According to Stanton, they feared for their reputations if they became associated with such a radical project. Influenced by Quakerism, spiritualism, and new thought, Stanton did not uphold

31. Ibid., 73.
32. For a detailed history of Stanton and the creation of *The Woman's Bible*, see Kathi Kern, *Mrs. Stanton's Bible* (Ithaca, NY: Cornell University Press, 2001).

the authority of the Bible as did many other women biblical interpreters. Thus, women who did not share Stanton's unorthodox views also chose not to participate. Stanton rejected the notion of "special inspiration," the idea that biblical texts were inspired by God. Instead, she treated biblical texts as works that were subject to the same critical scrutiny as any other. Some detractors of the project argued that it was not necessary to engage the Bible since it was outdated and no longer relevant. Stanton counters, "So long as tens of thousands of Bibles are printed every year, and circulated over the whole habitable globe, and the masses in all English-speaking nations revere it as the word of God, it is vain to belittle its influence."[33] Anticipating the so-called second-wave feminist biblical interpretation, these innovative readings underscore the enduring importance of the Bible both in efforts to maintain patriarchy and to improve the rights of women.

The Woman's Bible offers interpretations that counter those of traditional Christian biblical interpretation. For example, it argues for an understanding of the feminine divine. Many traditional Christian interpreters identify the plural subject in "Let us make man in our image" as referring to the Trinity, including God, the father; Jesus Christ, the son; and the Holy Spirit. In *The Woman's Bible*'s commentary on Genesis, these figures are identified as a father, mother, and son. It opposes the doctrine of the virgin birth as well as the immaculate conception. Yet it claims that "the best thing about the catholic church is the deification of Mary and yet this is denounced by protestantism as idolatry."[34] *The Woman's Bible* notes that the church is metaphorically referred to as female but cautions that "until the feminine is recognized in the divine being, and justice is established in the church by the complete equality of woman with man, the church cannot be thoroughly Christian."[35]

The Woman's Bible highlights several female biblical characters and offers a more positive perspective on their actions than typically found in traditional biblical interpretation. For example, it does not condemn Eve as causing the first sin. Instead, it regards Eve's decision to eat the fruit of the tree of good and evil as a courageous, laudable act since Eve eats in order to gain wisdom. It celebrates Deborah as judge and prophetess and points out that Barak refuses to go into battle without her, which proves her worthiness as a leader. Also, it claims that Deborah is the composer of the poem in Judges 5.

Arguments for gender equality are made throughout *The Woman's Bible*. Although it does not cite S. Grimké explicitly, it similarly argues that the creation accounts in Genesis do not support men's domination of women. Instead, both men and women have dominion over creation but not over each other. Also following Grimké, it refers to the so-called "curse" as a "prediction."[36] It notes the inconsistency in the New Testament epistles since they include texts

33. Elizabeth Cady Stanton, *The Woman's Bible* (New York: European Pub. Co., 1895–1898; reprt. with foreword by Maureen Fitzgerald (Boston: Northeastern University Press, 1993), 11.
34. Ibid., 144.
35. Ibid., 175.
36. Ibid., 27.

that limit women's religious leadership but also texts such as Galatians 3:28 that support equality.

Some anti-Judaism is present in *The Woman's Bible*. This is also a concern in later feminist biblical scholarship. In commenting on the second account of creation (Gen. 2–3), it claims that the second account "was manipulated by some Jew, in an endeavor to give 'heavenly authority' for requiring a woman to obey the man she married."[37] Also, it creates a motivation for Miriam's challenge to Aaron in Numbers 10. According to the commentary, she "saw the humiliating distinctions of sex in the Mosaic code and customs and longed for the power to make the needed amendments."[38]

The Woman's Bible was a political hot potato for women's rights advocates. Some felt that such a project was not politically expedient as it could alienate more religious advocates. In 1896, the National American Woman Suffrage Association passed a resolution distancing itself from *The Woman's Bible* and explaining that it had no affiliation with the project or its publication. Despite these concerns, the commentary became a classic work and sold in several printings. As discussed in chapter 6, the twentieth- and twenty-first-century feminist biblical scholarship commentary the *Women's Bible Commentary* alludes to and acknowledges its debt to the classic, *The Woman's Bible*.

CONCLUSION

These four documents, Harriet Livermore's *Scriptural Evidence in Favor of Female Testimony*, Sarah Moore Grimké's *Letters on the Equality of the Sexes and the Condition of Women*, the Seneca Falls Declaration of Rights and Sentiments, and *The Woman's Bible*, provide examples of nineteenth-century women activists' engagement with biblical texts. They illustrate the importance of biblical interpretation as a tool for upholding women's subordination and as a tool for empowering women. The status quo of women's subordination did not require biblically based arguments to support its continuation, but biblical texts were used to challenge it. Certainly, these documents do not have the same level of critical exegesis as that offered by professionally trained biblical scholars in later periods, but the foundations of that work are in the nineteenth century. Issues regarding differences between men and women and women's roles in society remain important topics in contemporary scholarship. These documents illustrate that since the time of so-called first-wave activism, the push for greater women's equality has been intertwined with biblical interpretation. Like feminism itself, feminist biblical interpretation begins with those who would not have used that term. As discussed in the following chapter, African American women had to argue for the importance of both race and gender among white

37. Ibid., 18.
38. Ibid., 102.

female and African American male activists. Facing racism and sexism, African American women offered new biblical interpretations that underscored the importance of both race and gender. These biblical interpretations anticipate the development of womanist biblical interpretation in the twentieth century.

RESOURCE LIST

Calvert-Koyzis, Nancy, and Heather E. Weir. *Strangely Familiar: Protofeminist Interpretations of Patriarchal Biblical Texts* (Boston: Brill, 2009). This edited volume includes an array of discussions of women interpreters on biblical texts used to support women's subordination.

Grimké, Sarah Moore. *Letters on the Equality of the Sexes and the Condition of Women, Addressed to Mary S. Parker.* Boston: Isaac Knapp, 1838. Edited and with an introduction by Elizabeth Ann Bartlett. New Haven, CT: Yale University Press, 1988. This collection of letters predates *The Woman's Bible* and provides examples of early efforts to argue for greater women's equality.

deGroot, Christiana, and Nancy Calvert-Koyzis. *Recovering Nineteenth-Century Women Interpreters of the Bible* (Atlanta: Society of Biblical Literature, 2007). This volume offers a collection of neglected nineteenth-century women's interpretations of biblical texts.

Stanton, Elizabeth Cady. *The Woman's Bible.* New York: European Pub. Co.,1895–1898. Reprinted with foreword by Maureen Fitzgerald. Boston: Northeastern University Press, 1993. This is a classic early commentary on biblical texts.

Wollstonecraft, Mary. *A Vindication of the Rights of Woman.* Edited by Eileen Hunt Botting. New Haven, CT: Yale University Press, 2014. Includes the influential text by classic British philosopher and writer Mary Wollstonecraft with essays by various contributors.

Chapter 3

Womanist Biblical Interpretation: Forerunners

INTRODUCTION

Theologian and mystic Howard Thurman relates a story involving his grand-mother in his work *Jesus and the Disinherited*. His grandmother was unable to read but asked her family to read the Bible to her. Thurman questions why she never asked him to read any of the Pauline epistles. She explains that when she was enslaved, white ministers preached routinely from Paul and sometimes used Ephesians 6:5 ("Slaves, obey your earthly masters with fear and trembling, in singleness of heart, as you obey Christ") as a text to support slavery. She says, "I promised my maker that if I ever learned to read and if freedom ever came, I would not read that part of the Bible."[1] Thurman's grandmother is reflecting a particular reading strategy that affirmed the importance of the Bible as a libera-tive force. Despite the myriad ways in which the Bible has been used to oppress African Americans, many African American Christian women developed their own interpretations of the Bible in ways that affirmed their humanity and served to combat their subjugation.

1. Howard Thurman, *Jesus and the Disinherited* (New York: Abingdon-Cokesbury Press, 1949), 30–31.

This chapter focuses on African American women's use of the Bible in nineteenth- and early-twentieth-century activism. Although these women are not typically included within the history of feminist biblical interpretation, they provide an important link to the development of womanist biblical interpretation in the twentieth and twenty-first centuries.[2] This chapter provides some historical context regarding the impact of biblical interpretation on the lives of African American women, and it analyzes selected examples of biblical interpretation by four African American women: Maria Stewart, Jarena Lee, Anna Julia Cooper, and Amanda Smith. This legacy of African American women's biblical engagement is part of African American women's history and activism.

HISTORICAL CONTEXT

African Americans and the Bible

The initial engagement between African peoples in the Americas and the Bible was marked by suspicion of the "book religion" from those Africans who relied on oral traditions within their religious practice.[3] Of course, some Africans who were enslaved were literate Muslims.[4] Still, the notion of the "talking book" emerges early within African American literature as African people encountered others who could "hear" the book talk by reading.[5] The Bible was introduced to enslaved persons in an effort to convert them to Christianity by preaching from and reading to them from biblical texts. In particular, the evangelical branch of the Protestant tradition emphasized the importance of both the Bible and one's personal experience of God. African Americans declared their own personal experiences of God and of the revelation of God's word to them.

African American women biblical interpreters are part of the African American literary tradition that made extensive use of biblical texts.[6] Since the colonial era, African American men and women wrote in a variety of literary genres

2. See Katherine Clay Bassard, *Transforming Scriptures: African American Women Writers and the Bible* (Athens: University of Georgia Press, 2010) and Valerie C. Cooper, *Word, Like Fire: Maria Stewart, the Bible, and the Rights of African Americans* (Charlottesville: University of Virginia Press, 2011).

3. See Milton C. Sernett, *African American Religious History: A Documentary Witness*, 2nd ed. (Durham, NC: Duke University Press, 1999); Albert J. Raboteau, *Slave Religion: The "Invisible Institution" in the Antebellum South*, rev. ed. (New York: Oxford University Press, 2004); and Timothy Earl Fulop and Albert J. Raboteau, *African-American Religion: Interpretive Essays in History and Culture* (New York: Routledge, 1997).

4. See Allan D. Austin, *African Muslims in Antebellum America: Transatlantic Stories and Spiritual Struggles*, rev. ed. (New York: Routledge, 1997) and Sylviane A. Diouf, *Servants of Allah: African Muslims Enslaved in the Americas*, 15th anniversary ed. (New York: New York University Press, 2013).

5. Henry Louis Gates, *The Signifying Monkey: A Theory of Afro-American Literary Criticism* (New York: Oxford University Press, 1988).

6. On the relationship of African Americans and biblical texts, see Vincent L. Wimbush, *The Bible and African Americans: A Brief History* (Minneapolis: Fortress Press, 2003).

and often included biblical quotations, allusions, and imagery in their writing. The first poem published by an African American was "An Evening Thought: Salvation by Christ," written by Jupiter Hammon. Phyllis Wheatley, a celebrated eighteenth-century writer, was the first African American writer to publish in *Poems on Various Subjects Religious and Moral* (1773). Absalom Jones, David Walker, Frederick Douglass, and many other African American writers used biblical texts in their work and highlighted the hypocrisy of White Christians who did not treat Africans and African Americans as equal to Whites.

African American Women as Biblical Interpreters

As discussed in chapter 2, the forerunners of contemporary feminist biblical interpretation engage biblical texts in their advocacy efforts. The women profiled and other African American women are not typically thought of as biblical interpreters in the same ways. The fact that African American women do not have documents such as *The Woman's Bible* and explicit biblical commentary on biblical texts plays a role in the neglect of their biblical engagement. African American women's use of biblical texts served to assert their agency, their humanity, and their legitimacy within ministry and leadership within a society that devalued them. They brought their lived experiences as African American women with them as they engaged biblical texts to address their unique situation as both women and as African Americans.

Certainly, personal experience was also an issue for white women. For instance, the Grimkés were popular speakers in part because they were part of a slaveholding family and spoke about their firsthand view of slavery. Their work is linked more easily to the so-called second-wave of feminist biblical interpretation. The biblical engagement of African American women, however, was not part of organized published efforts in the same way. Their more individualized efforts are connected to later womanist work that emphasizes the lived experience of the interpreter. Although these women did not provide an extended discourse on biblical texts like Grimké or Stanton and her committee, still they argued for their rights through their use of biblical quotations and allusions. Although these women would not have identified themselves as feminist or womanist as those terms were not popularly used at that time, their "both/and" concerns regarding race and gender connect to the development of both feminist and womanist biblical interpretation.

Furthermore, for those who were women preachers, evangelists, and ministers, they claimed the right to speak prophetically on behalf of and in the name of God. This was revolutionary in an era in which even white women were not generally permitted to teach, preach, or have active public lives. This effort to seek inclusion within their faith communities and within the wider society was considered a direct assault on the established social hierarchy. Also, these women were speaking during a time period in which persons of African descent were thought to be subhuman and women were considered inferior to men. These interpretations are acts of resistance that are in opposition to traditional main-stream interpretation of biblical texts. Without formal training in theology and often without support or credentials within religious denominational leadership, these African American women dared to claim that they could interpret biblical texts in ways that supported their humanity and their womanhood. They rein-terpreted biblical texts that had been used against them and found a liberating message that supported their public action.

These texts illustrate an early concern with using biblical texts in address-ing both race and gender oppression and highlighting experiences of African American women, including the lived experiences of the authors. Such con-cerns become a hallmark of womanist approaches to biblical interpretation in later periods. African American women's activism in the twentieth and twenty-first centuries was not just a reaction to white women's sometimes exclusionary practices and focused concerns. Furthermore, African American women's bibli-cal engagement was not simply a reaction to feminist biblical engagement but extends back to nineteenth-century African American women biblical interpret-ers. Their "both/and" concern for issues of gender and race provides the founda-tion for womanist scholarship in various academic disciplines in the twentieth century.

Masculinized African American Women

As discussed in chapter 2, understandings of the Bible as authoritative and normative shaped social norms and gender expectations in the United States and contributed to the notion of women as subordinate to men. Nineteenth-century white gendered ideals of "true womanhood" held up the vulnerable, fragile, upstanding white woman who was the "angel of the house." Yet African American women as well as other nonwhite and nonaffluent women were not considered to be "real" women in the same sense as wealthy white women. In particular, U.S. society did not grant to African American women the social status and courtesies granted to a civilized "lady," who was by definition a white woman. Even before the true womanhood ideals became prevalent in the United States, European colonizers regarded African women as uncivilized and hyper-sexual, which supported the persistent view of African American women as masculine, licentious, primitive, and without morals.[7] As well, enslaved women were masculinized by being forced to perform what were regarded as male-gendered tasks within the plantation economy.[8] Furthermore, enslaved women

7. On negative stereotypes and other views of African and African American women, see bell hooks, *Ain't I a Woman: Black Women and Feminism* (Boston: South End Press, 1981); Deborah Gray White, *Ar'n't I a Woman? Female Slaves in the Plantation South*, rev ed. (New York: W.W. Norton, 1999); and Melissa V. Harris-Perry, *Sister Citizen: Shame, Stereotypes, and Black Women in America* (New Haven, CT: Yale University Press, 2011).

8. Susan A. Mann, "Slavery, Sharecropping, and Sexual Inequality," *Signs* 14, no. 4 (1989): 774–98.

were dehumanized and regarded as "breeding stock." Their reproductive labor benefited the slaveholder since children of the enslaved mother followed the condition of the mother (*partus sequitur ventrem*) and were regarded as the property of the slaveholder.

African Americans were regarded as inferior to whites and even subhuman as part of the God-ordained, "natural" order. As abolitionists gained ground, proslavery advocates used biblical texts as the basis for theological and religious justifications of slavery.[9] For example, in Genesis 4:15, God puts a mark on Cain after Cain kills his brother Abel. The "curse of Cain" became interpreted as involving dark skin, with Africans regarded as the accursed descendants of Cain. Also in Genesis 9 Ham, one of the sons of Noah, sees Noah naked while his father is sleeping. When Noah awakes from his drunken stupor, Noah curses Canaan, son of Ham, and says, " 'Cursed be Canaan; lowest of slaves shall he be to his brothers'" (Genesis 9:25). African people were identified as the descendants of Ham in part because Genesis 10:6 associates some of his descendants with parts of Africa. The curse of Ham was used to justify the enslavement of African peoples. These and other texts (e.g., Eph. 6:5; Col. 3:22; 1 Tim. 6:1; and Philemon) were used to argue that slavery was sanctioned by the Bible and that it required obedience of slaves to masters. Even those who did not support slavery still upheld notions of white supremacy and black inferiority partly because of such biblical interpretations.

Within a social and historical context that supported the racial inferiority of African Americans and the gendered inferiority of women, African American women were regarded as subordinate to men and to whites due to both gender and race. Anna Julia Cooper explains at a train station that there are two rooms "for ladies" and "for colored people" and questions which door she should enter. Cooper states, "The colored woman . . . is confronted by both a woman question and a race problem, and is as yet an unknown or an unacknowledged factor in both."[10] Despite the efforts of some activists to separate racial and gender issues, African American women were both women and African Americans. They used biblical texts to argue for greater equality on issues regarding race and gender.

The Bible and African American Women's Witness

Elizabeth, A Colored Minister of the Gospel, Born in Slavery

The pamphlet *Elizabeth, A Colored Minister of the Gospel, Born in Slavery* was a spiritual autobiography of a formerly enslaved woman named Elizabeth (surname unknown). Published originally in 1863 and then in 1889, it recounts

9. On pro- and antislavery arguments using biblical texts, see Mark A. Noll, *The Civil War as a Theological Crisis* (Chapel Hill: University of North Carolina Press, 2006); Stephen R. Haynes, *Noah's Curse: The Biblical Justification of American Slavery* (New York: Oxford University Press, 2002); and Molly Oshatz, *Slavery and Sin: The Fight Against Slavery and the Rise of Liberal Protestantism* (New York: Oxford University Press, 2012).

10. Lemert and Bhan, *The Voice of Anna Julia Cooper*, 112–13.

Elizabeth's life and ministry in the United States and Canada and uses biblical allusion and citation to support her call to and service in Christian evangelism.

Elizabeth describes her early conversion experience by emphasizing her call from God. Born in 1766 to enslaved Methodist parents in Maryland, Elizabeth is sold away from her family. Although she has felt the presence of God since she was five, at around the age of eleven or twelve she has a conversion experience. Seen with her "spiritual eye," a "director, clothed in white raiment" appears to her.[11] This clothing may refer to the message to the church in Sardis in the book of Revelation in which the faithful are clothed in white robes (Rev. 3:5). As she seeks "mercy and salvation," Jesus appears to her and says, "Peace, peace, come unto me" and later asks "Art thou willing to be saved in my way?"[12] at which moment Elizabeth felt that she was forgiven of sin. In her vision, Jesus' words may have reflected his teaching to the disciples from John 6:65, which reads, "For this reason I have told you that no one can come to me unless it is granted by the Father." Because Elizabeth was a Methodist, salvation was not a personal choice to accept Jesus as Savior but a state initiated by God. Accepting salvation, Elizabeth is instructed to "call the people to repentance, for the day of the Lord was at hand," which she receives as a message with a "heavy yoke."[13] This call may reflect Matthew's call to discipleship in which Jesus says, "But go ye and learn what that meaneth, I will have mercy, and not sacrifice: for I am not come to call the righteous, but sinners to repentance (9:13 KJV; cf. Mark 2:17; Luke 5:32). In this text, Jesus cites Hosea 6:6, "For I desired mercy, and not sacrifice; and the knowledge of God more than burnt offerings" (KJV) in response to the Pharisees' question regarding Jesus' choice to eat with tax collectors and sinners, the people he has called to repentance. Several prophetic texts speak of "the day of the LORD" when God's wrath will be revealed (Isa. 13:9; Jer. 46:10; Ezek. 30:3) while the "heavy yoke" image refers to difficult burdens imposed (1 Kgs. 12; 2 Chr. 10). Elizabeth's use of biblical texts, language, and allusion support her call by God to salvation and to prophetic service.

In addressing the opposition that she faces as an African American woman who preaches, Elizabeth compares herself to various figures in biblical texts who faced opposition. Having been freed at age thirty, at age forty-two, Elizabeth moves into more active ministry as she feels that she must deliver the message that she has received despite her limited understanding of the Bible. She claims that she is rejected "as Christ was rejected by the Jews before me."[14] Also, she compares herself to the "speckled bird" of Jeremiah 12:9 who is persecuted by others and to Daniel and the persecutions that he faced. Despite opposition,

---

11. Elizabeth, *Elizabeth, A Colored Minister of the Gospel* (Philadelphia, 1889). Reprinted in Bert James Loewenberg and Ruth Bogin, *Black Women in Nineteenth-Century American Life: Their Words, Their Thoughts, Their Feelings* (University Park: Pennsylvania State University Press, 1976): 127–34.

12. Ibid., 129.

13. Ibid.

14. Ibid., 132.

she determines that she would go on "to prison and to death." Here, Elizabeth invokes Peter's words in Luke 22:33 in which Peter expresses his commitment to follow Jesus. After reasserting herself, Elizabeth feels that she is filled with light and that she "knew nothing but Jesus Christ, and Him crucified."[15] This reference echoes Paul's letter to the Corinthians in which he claims that he did not come to them with lofty words but preaching only "Jesus Christ, and him crucified" (1 Cor. 2:2). Her message, like that of Paul, will be only preaching about Jesus. She mentions taking the text "Woe to the rebellious city," which is from Zephaniah 3:1.[16]

Elizabeth faces opposition because of her race, gender, and message. She asserts that there were people who did not believe "that a colored woman could preach."[17] Also, she acknowledges that some sought to imprison her due to her antislavery sentiments. As an uneducated and nonordained woman, Elizabeth claims that she is ordained by God. She counters those who claim that there is no revelation by mentioning John at Patmos, who has a revelation of the risen Christ. Following this confrontation, she says in her "spirit," "Get thee behind me Satan," which echoes the words of Jesus following his temptation (Matt. 16:23; Mark 8:33; Luke 4:8).[18]

Elizabeth weaves biblical characters, allusions, and citations into her brief spiritual autobiography. At a time when white women were not public speakers, she is a formerly enslaved African American woman who dares to claim that she has been called by God to deliver a message to the people of God. She uses biblical texts not to argue chapter and verse regarding women's equality but to argue that she, an unlettered African American woman, can and must continue the ministry of Christian evangelism.

Farewell Address

Maria W. Stewart (1803–1879) was a nineteenth-century writer and public speaker. She was also an abolitionist and women's rights activist. Raised in Connecticut, she was a free African American woman born to free African American parents. She may have been the first woman political speaker to address publicly a "promiscuous" audience, a public audience of both men and women.[19] Due to the hostility that she faced as a public speaker, Stewart chose to retire from public life and became an educator. In saying goodbye to her public efforts, Stewart gave her "Farewell address to her friends in the city of Boston" (September 21, 1833) at the Belknap Baptist Church in Boston, Massachusetts.[20]

15. Ibid., 131.
16. Ibid., 133.
17. Ibid.
18. Ibid., 133–34.
19. The first woman speaker is likely Deborah Sampson Gannett, a woman who served in the American Revolutionary War while disguised as a man. See Judith Anderson, *Outspoken Women: Speeches by American Women Reformers*, 1635–1935 (Dubuque, IA: Kendall/Hunt, 1984), 135.
20. Garrison's *Liberator* published four of her public addresses. Her lectures were collected and published in *Productions of Mrs. Maria Stewart* (1835), and a revised and expanded edition was

In this address, she uses her personal experience along with numerous biblical quotations and allusions to justify her public speaking role while simultaneously retiring from that role and rebuking those who have opposed her. Her work is not typically considered biblical interpretation, but it provides an example of the link between biblical interpretation and African American women's activism.

Justifying her public service as divinely ordained, Stewart uses biblical texts to defend her public speaking career. She understands herself as doing the work of the Lord as called by God. For instance, during the course of her religious conversion and consecration she has a spiritual experience in which she is asked whether she is able "to drink of the cup that I have drank of? And to be baptized with the baptism that I have been baptized with?" (Mark 10:38; Matt. 20:22, her paraphrase).[21] These are the questions that Jesus asks of James and John, who have asked to sit on the right and left hand of Jesus. Jesus explains that although he will not grant their seating request, they will drink of his cup. That is, they will share in his suffering.

Stewart struggles to accept her calling. Although initially attempting to maintain her secular life, she signals her determination to continue with her religious life by quoting Matthew 6:24: "Ye cannot serve God and mammon." She paraphrases the figurative language of Mark 9:43 to indicate her choice. She writes, "And if thy hand offend thee, cut it off: it is better for thee to enter into life maimed, than having two hands to go into hell, into the fire that never shall be quenched."[22] In this passage from Mark, Jesus instructs his disciples regarding various temptations. Stewart rejects temptation that would prevent her from maintaining a religious life.

Also, in pursuing her Christian vocation, Stewart quotes Romans 8:38–39 to use Paul's encouragement of the church at Rome in distinguishing things of the "flesh" and things of the "spirit."[23] She believes that it is God through the Holy Spirit that guides her decisions. Furthermore, she understands her work as part of her "father's business" (Luke 2:49), as when Jesus' parents search for him in Jerusalem and find him in the temple. Also, she hears something within her that she understands as God telling her, "Press forward, I will be with thee."[24] Despite her struggles, Stewart determines to do zealously what she perceives as the work of the Lord.

Stewart positions herself as one who has suffered for a righteous cause. For example, at the start of her address, she begins with a quotation: "Is this vile world a friend to grace/to help me on to God?"[25] This is a line from the hymn "Am I a Soldier of the Cross?" by Isaac Watts. This militaristic hymn offers a

---

published as *Meditations from the Pen of Mrs. Maria W. Stewart* (1879). Text used here is from the 1835 version as reprinted in Sue E. Houchins, *Spiritual Narratives* (New York: Oxford University Press, 1988).
    21. Ibid., 73.
    22. Ibid.
    23. Ibid.
    24. Ibid., 74.
    25. Ibid., 72.

first-person description of the trials involved in being a follower of Christ. Yet despite these difficulties the speaker is determined to continue and hopes for the glorious return of Christ. Stewart follows the hymn quotation with a reference to Acts 14:22, "Ah no, for it is with great tribulation that any shall enter through the gates of the holy city."[26] In the literary context of Acts, the followers of Jesus face opposition from both Jews and Gentiles as they seek to spread the gospel of Jesus Christ. In particular, Paul and Barnabas encourage others to continue in their faith despite opposition. Stewart uses the Watts hymn and this text as the opening for her address in order to confront the opposition that she has faced from both whites and African Americans in her public speaking career.

In speaking of those who have opposed her public activism, Stewart shares her personal experiences of opposition from African Americans. Regarding her decision to step down from public life, she states, "For I find it is no use for me as an individual to try to make myself useful among my own color in this city." This quote may be an allusion to Jesus' response to his detractors: "A prophet is not without honor except in his hometown and in his own household" (Matt. 13:57; Mark 6:4; Luke 4:24). Furthermore, she charges, "Let us no longer talk of opposition, till we cease to oppose our own."[27] Stewart emphasizes her struggles as an African American woman but maintains that her efforts are honorable and righteous. She explains, "Men of eminence have mostly risen from obscurity; nor will I, although a female of a darker hue, and far more obscure than they, bend my head or hang my harp upon willows; for though poor I will virtuous prove." Here, Stewart invokes Psalm 137:2, in which the Israelites who are in exile in Babylon weep when they think of their destroyed former capital of Jerusalem. Defiantly, even as she is retiring, Stewart maintains that her public speaking was not out of order.

Stewart asks a series of stunning rhetorical questions to advocate for her right to public activism. First, she asks, "What if I am a woman; is not the God of ancient times the God of these modern days?"[28] Using additional rhetorical questions, Stewart compares herself with other historical and biblical women who were called to religious leadership. She stresses that women have been used in service to God and mentions Deborah, Esther, Mary Magdalene, and the adulterous woman (John 4:7–26). She rejects Paul's teachings on women keeping silent and notes that Jesus does not condemn the adulterous woman. Stewart claims that if Paul knew of the sufferings of women, he would have a different view. Also Stewart notes that Peter and James were not educated men but were still chosen by God. Drawing on *Sketches of the Fair Sex*, a nineteenth-century comparative study of the attitudes toward and treatment of women at different times and geographical locations, Stewart highlights the importance of women

26. Ibid.
27. Ibid., 78.
28. Ibid., 75.

in various parts of the world, including Jewish prophetesses, Greek women oracles, Roman sibyls, and Christian women as nuns and martyrs.

Continuing the comparison with other great women throughout history, Stewart asks, "What if such women as are here described should rise among our sable race? And it is not impossible; for it is not the color of the skin that makes the man or the woman, but the principle formed in the soul?"[29] Stewart argues that men and women of African descent are capable of great achievements. She was a pioneering public speaker whose work is not usually regarded as biblical interpretation, but she uses biblical texts to argue for her personhood and her public activism at a time when African Americans were denied personhood and when women were denied public roles. Furthermore, she justifies her actions as divinely sanctioned.

Religious Experience and Journal of Mrs. Jarena Lee

Using the tradition of the spiritual autobiography, nineteenth-century African American Christian missionary and preacher Jarena Lee discusses her religious encounters and her extensive travels and experiences as an itinerant preacher in *Religious Experience and Journal of Mrs. Jarena Lee, Giving an Account of Her Call to Preach the Gospel*.[30] Lee uses biblical texts and her personal experiences to support her calling and to argue for the equality of men and women before God. Born in 1783 in New Jersey, she was employed in domestic service at the age of seven. She was not raised as a Christian but experienced a conversion process later in life. Lee details the difficulties in her family life as a widow and mother and the hostility that she faces as an African American woman preacher.

In her autobiography, Lee uses biblical texts to justify her understanding of a divine call to preach. She uses Joel 2:28 as the epigram for her book: "And it shall come to pass . . . that I will pour out my Spirit upon all flesh; and your sons and your *daughters* shall prophesy."[31] Lee claims that she hears a voice telling her to preach, but she resists. The voice tells her, "Preach the Gospel; I will put words in your mouth, and will turn your enemies to become your friends."[32] Lee may have understood the voice as a theophany, an appearance of God, particularly if the words allude to Isaiah 51:16 ("I have put my words in your mouth"), a text in which the Lord offers comfort to the restored Israel. Later, she has a vision of a pulpit with a Bible and in which she sees herself preaching. She understands her call to preach as a command from God.

Following this initial call experience, Lee seeks permission from Rev. Richard Allen to pursue her call to preach. Allen was the first bishop and founder of

---

29. Ibid., 78.

30. Lee's spiritual autobiography, *Religious Experience and Journal of Mrs. Jarena Lee, Giving an Account of Her Call to Preach the Gospel*, was published in 1849, which was an expanded version of her 1836 publication *The Life and Religious Experience of Jarena Lee, a Coloured Lady*. Text used here is from the 1849 text as reprinted in Houchins, *Spiritual Narratives*.

31. Ibid., 3.

32. Ibid., 10.

the African Methodist Episcopal Church, the first African American Christian denomination. He informs Lee that Methodists permit women to offer exhortation and to hold prayer meetings but do not permit women to serve as preachers. Despite Allen's stand against racial discrimination in churches, he does not support equal opportunity of men and women in church leadership. Initially deflated by Allen, Lee realizes the dangers of responding to human authority rather than to divine authority. She warns, "O how careful ought we to be, lest through our by-law of church government and discipline, we bring into disrepute even the word of life."[33] Despite going against prevailing social standards for women and against her own denominational leadership, Lee contends that she must be faithful to God above all else.

Lee uses biblical texts to argue that men and women are equal before God and that both can be used as instruments of God. Lee asks rhetorically, "And why should it be thought impossible heterodox, or improper for a woman to preach? Seeing the Savior died for the woman as well as the man."[34] Here, Lee may be alluding to Luke 1:37 ("For nothing will be impossible with God") in which the angel Gabriel tells Mary of the pregnancy of Elizabeth, despite Elizabeth's age. Lee uses male and female characters from biblical texts to support her position. For example, she refers to Mary as the first to preach the resurrection of Christ (Matt. 28:1–10; Mark 9:11; Luke 24:1–12; John 20:11–18). Lee compares herself to the prophet Jonah (Jonah 2:9) as one who had been reluctant to accept a call. She also writes of feeling suicidal at points in her journey and thus compares herself to Noah as "a fanatic, deluded, and beside himself."[35] Not limiting herself to women leaders, Lee parallels her own call with biblical narratives of both men and women called by God.

Lee acknowledges both her race and gender in her struggles and successes as a preacher. For example, she mentions an old slaveholder who did not believe that "coloured people had any souls,"[36] who is won over and states his public support of preaching. In detailing her extensive travels and her effectiveness in preaching to both whites and blacks, she writes, "Here by the instrumentality of a poor colored woman, the Lord poured forth his spirit among the people."[37] Lee refers back to her epigram of Joel 2:29 while explicitly stating her position as an African American woman. She underscores the work of God in using her as a tool for ministry. For instance, she expands on Acts 10:35 by writing, "He that feareth God and worketh righteousness shall be accepted of Him—not he who hath a different skin—not he who belongs to this denomination, or, to that—but he that feareth God." Lee contends that God has chosen her to preach regardless of her skin color or denomination.

33. Ibid., 11.
34. Ibid.
35. Ibid.
36. Ibid., 19.
37. Ibid., 18.

In addition to noting her race and gender, Lee acknowledges education as another element that would seem to disqualify her from preaching. She has not received a formal education and claims that she has had only three months of schooling. Yet she notes that although the disciples of Jesus were not learned men, Jesus still called them to preach the gospel. Furthermore, Lee uses the popular misconception that blind persons have additional sensory powers in other areas in order to support her fitness for ministry. She quotes Romans 13:14: "For as many as are led by the *Spirit* of God are the sons of God."[38] She claims that without education she has been more open and in tune with the Spirit of God and uses this verse in Romans to contend that she is ordained by God, despite the gender-specific language in this verse. For Lee, neither her gender, race, nor lack of education should be deterrents in following the will of God.

Lee highlights her ability to win over detractors who oppose her due to both her race and gender. She recounts a response to such opposition: "If an ass reproved Balaam, and a barn-door fowl reproved Peter, why should not a woman reprove sin?" This response uses the story of a talking donkey (Num. 22:21–38) and the crowing of the cock in Matthew 26:34; 74–75 when Peter denies Jesus. In the story of Balaam's ass, Balaam is a prophet who is on his way to Balak, king of Moab. The angel of the Lord impedes his path, but Balaam is unable to see the angel, although his ass does. After resisting Balaam three times, the ass speaks to Balaam after the Lord opens its mouth. Then, the Lord opens Balaam's eyes to see the angel. Lee offers the comment of an unnamed "poor woman, who had once been a slave" who, hearing objections regarding women preachers, replied, "Maybe a speaking woman is like an ass —but I can tell you one thing, the ass seen the angel when Balaam didn't."[39] Lee notes the uncomplimentary linking of women with animals but points out that the ass was able to do what Balaam was not. Lee uses these stories to support not only her call but her successful ministry.

Although she is not thought of as a biblical interpreter, Lee's insistence on her call to preach is a form of biblical interpretation and a form of protest. Despite the pervasive view of white superiority and the social and religious prohibitions against women speaking publically and preaching, she embodies and offers a message of equality and freedom. She uses biblical texts alongside of her personal experience to support greater opportunities for African American women. Lee acknowledges the typical view of the impropriety of women's speaking and preaching in public, but she argues that even if her call to preach is not sanctioned by church or society, it comes from God, who is a higher authority than any human or institution.

38. Ibid., 97.
39. Ibid., 23.

Womanhood: A Vital Element in the Regeneration and Progress of a Race

Anna Julia Cooper was an educator, writer, and social activist who was the fourth African American woman to earn a doctoral degree. Cooper received her doctorate in French from the Sorbonne in Paris, France.[40] In 1892, Cooper published *A Voice from the South: By a Black Woman from the South*, a wide-ranging collection of speeches and essays that addresses the plight of African American women. In her speech "Womanhood: A Vital Element in the Regeneration and Progress of a Race" (1886), Cooper expresses the importance of African American women in the struggle for racial progress and uses biblical texts to make claims for greater equality.[41] Delivered to the Washington D.C. convocation of colored clergy of the Protestant Episcopal Church, her speech is not a sermon or an explicitly religious speech. Still, Cooper, although not a minister or missionary, engages the Bible in expressing her concern for both race and gender issues.

In "Womanhood," Cooper uses biblical texts to argue for equality of men and women, especially in the sense of a moral code. Without citing the particular biblical text explicitly or describing the details of the text, Cooper notes Jesus' refusal to condemn the woman caught in adultery (John 8:1–11). Also, without naming Mary and Martha, she notes that Jesus enjoyed their friendship and hospitality (Luke 10:38–42). Cooper notes Jesus' command to Peter, "the disciple whom he loved": "Behold thy mother!" (John 19:26–27 KJV) and argues Jesus' entrusting his mother into the hands of Peter illustrates Jesus' concern not only for his own family but for women in general. Perhaps alluding to the creation of woman in Genesis 2:18, Cooper contends that Jesus considers women "as an equal, as a helper, as a friend, and as a sacred charge to be sheltered and cared for with a brother's love and sympathy."[42] Cooper uses Jesus' actions in order to position women as needing the care and support of men while remaining their equals.

Cooper attacks the masculinization of African American women, which she calls "that supercilious caste spirit in America which cynically assumes 'a Negro woman cannot be a lady.'"[43] In arguing for the importance of caring for African American women because they are "mothers of the next generation," Cooper reworks the story of Cain and Abel (Genesis 4) and states, "I am my sister's keeper."[44] In Genesis, after Cain kills Abel, Cain responds to God's query with a question: "Am I my brother's keeper?" (Genesis 4:9). Cooper changes Cain's question into a declarative and affirmative statement. This innovative

40. For online information, see the Anna Julia Cooper Center on Gender, Race, and Politics in the South. The center is led by political scientist and media commentator Melissa Harris-Perry, http://cooperproject.org/.

41. Cooper's "Womanhood" essay appears in Lemert and Bhan, *The Voice of Anna Julia Cooper*, 53–71.

42. Ibid., 57.

43. Ibid., 64.

44. Ibid.

interpretation supports Cooper's claim that women's importance derives primarily from their roles as mothers who are responsible for the education and Christian training of the young. She is advocating for the collective responsibility of both men and women to care for African American women. While individual efforts are important, she argues that the future of the "Negro" race collectively depends on its women. To argue that African American women require nurture and protection counters the prevailing view of African American women as sub-human breeding stock. Although Cooper includes notions of separate spheres and complementary roles for women, she still advocates for gender equality and in particular for the rights of African American girls and women.

In addition to their roles as mothers, Cooper claims that African American women have an essential role to play in Christian evangelism. She tells the clergymen that we "must be about our father's business" (Luke 2:49) using Jesus' reply to his parents who were searching for him at the Passover festival in Jerusalem. She points out that successful evangelism to African Americans will require a human touch. In stressing the importance of this personal connection, Cooper notes that "the Word was made flesh, and dwelt among us" (John 1:14 KJV) and that Jesus "drew" (perhaps an allusion to John 12:32) humanity toward God.

Cooper's speech is only sprinkled with biblical allusions, but it still provides an example of the use of biblical texts in supporting equality of men and women. In a period in which mainstream white society held that women were inferior to men and that African Americans were inferior to whites, Cooper's claim of the importance of African American women to their race and to the church in front of an audience of African American clergymen provides an early and innovative use of biblical texts within African American women's activism.

CONCLUSION

The African American women profiled here are not typically thought of as biblical interpreters, but they provide an important link to the development of womanist biblical interpretation in the twentieth century by demonstrating a legacy of African American women's biblical engagement. Despite mainstream racist and sexist ideologies, some African American women activists interpreted biblical texts in new ways that challenged standard views of the public role of women. This effort to seek inclusion within their faith communities and within the wider society was considered a direct assault on the established social hierarchy. It is not an encounter with white women in the 1960s that brought African American women to these issues or that brought about womanist biblical interpretation. Their concern for issues of gender and race provides an important link to the development of womanist biblical interpretation in the twentieth century by demonstrating a legacy of African American women's biblical engagement.

RESOURCE LIST

Bassard, Katherine Clay. *Transforming Scriptures: African American Women Writers and the Bible*. Athens: University of Georgia Press, 2010. Discusses the literary production of African American women and its connections with biblical texts.

Foster, Frances Smith. *Written by Herself: Literary Production by African American Women, 1746–1892*. Bloomington: Indiana University Press, 1993. This volume highlights African American women's writings in the eighteenth and nineteenth centuries.

Harper, Frances Ellen Watkins, and Frances Smith Foster. *A Brighter Coming Day: A Frances Ellen Watkins Harper Reader*. New York: Feminist Press at the City University of New York, 1990. This volume is a collection of varied writings by Frances Ellen Watkins Harper, including fiction and nonfiction.

Loewenberg, Bert James, and Ruth Bogin. *Black Women in Nineteenth-Century American Life: Their Words, Their Thoughts, Their Feelings*. University Park: Pennsylvania State University Press, 1976. This edited volume provides introductory essays and a collection of various writings by nineteenth-century African American women.

Waters, Kristin, and Carol B. Conaway, eds. *Black Women's Intellectual Traditions: Speaking Their Minds*. Lebanon, NH: University Press of New England, 2007. This edited volume highlights the contributions of African American women as activists and intellectuals.

PART II
CONTEMPORARY
SCHOLARSHIP

Chapter 4

Womanism in Religious-Studies-Related Fields

The $60,000 Pyramid is an old game show in which the contestants work with a partner. One person names a list of items while the second person attempts to guess what they all have in common. It is a game of categorization. The sky, Smurfs, 1960s eye shadow. Things that are blue. If I name a list of scholars in religious studies, such as James Cone, Stanley Hauerwas, Walter Bruggemann, and Diana Eck, it is not assumed that they have anything in common except the study of religion. Most people familiar with religious studies would not think that they do the same type of scholarship or work in the same areas or have the same interests. Scholars identify themselves in particular ways. For instance, a scholar may self-identify as a theologian, an ethicist, or a historian. Of course, each person should be able to identify as he or she wishes, but within the academy, labeling has significant consequences because it affects the academy's perception of someone as a scholar.

Yet if I name Emilie Townes, Delores Williams, and Cheryl Townsend Gilkes, although they are scholars in ethics, theology, and sociology, respectively, many academics would categorize them as womanists. The use of the term *womanist* links together these three scholars although they may not use the term in the same ways or use the same types of sources or methods. Given the relatively few numbers of African American women in academic religious studies and the loose use of the term *womanist*, African American women scholars are presumed to be womanists regardless of their personal identification or scholarly training.

In this chapter, I discuss selected contemporary womanist work in religious-studies-related fields with an emphasis on how these works engage with Walker's definition of *womanist* as discussed in the introduction as well as the features of their womanist approach and their use of biblical texts. This discussion demonstrates important links with African American women's activism (discussed in chapter 3), particularly regarding its emphasis on lived experience, which predates modern feminist and womanist scholarship. Also, it provides background for the treatment of womanist scholarship in biblical studies in chapter 6. This survey is not a representative sample of womanist scholarship, and the discussion does not represent the full body of each scholar's work. The scholars reviewed in this chapter are not biblical scholars in the academic sense of the term, and their primary aim is not to develop a womanist biblical hermeneutic or womanist readings of biblical texts. To be clear, my aim is not to offer a substantive scholarly critique of their work or to disparage their use or nonuse of biblical texts. Rather, this chapter serves to distinguish the work of those using womanist approaches in religious-studies-related fields from that of biblical studies. This chapter provides background regarding womanist approaches in religious-studies-related fields and highlights the work of pioneering scholars.

BACKGROUND

Womanist Approaches

In the 1980s some African American women began to self-identify as womanist in preference to feminist, and within the academy, some African American women started to develop black feminist and womanist approaches to their scholarship. Although womanist scholars in religious-studies-related fields (e.g., theology, ethics, and practical theology) are often grouped together as womanists, there is considerable disciplinary diversity among these scholars. They differ in terms of their academic training, and they use discipline-specific types of evidence, methods, and scholarly conventions. Despite disciplinary differences, womanist scholars in various fields in religious studies cite one another's work, critique one another, and engage in conversation across disciplines and across scholarly generations.[1]

1. Some scholars treat the developments within womanist religious thought as first, second, and third waves. Unlike treatments of the first wave as nineteenth-century pioneers, these three waves involve twentieth- and twenty-first-century scholars. For example, Stacy Floyd-Thomas refers to Katie Cannon, Jacquelyn Grant, and Delores Williams as "matriarchs" and refers to a second and third generation of scholars. Monica Coleman also refers to three waves of womanist religious thought.

In general, womanist scholars in religious-studies-related fields do not offer readings of biblical texts or engage biblical scholarship in ways that one would anticipate from biblical scholars. This is to be expected given their respective disciplines. What is problematic is when womanist scholars from these fields and from biblical studies are grouped together. For example, African American anthropologist Linda Thomas writes, "Names associated with the emergence of womanist theology in the U.S.A. are Katie Cannon, Emilie Townes, Jacqueline Grant, Delores Williams, Cheryl Townsend Gilkes, Kelly Brown Douglas, Renita Weems, Shawn Copeland, Clarice Martin, Francis Wood, Karen Baker-Fletcher, Jamie Phelps, Marcia Riggs, and Cheryl Kirk-Duggan."[2] By grouping together these fourteen African American women scholars, Thomas gives the mistaken impression that they are all theologians who use womanist approaches. Yet they are in different fields, including but not limited to theology, ethics, and biblical studies.

In *Introducing Womanist Theology*, Stephanie Mitchem explains, "If black women's lives and religious meanings have been deemed unworthy of serious study, then womanist theologians must employ the interdisciplinary tools of history, ethnography, literary criticism, folklore, sociology, economics, and medicine. Uses of different disciplines are liberatory practices. The rich textures and gifts of African American religious lives, from women's perspectives, need exploration."[3] Mitchem calls on womanist theologians to embrace interdisciplinary approaches. Such cross-disciplinary work can be fruitful in developing new avenues for research and collaboration, but it becomes problematic when the term *womanist* is used to group together scholars whose work shares little other than its being labeled with that term.

Womanist Sources

Despite their disciplinary differences, womanist scholarship in religious studies shares some commonalities regarding the sources it uses, including its limited use of biblical texts and its frequent use of the lived experiences of African American women. The use of the Bible as a source in womanist religious studies scholarship varies greatly. While some of these scholars acknowledge the historical and ongoing importance of the Bible in African American Christian communities, they do not commonly use biblical texts as source material. Even among those scholars who engage biblical texts, most do so in very limited ways. That is, they often discuss particular biblical characters or traditional Christian interpretations of biblical texts without offering their own detailed, exegetical treatment of texts. Of course, it is important to acknowledge that these scholars are not biblical scholars and that their research questions do not require extensive

2. Linda E. Thomas, "Womanist Theology, Epistemology, and a New Anthropological Paradigm," *Cross Currents* 48, no. 4 (1998), http://crosscurrents.org/thomas.
3. Stephanie Y. Mitchem, *Introducing Womanist Theology* (Maryknoll, NY: Orbis Books, 2002), 61.

engagement with biblical texts. In contrast, biblical studies treats biblical texts along with other ancient Near Eastern literature and material culture as its principal source material.

Another of the distinctive features of womanist scholarship in religious studies is the frequent use of the lived experience of African American women as a source. Contemporary womanist scholars in religious-studies-related fields mine African American women's history, art, and literature and use them as important sources for their explorations. Novels, sermons, speeches, autobiographies, and data on the lives of African American women provide foundational material that these scholars analyze and use for reflection within their work. In some instances scholars use work of individual writers and activists while in other instances they refer to the collective experiences of African American women. Also, many of these scholars include personal anecdotes and cite their own personal experiences as African American women. Although the terminology regarding womanist work developed in the 1980s, African American women's emphasis on their lived experience as women and as African Americans predates the use of the term *womanist*, as discussed in chapter 3. In this sense, contemporary womanist scholarship is not simply a by-product of feminist scholarship but grows out of a distinctive tradition of African American women's activism.

Terminology Controversies

Among womanist scholars in religious studies, most use *womanist* as a descriptive term in conjunction with their particular disciplinary identification. For example, the scholars profiled in this chapter identify as womanist theologians or womanist ethicists. In general, these scholars use *womanist* to refer to both themselves and their scholarly work. Yet not all African American women use the word *womanist*. Of course, there is no reason that African American women should feel in any way obligated to use the term *womanist* to identify themselves. Yet, due to the popularity of the term inside and outside of the academy, many people assume that *womanist* is synonymous with African American woman. Such usage conflates the scholar and her scholarship.

As discussed in chapter 1, there is a long history regarding African American women's involvement in mainstream feminist activities and their self-identifying as either feminist or womanist. This remains a live-wire issue within religious studies. Scholars have many different reasons for their choices to identify with particular terms or not. Yet due to the popularity of the term, many people assume that an African American female scholar identifies herself and her work as womanist regardless of the subject of such work. To identify oneself and/or one's work differently is often perceived as opting out of the default womanist position.

For example, social ethicist Traci West identifies as a "black feminist scholar/activist" and offers a response to self-identified womanists in an edited volume on womanism in religion and society.[4] West acknowledges the contributions of womanist scholarship but explores some of the problematic ways in which *womanist* is used in religious studies. She questions the potential "dangers of parochialism that might be inherent in this [womanist] project." That is, womanists may have the potential to become cliquish and overly narrow in scope. Also, after relating an anecdote in which a friend chided her for identifying as feminist by explaining, "We aren't feminists; we're womanists," West asks, "But, if there is such a consensus being promoted by womanists, how can they avoid the contradiction of circumscribing conformity and policing black womanhood while claiming to free it from the bondage of too few acceptable forms?"[5] For West, one of the dangers of accepting the notion that African American women religious scholars should identify as womanists is that it narrowly construes and limits African American women's scholarly contributions. To require a particular self-identification of scholars of a particular race and gender confines African American women to a marginalized space within the academy.

In a well-cited roundtable discussion, ethicist Cheryl Sanders questions the appropriation of *womanist* within the academy and particularly within ethical and theological conversations.[6] She critiques the selective and what she considers to be distorted uses of Walker's definition, particularly within religious studies. Due to its development outside of Christianity, Sanders considers womanist approaches to involve the secular rather than the sacred and questions its use within Christian theology and ethics.

Furthermore, Sanders contends that the inclusion of homosexuality within Walker's definition makes it incompatible with Christian faith and practice. Sanders writes, "In my view there is a fundamental discrepancy between the womanist criteria that would affirm and/or advocate homosexual practice, and the ethical norms the black church might employ to promote the survival and wholeness of black families."[7] Thus, the segment "a woman who loves other women, sexually and/or nonsexually" and the segment "committed to survival and wholeness of entire people, male *and* female" within part 2 of Walker's definition[8] are incompatible with Sanders's notion that African American marriages and families do not include same-gender loving couples. Sanders asserts, "The term 'womanist theology' is in my view a forced hybridization of two disparate concepts and may come to resemble another familiar hybrid, the mule, in being incapable of producing offspring."[9]

4. Traci C. West, "Is a Womanist a Black Feminist? Marking the Distinctions and Defying Term," in *Deeper Shades of Purple: Womanism in Religion and Society*, ed. Stacey M. Floyd-Thomas (New York: New York University Press, 2006), 291–95.

5. Ibid., 294–95.

6. Cheryl Sanders, "Roundtable Discussion: Christian Ethics and Theology in Womanist Perspective," *Journal of Feminist Studies in Religion* 5, no. 2 (Fall 1989): 83–91.

7. Ibid., 90.

8. Walker, *In Search of Our Mothers' Gardens: Womanist Prose* (Orlando, FL: Harcourt, Inc., 1983), xi.

9. Sanders, "Roundtable Discussion," 89.

The scholars who respond to Sanders in the same volume offer varied perspectives on Sanders' charges against the term *womanism*.[10] Some scholars find that Sanders has focused narrowly on Walker's definition without acknowledging the importance of black feminist thought that predates Walker's 1983 definition or the importance of womanist work that has evolved beyond Walker's definition. Others note the ways in which womanism has been embraced due to its resonance with many African American women who feel alienated from white feminism. Also, some contend that Sanders has exaggerated the link between womanism and same-gender loving sexuality and that her macrocritique makes generalizations regarding the use of the term *womanism* without offering substantive engagement with the work of particular womanist scholars. Although the responses differ with Sanders regarding specific arguments, there is some agreement regarding the importance of raising pertinent questions about identity, labeling, appropriation, and methodology.

The question of naming continued in another roundtable discussion in the *Journal of Feminist Studies in Religion*, which focused on the issue of naming with a lead essay "Must I Be a Womanist?" (2006) by theologian Monica Coleman.[11] Coleman identifies herself as a black, female, religious scholar and provides a thorough discussion of key issues and challenges relating to the identification of womanists within religious studies. Coleman notes that womanist scholarship within religious studies has been dominated by Christians, especially those with commitments to produce work for both the church and the academy. Coleman claims that this "Christian hegemonic discourse" has had a great influence on the development of the field and has contributed to its failure to address religious pluralism among African Americans.[12]

While some scholars, such as Brown Douglas, address issues of sexuality as discussed later in this chapter, Coleman notes the relative silence of womanist scholars regarding homosexuality and the heteronormative assumptions made in their work. She charges womanist scholars with a lack of engagement in contemporary political agendas and describes their work as largely descriptive but not engaged in particular issues. Coleman questions the exclusivism and usefulness of womanist religious scholarship if it is only "by and for and about black women."[13] Furthermore, she highlights what she perceives as the "commodification and commercialization" of womanist work within academy.[14] She contends that some African American women may feel pressured to label themselves and their scholarly output as *womanist* in order to

10. For responses to Sanders by Katie G. Cannon, Emilie M. Townes, M. Shawn Copeland, bell hooks, and Cheryl Townsend Gilkes, see ibid., 92–112. Also, see Sanders's response, ibid., 109–12.
11. Monica A. Coleman, "Must I Be a Womanist?" *Journal of Feminist Studies in Religion* 22, no. 1 (2006): 85–96.
12. Ibid., 89.
13. Ibid., 91.
14. Ibid., 93.

fulfill expectations by editors, colleagues, and potential employers regarding African-American women scholars. Finally, Coleman anticipates a third wave of womanist religious scholarship that will perhaps redefine notions of the term *womanism*.

In seven response essays, religious scholars and activists raise numerous objections to Coleman's articulation of concerns regarding the use of the term *womanism* in religious studies, although not all of the essays address Coleman's arguments directly.[15] Some of the responses applaud Coleman's efforts to question the use of this term within religious studies and her attention to the focus on Christianity within womanist religious scholarship. Others celebrate the success of African American women in building a body of work and establishing womanist work within the academy. In response to the issue regarding external pressure to identify oneself or one's work as womanist, some respondents point out that some African American women scholars do not identify as womanists and that their careers and publications have been successful without the relying on that term.

Coleman revisits her 2006 essay in the introduction to an edited volume *Ain't I a Womanist Too: Third Wave Womanist Religious Thought*. Here Coleman claims that African American women are not owners of the term *womanist*. She explains, "I'd like to take the radical position that black women relinquished ownership of the term 'womanism' when they published it and brought it into the academy, just as Walker loses definitional rights to her term 'womanist' to the 'womanisms' that developed from her term."[16] Coleman suggests that womanist religious scholarship needs to shift "from identity of the scholar that centers black women's religious experiences and onto the work that is grounded in black women's religious experience."[17] Her work may reflect the growth of womanist religious thought to be more inclusive and to focus less on the scholar and more on the sources with which that scholar engages.

The terminology controversies within womanist religious-studies-related fields are related to an emphasis on personal identity within womanist scholarship, which remains a concern in womanist biblical scholarship. In order to compare and contrast the work of womanist religious-studies-related scholarship and womanist biblical studies in chapter 6, the following discussion focuses on each scholar's womanist approach, engagement with Walker's 1983 definition of *womanism*, and engagement with biblical texts.

15. Monica A. Coleman, "'Must I Be a Womanist?': Roundtable Discussion and Responses," *Journal of Feminist Studies in Religion* 22, no. 1 (2006): 85–134. Includes responses by Katie G. Cannon, Arisika Razak, Irene Monroe, Debra Mubashshir Majeed, Stephanie Y. Mitchem, and Traci C. West.
16. Monica A. Coleman, *Ain't I a Womanist, Too? Third-Wave Womanist Religious Thought* (Minneapolis: Fortress Press, 2013), 18.
17. Ibid.

PIONEERING SCHOLARSHIP

Black Womanist Ethics

Katie G. Cannon's *Black Womanist Ethics* (1988) was one of the first womanist publications in a religious studies field. Cannon's groundbreaking work exposes the unique ways in which African American women provide moral wisdom and express moral agency. Based on her 1983 dissertation from Union Theological Seminary (New York City), "Resources for a Constructive Ethic for Women with Special Attention to the Life and Work of Zora Neale Hurston," Cannon's work illustrates how African American women live as moral agents outside of the norms and values of white, male-dominated society. Cannon uses as her source material literary texts created by African American women with particular emphasis on the work of Zora Neale Hurston. Cannon stresses the importance of drawing on a resource in which African American women define and control images of themselves and their experiences. Cannon does not use the Bible as one of her sources for ethical reflection although she acknowledges its importance within African American culture.[18]

Cannon does not cite Alice Walker's definition of *womanist* but instead makes *black feminist* synonymous with *womanist*, which links to part of section 1 of Walker's definition: "a black feminist or feminist of color."[19] Cannon contends, "Black feminist consciousness may be more accurately identified as Black womanist consciousness, to use Alice Walker's concept and definition."[20] Still, Cannon uses the terms *black* and *womanist* without explanation. Cannon addresses the triple oppression faced by African American women due to race, gender, and class, but she does not articulate explicitly how her womanist approach informs her work.

Although *Black Womanist Ethics* is one of Cannon's most well-known works, her 1985 article "The Emergence of Black Feminist Consciousness" is more important for our purposes because of its links to biblical studies.[21] This article appears in the edited volume *Feminist Interpretation of the Bible*, a classic work in feminist biblical interpretation, although edited by Letty Russell, a theologian. It is likely that Cannon's essay is more well-known in biblical studies because it appears in a volume on feminist biblical interpretation and would probably be read by more biblical scholars than Cannon's ethics volume. Cannon's contribution in *Feminist Interpretation of the Bible* is the only one by an African American scholar, whether man or woman.[22]

18. Katie G. Cannon, *Black Womanist Ethics*, American Academy of Religion Academy 60 (Atlanta: Scholars Press, 1988).

19. Walker, *In Search of Our Mothers' Gardens*, xi.

20. Katie G. Cannon, "The Emergence of Black Feminist Consciousness," in *Feminist Interpretation of the Bible*, ed. Letty M. Russell (Louisville, KY: Westminster John Knox Press, 1985), 40.

21. Ibid.

22. While I cannot speak to the editor's considerations regarding those who were invited to contribute to the volume, in 1985 there were no formally trained African American female biblical scholars.

In this essay, Cannon argues for the importance of the Bible in preserving hope and dignity for African American women. She writes, "The Bible is the highest source of authority for most Black women."[23] She contends that biblical texts are a resource for African American women. Although Cannon speaks of African American women's experiences, she operates from the assumption that most African American women are Christian. Her womanist work highlights the experiences of African American women but makes generalizations regarding those experiences. While her essay is included in a volume on feminist biblical interpretation, Cannon's graduate training included work in biblical studies, but she does not provide any detailed exegesis or in-depth treatment of biblical texts as a biblical scholar might do. Cannon does not provide any principles or methods for a black feminist or womanist reading of biblical texts. In other words, she is not aiming to establish a womanist biblical hermeneutic. To be fair, she is an ethicist writing on the Bible and does not claim to be writing as a biblical scholar.

White Women's Christ and Black Women's Jesus

Jacqueline Grant's *White Women's Christ and Black Women's Jesus: Feminist Christology and Womanist Response* (1989) discusses the figure of Jesus with minimal engagement with biblical texts.[24] In this classic work in womanist theology, Grant does not use the Bible as an authoritative source. Instead, she focuses on African American women's experience as a key source for theological reflection. Although Grant acknowledges that biblical texts serve as a source for theological reflection within feminist theology, she identifies the Bible as one of the tools used in the oppression of women. Grant contends that the Bible must be read within the context of African American women's experiences. Arguing that the Bible has historically been an important part of black women's religious experience, she holds up Howard Thurman's grandmother (mentioned in chap. 3) as a model for black women's biblical engagement. His grandmother was a former slave woman who rejected proslavery texts. Grant discusses the role of Jesus in Christology, but she does not offer a detailed exegetical treatment of any biblical text. Her discussion of Jesus is in the abstract rather than based in a particular biblical representation of Jesus. She focuses primarily on the life of Jesus and his humanity, but she engages Christian concepts of Jesus Christ without focusing on biblical texts.

In dialogue with feminist theology and Christology as well as liberation theology, Grant offers a response from a womanist perspective. She provides an overview of feminist perspectives on Christology and contends that there are two problems with feminist theology: that it is "*White* and *racist*" (Grant's

23. Ibid., 39–40.
24. Jacquelyn Grant, *White Women's Christ and Black Women's Jesus: Feminist Christology and Womanist Response*, American Academy of Religion Academy 64 (Atlanta: Scholars Press, 1989).

italics).[25] She asks, "In light of the struggle of women today, what is the meaning of Jesus Christ?"[26] Reflecting on this question is important because Grant argues that one's perception of Jesus Christ is linked with one's perception of oneself.[27]

Grant claims that feminist theology focuses on white women's experiences. Thus, she chooses to use African American women's experience as a primary source for theological reflection. Grant does not identify her methodology explicitly as womanist but as involving contextualization. She critiques the single-issue focus of white feminist Christology on gender and argues for an analysis of race, sex, and class.

Grant does not mention Alice Walker's definition of *womanist* until the last chapter of the book, "Women's Experience Revisited: The Challenge of the Darker Sister." She does not cite Walker's full four-part definition but mentions Walker's notion of *womanist* as distinct from *feminist* and as referring to "feminists of color."[28] Furthermore, Grant offers her own definitions of *womanist*, including "a strong Black woman who has sometimes been mislabeled as a domineering castrating matriarch . . . one who has developed survival strategies in spite of the oppression of her race and sex in order to save her family and her people" and as "*being* and *acting* out who you are" (Grant's italics).[29] She identifies women of previous eras as womanists, including Sojourner Truth and Jarena Lee. Grant argues, "Black women must do theology out of their tri-dimensional experience of racism/sexism/classism."[30] Although Grant does not explicitly label her approach as womanist from the outset, her focus on the lived experience of black women and on race, gender, and class constitute elements of what she understands as a womanist approach.

Sisters in the Wilderness

A self-identified womanist theologian, Delores Williams's *Sisters in the Wilderness: The Challenge of Womanist God-Talk* (1993) is one of the most well-known works of womanist theology.[31] Delores Williams cites Walker's full four-part definition of *womanist* in a footnote and includes a discussion of differences between womanist and feminist thought. Expanding on the part of Walker's definition that emphasizes survival and wholeness, Williams understands womanist theology as particularly concerned with the "faith, survival and freedom-struggle of African-American women."[32] While her work is in conversation with liberation theology and feminist theology, Williams offers womanist theology

25. Ibid., 195.
26. Ibid., 9.
27. Ibid., 63.
28. Ibid.
29. Ibid., 205.
30. Ibid., 209.
31. Delores S. Williams, *Sisters in the Wilderness: The Challenge of Womanist God-Talk* (Maryknoll, NY: Orbis Books, 1993).
32. Ibid., xiv.

as a corrective that is in dialogue with black churchwomen and that brings the experiences of black women into the larger dialogue of Christian theology.

The Bible is an essential element of Williams's work. Building on Walker's definition's emphasis on survival, Williams identifies a "survival/quality-of-life tradition of African-American biblical appropriation," which serves as the starting point of her development of womanist theology.[33] She derives this survival tradition from two other traditions that she identifies: 1) the liberation tradition of African American biblical interpretation, which emphasizes the importance of the Exodus and the notion of God as being on the side of the oppressed; and 2) a tradition that highlights the importance of female action in the biblical text.

Williams discusses biblical texts in three key segments that focus on the exodus, the life of Jesus, and the story of Hagar. The major biblical engagement in *Sisters in the Wilderness* involves texts on Hagar, which are foundational for the construction of Williams's womanist theology. Treating the story of Hagar (Gen. 16, 21; Gal. 4) and her wilderness experience in particular as parallel to the experience of African American women, Williams highlights the importance of Hagar in African American life and culture, including the Universal Hagar's Spiritual Church.[34] Relying heavily on secondary literature, Williams provides basic background on Genesis 16 and 21, but she does not offer an exegetical reading of Hagar's story or provide a detailed history of biblical interpretation. Furthermore, she does not clearly distinguish the literary portrait of Hagar as a character within the biblical text and historical evidence regarding slavery in the ancient Near East. That is, she does not make clear that biblical Hagar is a literary construction and not a historical figure as would typically be made clear within biblical scholarship. Offering parallels between Hagar's experiences as an enslaved woman and the historical experiences of African American women, Williams treats Hagar as a symbolic figure who serves as a model of resistance and survival for African American women. Her engagement with biblical texts functions primarily to link biblical Hagar with African American women. Williams does not offer the type of focused attention on the text itself that a biblical scholar might provide.

In chapter 6 of *Sisters in the Wilderness*, "Womanist God-Talk and Black Liberation Theology," Williams critiques liberation theology's focus on Exodus and its emphasis on the God of the oppressed. She claims that uncritical regard for biblical texts as liberative is problematic and notes that many biblical texts are clearly nonliberative but supportive of violence, slavery, and other forms of oppression. She encourages the use of the exodus story as a "*holistic story* rather than *event* [Williams's italics]."[35] Despite these critiques, Williams does not offer her own exegetical analysis of Exodus texts nor does she discuss the importance of the exodus metaphor in other biblical texts.

33. Ibid., 6.
34. This is a spiritualist church founded in 1923 in Detroit, Michigan. See Universal Hagar's Spiritual Church Association at http://www.uhsca.org/.
35. Ibid., 150.

Elsewhere in her book, Williams problematizes the Christian notion of Jesus Christ's suffering and death on the cross as redemption for human sin. Informed by her discussion of African American women facing both coerced and voluntary surrogacy, she rejects traditional Christian notions of atonement theology, which hold that salvation is made possible through the sacrifice of Jesus with his death on the cross. Williams contends that humanity is redeemed through the life and ministry of Jesus rather than through his death.[36]

Within this wide-ranging book that discusses African American history, surrogacy, colorism, and theology, Williams acknowledges the importance of biblical texts in African American life and culture. She uses elements of Walker's definition in her emphasis on survival and quality of life for African American women when discussing biblical texts on Hagar, the exodus, and Jesus. Although she is not attempting to construct a womanist biblical hermeneutic, she claims that womanist hermeneutics must understand the Bible as androcentric and that womanists must adopt a "hermeneutical posture of suspicion" as many feminists have done (e.g., see chap. 5 of this book).[37] Furthermore, they must develop a "hermeneutical posture of affirmation" that embraces the liberative message of biblical texts and that appreciates the importance of biblical stories, themes, and motifs for African Americans.[38] As a theologian, Williams cites biblical texts and explores the representation of Hagar, Jesus, and the exodus for their theological importance, but she does not offer a sustained analysis of biblical texts.

Womanist Justice, Womanist Hope

In *Womanist Justice, Womanist Hope* (1993) Emilie Townes, a womanist ethicist, uses the life of Ida B. Wells-Barnett, an African American social justice activist, churchwoman, speaker, and writer, as a starting point for "substantial scholarly historical and ethical inquiry into the social and moral lives of African-American women in the contemporary church."[39] Acknowledging the importance of the Bible within the African American Christian experience, she notes Wells-Barnett's experience as a Sunday school teacher and her engagement with biblical texts within her activism. Nevertheless, Townes rejects the primacy of the Protestant Reformation doctrine of "Scripture alone." She writes, "From

36. Ibid., 167.
37. The notion of a "hermeneutics of suspicion" stems from the work of philosopher Paul Ricoeur, who identifies Karl Marx, Friedrich Nietzsche, and Sigmund Freud as thinkers within a school of suspicion that examines the ways in which discourse both reveals and conceals meaning. Feminist scholars, including Elisabeth Schüssler Fiorenza and others, employ this notion to argue for the ways in which texts may seem liberative but still serve patriarchal functions. See Elisabeth Schüssler Fiorenza, *But She Said: Feminist Practices of Biblical Interpretation* (Boston: Beacon Press, 1992).
38. Williams, *Sisters in the Wilderness*, 188.
39. Emilie M. Townes, *Womanist Justice, Womanist Hope*, American Academy of Religion Academy 79 (Atlanta: Scholars Press, 1993). Townes's 1989 Garrett Evangelical Theological Seminary/Northwestern University dissertation was titled *The Social and Moral Perspectives of Ida B. Wells-Barnett as a Resource for Contemporary Afro-American Christian Social Ethic*.

such a rich history of lived experience and biblical witness, womanists must be open to God's ongoing revelation in the world."[40] For Townes, biblical texts must be used in conjunction with other sources, including experience, tradition, and science, reflecting a Methodist quadrilateral.

Utilizing Wells-Barnett's autobiography and biographies of Wells-Barnett, Townes explores nineteenth- and early-twentieth-century African American women's activism, which she uses as a foundation for the development of a womanist Christian social ethic. In her work, Townes cites Alice Walker but quotes only section 1 of Walker's four-part definition. Although Townes does not articulate the particular ways in which she is using a womanist approach, she highlights Katie Cannon's scholarship in ethics and emphasizes the importance of race, sex, class, and other factors in ethical reflection.

Sexuality and the Black Church: A Womanist Perspective

Kelly Brown Douglas offers a womanist perspective on issues of sexuality in the black church and discusses the importance of the Bible within the black church in *Sexuality and the Black Church: A Womanist Perspective* (1999).[41] In her discussion of womanist theology, Brown Douglas discusses issues related to the interpretation of biblical texts but does not offer her own exegesis of particular biblical texts. For example, her treatment of the incarnation of Jesus Christ focuses on creedal statements, theological doctrine, and the scholarship of other theologians rather than biblical texts or secondary biblical scholarship. Also, she highlights the biblical figure of Jezebel and how the Jezebel stereotype is used against African American women but does not provide a detailed analysis of the biblical texts or biblical scholarship involving Jezebel. Rather, Brown Douglas offers an extensive discussion on the use of biblical texts within the black church and discusses how the black church appeals to biblical texts in order to oppose homosexuality.

Brown Douglas does not offer a womanist approach to biblical interpretation, but she discusses the work of African American biblical scholars Renita Weems and Vincent Wimbush. She seems to assume that African American biblical scholars are part of Christian communities by calling for African American biblical scholars to have a greater role in the black church. She claims that they have a responsibility to the black church to identify a "biblical tradition of terror" for African Americans; to employ a "hermeneutic of suspicion"; to discuss sexuality from within the "Black biblical oral/aural tradition" rather than only in written form, since the latter is privileged within biblical scholarship; and to address interpretations that have gained authority within the black church, particularly surrounding homosexuality.[42]

40. Ibid., 185.
41. Kelly Brown Douglas, *Sexuality and the Black Church: A Womanist Perspective* (Maryknoll, NY: Orbis Books, 1999).
42. Ibid., 96–97.

Brown Douglas acknowledges that womanist theologians have neglected to address the homophobia of many African American churches and that many African American churches have been slow to respond to the HIV/AIDS epidemic. She admits that womanist theologians have been selective in their use of Walker's definition and have failed to address issues of sexuality as directly as Walker does in her definition. Brown Douglas seeks to uncover reasons why sexuality is a taboo subject, to foster womanist discourse on sexuality, and to support healthier attitudes and behaviors regarding sexuality, including the black church's homophobia and heterosexism.[43]

Brown Douglas does not cite Alice Walker's full definition, but, like Williams, she highlights the segment of Walker's definition that emphasizes a commitment to "survival and wholeness."[44] Although she does not offer citations, she contends that this portion of Walker's definition, "committed to survival and wholeness of entire people, male *and* female" (Walker's italics) "is the one that has been unanimously affirmed" by womanist religious scholars.[45]

Exorcising Evil: A Womanist Perspective on the Spirituals

Musician and theologian Cheryl Kirk-Duggan's *Exorcising Evil: A Womanist Perspective on the Spirituals* (2000) provides a womanist approach to the indigenous musical art form created by African American slave men and women, often called Negro spirituals or just spirituals.[46] These communal, religious songs developed into a concert tradition that was popularized by the Fisk Jubilee Singers of Fisk University in the 1870s. Kirk-Duggan uses the spirituals "as a resource for doing narrative theology, specifically theodicy,"[47] which questions the existence and benevolence of God in the presence of evil. In an extensive revisiting of the religious, musical, cultural history of African Americans through the spirituals, she examines these songs as affirming the existence of God and as providing survival strategies from the antebellum period through their reinterpretation as part of the nonviolent protests of the civil rights movement in the 1950s and 1960s. Kirk-Duggan provides a multidimensional analysis of "naming, unmasking and engaging" particular areas of the spirituals, including "context, story, creative spirit, and faith and thought."[48] She identifies similarities between spirituals and biblical psalms of lament and also mentions significant biblical texts in the life of African American communities, including the so-called curse of Ham (Gen. 9:18–27) and the exodus. Kirk-Duggan discusses the

43. Ibid., 5.
44. Ibid.
45. Ibid., 128.
46. Cheryl A. Kirk-Duggan, *Exorcizing Evil: A Womanist Perspective on the Spirituals*, Bishop Henry McNeal Turner/Sojourner Truth Series in Black Religion 14 (Maryknoll, NY: Orbis Books, 1997), 96–97.
47. Ibid., xvii.
48. Ibid., 77.

importance of biblical images, characters, and allusion in spirituals, but biblical texts do not constitute her primary source material.

In chapter 7 of *Exorcising Evil* Kirk-Duggan explores the term *womanist* and its usage. Kirk-Duggan cites only a portion of Alice Walker's definition when she writes, "*Womanist*, derived by Alice Walker from the term *Womanish*, refers to Black women who are audacious, outrageous, in charge, and responsible; in other words, to Black feminists."[49] Later, she continues, "As Walker says, Womanists are serious and commit to the survival and wholeness of all people."[50] This partial citation provides a focal point for Kirk-Duggan's explorations of African American women's experiences. She claims, "Theologically, from narratives and from life itself, Womanists seek to identify relevant issues and resources, to uncover discrepancies, to right the wrongs of gender, class, and race oppression, and to make Black women visible."[51] Kirk-Duggan highlights the work such womanist scholars and writers as Delores Williams and Audre Lorde, and like Brown Douglas she makes some generalizations regarding womanist views. For example, she writes, "Womanists love God and life, living from a perspective of sacrality."[52]

If It Wasn't for the Women

Sociologist Cheryl Townsend Gilkes's *If It Wasn't for the Women...: Black Women's Experience and Womanist Culture in Church and Community* (2001) is a collection of her previously published essays.[53] Although there is no single approach or topic in this collection, Gilkes's work exposes the intersections of race and class and highlights the importance of economic and political power. In general, she emphasizes the neglected history of African American women's activism and influence in African American communities, particularly within churches. Gilkes counters negative stereotypes of African American women and stresses the important role of women as community builders. She writes, "If it wasn't for the women, racially oppressed communities would not have the institutions, organizations, strategies, and ethics that enable the group not only to survive or to maintain itself as an integral whole, but also to develop in an alien, hostile, oppressive situation and to challenge it."[54] Gilkes highlights African American women's agency as unsung community leaders who were not highly visible in mainstream white women's movements. Gilkes's work as a sociologist highlights the varied ways in which African American women provide leadership and demonstrate agency in their communities.

49. Ibid., xix.
50. Ibid.
51. Ibid., 139.
52. Ibid., 157.
53. Cheryl Townsend Gilkes, *If It Wasn't for the Women...: Black Women's Experience and Womanist Culture in Church and Community* (Maryknoll, NY: Orbis Books, 2001).
54. Ibid., 26.

Gilkes explains the importance of the Bible but does not offer any particular biblical engagement. In her article "Some Mother's Son and Some Father's Daughter," she discusses the importance of biblical imagery and characters in African American culture and religious experience. Not included in *If It Wasn't for the Women*, Gilkes's article "'Mother to the Motherless, Father to the Fatherless:' Power, Gender, and Community in an Afrocentric Biblical Tradition" (1989) discusses the usage of "father to the fatherless" (Ps. 68:5) and fragments of other biblical texts within African American Christian worship traditions. For instance, Gilkes looks at the links of "father to the fatherless" and "mother to the motherless" within the gospel song "Surely God Is Able," which highlights God's miraculous works. She argues that African Americans construct Afrocentric and liberative messages from their engagement with biblical texts by expressing resistance to oppression and belief in God.[55] Primarily, Gilkes does not offer her own readings of biblical texts but describes the use of biblical texts among African Americans.

In the introduction to the collection, Gilkes explains that Alice Walker coined the word *womanist* and mentions several elements of Walker's definition, including "survival and wholeness" and "womanist" as "black feminist."[56] In several of the essays, Gilkes introduces the notion of womanism and cites Deborah King's concepts of "multiple jeopardy" (discussed in the introduction to this book). Borrowing from Alice Walker's short story collection *In Love and Trouble: Stories of Black Women*, Gilkes notes that most African American women would not define themselves as feminist and argues in "The 'Loves' and 'Troubles' of African-American Women's Bodies: The Womanist Challenge to Cultural Humiliation and Community Ambivalence" that *womanist* should not be used simply as a way to distinguish black and white feminists. She contends, "Not all black women are womanist, but the womanist potential is embedded in all black women's experiences."[57]

Making a Way Out of No Way: A Womanist Theology

In *Making a Way Out of No Way: A Womanist Theology* (2008) Monica Coleman offers a constructive postmodern womanist theology that focuses on black women's lived experiences.[58] While she acknowledges Christianity's dominance within theology, Coleman does not use biblical texts as a source for her womanist theology. Instead, she seeks to be more inclusive of the religious pluralism within African American religious communities, including African traditional

---

55. Cheryl Townsend Gilkes, "'Mother to the Motherless, Father to the Fatherless': Power, Gender, and Community in an Afrocentric Biblical Tradition," *Semeia* 47 (1989): 57–85.

56. Gilkes, *If It Wasn't for the Women*, 10.

57. Ibid., 186.

58. Monica A. Coleman, *Making a Way Out of No Way: A Womanist Theology* (Minneapolis: Fortress Press, 2008).

religions.[59] For example, she uses African American writer Octavia Butler's novel *Parable of the Sower* as a source for theological reflection due to the novel's emphasis on traditional Yoruba traditions from Nigeria, Benin, and Togo.

Coleman's work is informed by womanist theology, process theology, and philosophical metaphysics. For Coleman, metaphysics focuses on "human experience as the source of religious knowledge." She defines *metaphysics* as "our best ideas given what we know."[60] Coleman acknowledges the critiques of black theology and feminist theology that contributed to the development of womanist theology. She mentions Walker's 1983 definition of *womanist* without citing the full definition, yet she emphasizes the importance of addressing racism, sexism, and classism, which is a key element in womanist approaches. Coleman uses black women's experiences as the starting point for womanist theology as well as the theme of "making a way out of no way" for black women's "struggles and God's assistance in helping them to overcome oppression."[61]

CONCLUSION

The scholars discussed above represent only a portion of the diverse approaches to womanist religious thought. More recent scholarship by an array of scholars appears in the edited volume *Deeper Shades of Purple: Womanism in Religion and Society*.[62] Furthermore, a potential "third Wave" of scholarship is collected in another edited volume, *Ain't I a Womanist Too? Third-Wave Womanist Religious Thought*.[63] There are numerous monographs, edited volumes, and journal articles with varying approaches and understandings of womanist thought. This discussion of selected womanist texts does not do justice to the body of work that each scholar has produced nor to the much larger body of womanist work in religious studies and beyond.

Still, this discussion highlights some of the key issues raised by this brief survey, including the limited use of biblical texts as sources and key features of womanist approaches in religious-studies-related fields. These womanist scholars provide an important link to twentieth- and twenty-first-century womanist biblical scholarship and to nineteenth-century writings by African American women due to their emphasis on the lived experience of African American women. Yet while womanist scholarship in religious thought and womanist scholarship in biblical studies share some similarities, they differ in fundamental ways.

---

59. African traditional or indigenous religion includes a variety of beliefs and practices among African peoples, such as the Yoruba or the Bantu.

60. Ibid., 42–43.

61. Ibid., 9.

62. Stacey M. Floyd-Thomas, ed., *Deeper Shades of Purple: Womanism in Religion and Society* (New York: New York University Press, 2006).

63. Monica A. Coleman, *Ain't I a Womanist, Too? Third-Wave Womanist Religious Thought* (Minneapolis: Fortress Press, 2013).

As this brief survey of womanist work in religious-studies-related fields demonstrates, there is no single, clear approach to womanist work within religious studies, partly because religious studies includes a range of discrete disciplines.[64] For example, Jacquelyn Grant, Delores Williams, and Monica Coleman are all theologians, but they have different conversation partners. Grant is in conversation with white feminist theology and Christology. While Delores Williams engages black liberation theology, Monica Coleman relies on process theology. The standing that these scholars have within theology may be taken to mean that African American women's contributions have gained some acceptance and legitimacy in the academy and that African American women have named and claimed a space for themselves and their work in the academy. Yet the grouping of these scholars together as womanists and the assumption that all African American women scholars are womanists may contribute to the marginalization of African American women in the academy by not allowing them to label themselves and their work as they wish but instead pigeon-holing them by their gender and ethnicity.

Nonetheless, there are some distinctive features of womanist scholarship in religious studies, including the use of the term *womanist* and engagement with the lived experience of African American women. At a minimum, the scholarship labeled as womanist mentions Alice Walker and her definition of *womanist*. Yet scholars offer their own notions of womanism beyond Walker's definition. Moreover, these scholars differ greatly in the degree to which they engage Walker's definition, for they tend to highlight and to engage only particular elements of her definition.

These scholars use Alice Walker's definition of *womanist* in multiple ways and use African American women's lived experiences as source material for their research. Scholars in religious-studies-related fields mention the importance of the Bible for many African American women, although unlike their counterparts in biblical studies, they have relatively limited exegetical engagement with biblical texts. Nevertheless, womanist scholars in religious studies have become conversation partners for womanist biblical scholars. As explained in chapter 6, many of the issues and challenges facing womanist religious studies scholarship remain relevant for womanist biblical studies because womanist scholarship in religious studies is frequently cited in womanist biblical scholarship.

64. Ethicist Stacey M. Floyd-Thomas argues for four tenets of womanism: radical subjectivity, traditional communalism, redemptive self-love, and critical engagement. See Stacey M. Floyd-Thomas, *Mining the Motherlode: Methods in Womanist Ethics* (Cleveland, OH: Pilgrim Press, 2006). Psychologist Layli Phillips finds five characteristics of womanism: antioppressionist, vernacular, nonideological, communitarian, and spiritualized. See Layli Phillips, "Womanism: On Its Own," in *The Womanist Reader* (New York: Routledge, 2006), xix–lv.

Theologian Monica Coleman offers four "marks" of womanist thought: "engages, the religious lives of women of African descent; maintains a goal of justice, survival, freedom, liberation, and/or quality of life; understands itself to both draw upon *and also depart from* a tradition of womanist religious scholarship; and engages work and thinkers both inside and outside of black religious scholarship" (Coleman's italics). Coleman, *Ain't I a Womanist Too?*, 19.

RESOURCE LIST

Coleman, Monica A., ed. *Ain't I a Womanist, Too? Third-Wave Womanist Religious Thought.* Minneapolis: Fortress Press, 2013. This edited volume brings together a new generation of religion scholars engaging womanist thought.

Floyd-Thomas, Stacey M., ed. *Deeper Shades of Purple: Womanism in Religion and Society.* Religion, Race, and Ethnicity. New York: New York University Press, 2006. This edited volume offers new perspectives on religious-studies-related womanist thought.

Grant, Jacquelyn. *White Women's Christ and Black Women's Jesus: Feminist Christology and Womanist Response.* American Academy of Religion Academy 64. Atlanta: Scholars Press, 1989. Grant's pioneering work on womanist theology is an excellent starting place for understanding the development of religious-studies-related womanist work.

Mitchem, Stephanie Y. *Introducing Womanist Theology.* Maryknoll, NY: Orbis Books, 2002 This book provides an overview of womanist theology and its origins.

Williams, Delores S. *Sisters in the Wilderness: The Challenge of Womanist God-Talk.* Maryknoll, NY: Orbis Books, 1993. This is a classic womanist theology text that highlights the Hagar story in Genesis.

Chapter 5

Feminist Biblical
Interpretation

As discussed in chapter 2, some nineteenth-century women offered new biblical interpretations that supported greater equality for women. These interpretations are often retroactively labeled as first-wave feminism. In the 1970s, some scholars began to develop feminist approaches to biblical studies or what is often called second-wave feminist biblical criticism. Linking these two periods by referring to them as waves creates a longer history of women's engagement with biblical texts. Yet these two periods differ considerably in that nineteenth-century efforts were more explicitly tied to specific political causes and directed toward advancing efforts for greater women's equality. Also, they were conducted primarily by laypersons and by those outside of mainstream faith communities. In contrast, the twentieth-century scholarship involves the work of professionally trained biblical scholars.

The purpose of this chapter is to provide background on this so-called second wave of feminist biblical interpretation. It surveys key issues in the development of feminist biblical interpretation starting in the 1970s to illustrate the significant contrast between feminist biblical scholarship and womanist biblical scholarship. As discussed in chapter 6, although feminist and womanist approaches in biblical studies are consistently linked together as if they are parallel in their development, they differ significantly in terms of output and approach. This chapter does not provide a thorough history of the voluminous body of feminist scholarship in biblical studies. Rather, it sketches the considerable diversity of feminist biblical interpretation. It provides background on key stages in the development of feminist biblical scholarship and discusses its impact on the discipline of biblical studies in order to contrast it with womanist biblical interpretation in chapter 6.

BACKGROUND

As discussed in the introduction, feminist approaches within biblical studies address issues of gender and power relations within biblical texts and related material, but what constitutes a feminist approach is highly contested. I refer to feminist approaches or perspectives rather than methods because feminist approaches do not involve a single set of procedures for conducting one's inquiry. In contrast, other methods used in biblical studies have recognized steps or actions. For example, source criticism has developed a set of principles and procedures that relate to its use as a method. In basic terms, source criticism is a critical method used to analyze texts that are assumed not to be the work of a single author but result from a combination of originally separate documents.[1] Of course, scholars may have disagreements regarding their source-critical analysis of certain biblical texts and the specific features of their method. Still, among professionally trained biblical scholars, even if there is not a scholarly consensus regarding a particular critical argument, there is a widespread understanding of what is involved in a source-critical reading.

In contrast, if a scholar labels a work as feminist biblical interpretation, it requires further clarification in a way that a work labeled as source criticism will not. A feminist approach could involve an array of types of engagement with the text because it does not constitute a stand-alone method. There is no agreed-on set of principles, procedures, preconditions, or intentions for feminist work. Instead, feminist approaches are used in combination with a variety of scholarly methods, including historical-critical, literary, theological, and postmodern methods.[2] For example, a scholar may use rhetorical criticism in concert with

1. See Joel S. Baden, *The Composition of the Pentateuch: Renewing the Documentary Hypothesis* (New Haven, CT: Yale University Press, 2012); Pauline A. Viviano, "Source Criticism," in *To Each Its Own Meaning*, ed. Steven L. McKenzie and Stephen R. Hayes, rev. ed. (Louisville, KY: Westminster John Knox Press, 1999), 35–57; and Christopher Levin, "Source Criticism: The Miracle at the Sea," in *Method Matters: Essays on the Interpretation of the Hebrew Bible in Honor of David L. Petersen*, ed. David L. Petersen, Joel M. LeMon, and Kent Harold Richards, Society of Biblical Literature Resources for Biblical Study, vol. 56 (Atlanta: Society of Biblical Literature, 2009), 39–61.

2. See Richard N. Soulen and R. Kendall Soulen, *Handbook of Biblical Criticism*, 4th ed. (Louisville, KY: Westminster John Knox Press, 2011); John Barton, *Reading the Old Testament: Method in Biblical Study*, rev. ed. (Louisville, KY: Westminster John Knox Press, 1996); and Petersen et al., eds., *Method Matters*.

feminist approaches to consider the use of gendered language within a text. In *Texts of Terror: Literary-Feminist Readings of Biblical Narratives*, Hebrew Bible scholar Phyllis Trible claims Jacob's wrestling at the Jabbok (Gen. 32:22–32) as a story of journey for her work, but she separates her method from her feminist perspective in identifying influences in her work. She writes, "Jacob's wrestling at the Jabbok is the story; literary criticism, the methodology; and feminism, the perspective."[3] Also, a scholar may use the historical-critical method in combination with feminist approaches in order to examine women's leadership roles in ancient Israelite society. Furthermore, feminist approaches may be used alongside other approaches that are not stand-alone methods. For instance, scholars may offer a postcolonial-feminist or queer-feminist reading.[4]

Due to the lack of a defined methodology of feminist biblical scholarship and due to some feminist scholars' disclosure of a feminist agenda within their work, some other scholars have dismissed feminist biblical scholarship as subjective. Feminist interpreters would argue that their work is not more subjective than the work of other interpreters. It is simply more transparent about its agenda. Although most scholars understand that no method is entirely objective, many feminist biblical scholars concede their nonobjective stance and their aims and interests in conducting their scholarship. They reject claims of objectivity and neutrality that underlie much of what is often regarded as traditional, mainstream biblical scholarship.[5] Regardless of the specific method or agenda, how a scholar uses feminist approaches depends on that scholar's research questions and how he or she understands the features of a feminist approach.

SURVEY OF FEMINIST RESEARCH

Early Development

Feminist approaches have been characterized by their diversity since their early development. In the 1970s, influenced by developments in liberation theology, women's studies, religious studies, and other fields, some biblical scholars began to develop feminist approaches to biblical criticism. They used a variety of scholarly methodologies, and they did not necessarily use the term *feminist* in the title or in the body of their work or situate themselves within a feminist agenda. Still,

3. Phyllis Trible, *Texts of Terror: Literary-Feminist Readings of Biblical Narratives* (Philadelphia: Fortress Press, 1984), 3.

4. See Musa W. Dube, *Postcolonial Feminist Interpretation of the Bible* (St. Louis: Chalice Press, 2000); and Deryn Guest, *When Deborah Met Jael: Lesbian Biblical Hermeneutics* (London: SCM Press, 2005).

5. See Adele Reinhartz, "Feminist Criticism and Biblical Studies on the Verge of the Twenty-First Century," in *A Feminist Companion to Reading the Bible: Approaches, Methods and Strategies,* ed. Athalya Brenner and Carole Fontaine (Sheffield: Sheffield Academic Press, 1997), 30–38; and Mary Ann Tolbert, "Defining the Problem: The Bible and Feminist Hermeneutics," *Semeia* 28 (1983b), 113–26.

some of the common features of this work included interrogating biblical texts with particular attention to female characters and to gender-related issues. Also, they reexamined traditional interpretations that were used to support women's subordination.

For example, in "Depatriarchalizing in Biblical Interpretation" (1973), Phyllis Trible counters other scholars who find the creation story in Genesis 2–3 to be irredeemable for women.[6] Although she locates herself within debates regarding the Bible and the women's liberation movement, she does not label her approach as a feminist one at this point in her career. She admits that biblical texts and biblical religion are patriarchal, but she contends that it was possible to read these texts from a new perspective. Trible claims equality of the sexes in Genesis 2–3 and finds mutuality in the erotic love poetry of Song of Songs. Trible writes of her goal, "The hermeneutical challenge is to translate biblical faith without sexism."[7] Trible refuses to reject the Bible as hopelessly oppressive to women, for she contends that it is not the text but interpretations of biblical texts that support patriarchy.

Religion and Sexism: Images of Woman in the Jewish and Christian Traditions (1974) was an important volume in the development of feminist approaches to biblical studies.[8] Edited by theologian Rosemary Radford Reuther, this volume includes essays by scholars in a variety of fields who address the role of religion in the oppression of women, but these essays provide new perspectives on the role of women in multiple textual traditions, theology, and church history. For example, Hebrew Bible scholar Phyllis Bird's essay "Images of Women in the Old Testament" looks at the diversity of female characters in the Old Testament, but it does not include the term *feminist*.

Trible's first full-length monograph *God and the Rhetoric of Sexuality* (1978) was one of the first books identified as contemporary feminist biblical scholarship.[9] Here Trible labels her work as feminist hermeneutics, but she clarifies her understanding of feminism. She writes, "By feminism I do not mean a narrow focus upon women, but rather a critique of culture in light of misogyny."[10] Although Trible understands her work as feminist, she identifies her methodology as rhetorical criticism, a method in biblical studies related to form criticism. Furthermore, Trible considers her work to be interdisciplinary and cites multiple influences, including literary criticism, psychoanalytic criticism, and Zen Buddhism. She focuses on Genesis 1:27 and "the image of God" in order to study God in relation to the rhetoric of sexuality. Trible also investigates the biblical Hebrew word for "womb," female metaphors for God, and Genesis

---

6. Phyllis Trible, "Depatriarchalizing in Biblical Interpretation," *Journal of the American Academy of Religion* 41 (1973): 30–48.

7. Ibid., 31.

8. Rosemary Radford Ruether, ed., *Religion and Sexism: Images of Woman in the Jewish and Christian Traditions* (New York: Simon & Schuster, 1974).

9. Phyllis Trible, *God and the Rhetoric of Sexuality* (Philadelphia: Fortress Press, 1978).

10. Ibid., 7.

2:7–3:24, Song of Songs, and Ruth. Despite their nonuse of the term, both Trible's and Bird's early works are grouped together with the work of other scholars who identified their work as feminist.

In the 1980s, four early works highlight the nascent development of feminist biblical scholarship and illustrate a range of feminist approaches: a 1982 *Journal for the Study of the Old Testament* (*JSOT*) volume;[11] the 1983 Semeia volume 28, *The Bible and Feminist Hermeneutics*, edited by New Testament scholar Mary Ann Tolbert;[12] the 1985 volume *Feminist Perspectives on Biblical Scholarship*, edited by New Testament scholar Adela Yarbro Collins;[13] and the 1985 collection of essays *Feminist Interpretation of the Bible*, edited by theologian Letty Russell.[14] These volumes provide examples of the diversity of feminist biblical interpretation and its varied uses of feminist approaches.

The *JSOT* (1982) volume resulted from the absence of women's contributions or mention of feminist approaches in the 1980 centennial celebration program of the Society of Biblical Literature (SBL). Trible explains that the SBL program committee had recommended one session on women and the Bible within "The History and Sociology of Biblical Scholarship," but some women scholars seized the opportunity to organize a panel titled "The Effects of Women's Studies on Biblical Studies."[15] The oral presentations from the panel were collected and published in the *JSOT* volume.

The contributors to the *JSOT* volume worked in various fields. All of them did not identify their approach or their concerns as explicitly feminist, and they engaged the intersection of women's studies and biblical studies from different angles. For example, ancient Near Eastern specialist Mary K. Wakeman investigated sacred marriage in ancient Sumer and examined how changes in the view of the goddess Inanna and her consort reflected changes in political power relations.[16] Also, several contributors operated from a confessional stance and included theological concerns. For instance, New Testament scholar Adela Yarbro Collins offered a Christian feminist reading of the Gospel of John that highlighted masculine and feminine elements in the text.[17] Also, in her essay, Trible used theologically loaded words such as "prophetic" and "sin" when she wrote, "We speak from the shared perspective of feminism as a prophetic movement naming the sin of patriarchy. If to date the effects of women's studies on

---

11. *Journal for the Study of the Old Testament* 7 (1982).

12. Mary Ann Tolbert, ed., *The Bible and Feminist Hermeneutics*, vol. 28 (Atlanta: Scholars Press, 1983).

13. Adela Yarbro Collins, ed., *Feminist Perspectives on Biblical Scholarship* (Chico, CA: Scholars Press, 1985).

14. Letty M. Russell, *Feminist Interpretation of the Bible* (Louisville, KY: Westminster/John Knox Press, 1985).

15. Phyllis Trible, "The Effects of Women's Studies on Biblical Studies," *Journal for the Study of the Old Testament* 22 (1982): 3–5.

16. Mary K. Wakeman, "Sacred Marriage," *Journal for the Study of the Old Testament* 7 (1982), 21–31.

17. Adela Yarbro Collins, "New Testament Perspectives: The Gospel of John," *Journal for the Study of the Old Testament* 7 (1982): 47–53.

biblical studies have been small, we despair not."[18] This collection of articles demonstrated the importance of women's studies for biblical studies as well as the growing momentum of feminist biblical criticism by the early 1980s.

According to Tolbert, the aim of the Semeia volume *The Bible and Feminist Hermeneutics* was to offer biblical interpretation "in light of the feminist critique of patriarchal culture" and to link biblical studies with various "liberation movements."[19] All of the essays, except Tolbert's programmatic essay, address either particular texts with female characters or texts that address the roles and behavior of women. Another product of conversations surrounding the SBL Centennial, *Feminist Perspectives on Biblical Scholarship* was a volume edited by Adela Yarbro Collins. Published in 1985, it includes contributions by eight women in various fields. For example, New Testament scholar Bernadette Brooten addresses critical issues in the study of early Christian women's history,[20] and Hebrew Bible scholar Esther Fuchs examines the literary characterization of mothers in the Hebrew Bible.[21] Also published in 1985, *Feminist Interpretation of the Bible*, edited by theologian Letty Russell, includes contributions by twelve women in different disciplines. In this volume, New Testament scholar Sharon H. Ringe revisits the Gentile woman in Mark 7:24–30 and Matthew 15:20–28,[22] and Jewish educator T. Drorah Setel examines the female sexual imagery in Hosea.[23] In the 1970s to 1980s the work of biblical scholars who drew attention to issues of gender and to female characters was innovative within biblical studies. Not all of these scholars identified their work as feminist, but their work was foundational for much of the feminist work that developed later.

Categorization Efforts

In some ways, the notion of feminist approaches to biblical studies is used so loosely that the term *feminist* is not a precise definition as much as an umbrella category. As more feminist biblical criticism was published, by the mid-1980s some scholars attempted to describe and to categorize the wide range of feminist work. These efforts at categorization demonstrate the variety of ways in which feminist biblical criticism was employed. These scholars did not seek to delineate the contours of a feminist method but only classified current work. Such work was more dissimilar than alike, but it did include a focused attention on

18. Trible, "The Effects of Women's Studies," 3–5.

19. Mary Ann Tolbert, "Introduction," *Semeia* 28 (1983), [n.p.].

20. Bernadette J. Brooten, "Early Christian Women and their Cultural Context: Issues of Method in Historical Reconstruction," in Collins, ed., *Feminist Perspectives on Biblical Scholarship*, 65–91.

21. Esther Fuchs, "Who Is Hiding the Truth? Deceptive Women and Biblical Androcentrism," in Collins, ed., *Feminist Perspectives on Biblical Scholarship*, 137–44.

22. Sharon H. Ringe, "A Gentile Woman's Story," in *Feminist Interpretation of the Bible*, ed. Letty M. Russell (Philadelphia: Westminster Press, 1985), 65–72.

23. T. Drorah Setel, "Prophets and Pornography: Female Sexual Imagery in Hosea," in Russell, ed., *Feminist Interpretation of the Bible*, 86–95.

gender that had not been a significant part of biblical scholarship previously. It is a significant development within feminist biblical scholarship because it demonstrates that a critical mass of feminist biblical scholarship had matured to the point of self-examination.

In the *JSOT* volume, Hebrew Bible scholar Katherine Doob Sakenfeld's essay analyzes the impact of women's studies on biblical studies.[24] Sakenfeld does not identify these issues as explicitly feminist issues, but she notes five areas of impact:

1. The status and role of women in ancient Israelite culture
2. Rediscovery and reassessment of Old Testament traditions
3. Reassessment of female biblical characters
4. Variety of imagery for God
5. Translation and inclusive language

Sakenfeld acknowledges the minimal but growing development of these types of inquiries into biblical studies through women's studies. Furthermore, she admits that the work of exploring the complexities of racism, classism, and sexism had begun in theological circles but had yet to be explored in biblical studies.

In her essay "Defining the Problem: The Bible and Feminist Hermeneutics" in the Semeia volume (1983), Mary Ann Tolbert offers her own explanation of feminism. While noting the lack of a single definition of the term *feminism*, she writes, "Feminism, like other liberation movements, attempts a critique of the oppressive structures of society."[25] Using this definition, Tolbert describes feminist hermeneutics as "a reading of a text (or writing of analysis, or the reconstructing of history) in light of the oppressive structures of a patriarchal society."[26] She identifies three ways in which feminist biblical hermeneutics are employed. Within what she calls the reformist position,[27] she notes three types of engagement with biblical texts: liberative, remnant, and reconstruction.[28] The liberative position seeks the liberation of oppressed peoples. The remnant position attempts to recover overlooked and neglected texts and characters and to find antipatriarchal texts as a counter to patriarchal texts. Historical reconstruction makes an effort to reconstruct the lives of early women and their societies. Like Sakenfeld, Tolbert raises questions regarding the ongoing use of the Bible for Christians. Also, she acknowledges her focus on Christian feminists as well as the different experiences of Jewish feminists.

24. Katharine Doob Sakenfeld, "Old Testament Perspectives: Methodological Considerations," *Journal for the Study of the Old Testament* 22 (1982): 13–20.

25. Tolbert, "Defining the Problem," 115.

26. Ibid., 119.

27. Tolbert does not cite a source regarding her use of the term *reformist*. She may be referring to Carol Christ's description of "reformist" and "revolutionary" as two positions relating to feminist approaches. See Carol P. Christ, "The New Feminist Theology: A Review of the Literature," *Religious Studies Review* 3 (1977): 203–12.

28. Tolbert, "Defining the Problem," 122–23.

In *Feminist Perspectives on Biblical Scholarship*, Carolyn Osiek's essay "The Feminist and the Bible: Hermeneutical Alternatives" offers five different strategies for feminist hermeneutics: rejectionist, loyalist, revisionist, sublimationist, and liberationist.[29] Osiek, in conversation with Sakenfeld and others, attempts to describe the types of feminist engagement with biblical texts along with examples of the scholars that she contends are using each particular approach. For Osiek, the rejectionist readers reject the authority of the Bible. The loyalist approach could be considered "biblical feminism." These readers contend that the Bible itself is not oppressive to women but that the misinterpretation of biblical texts has created the oppression. The revisionist approach is a moderate approach between the rejectionist and loyalist positions. These scholars find that some biblical traditions and texts are worth saving. The sublimationists focus on female imagery and symbols. Influenced by liberation theology, the liberationists highlight what they consider to be the liberative elements of the biblical text. Like Sakenfeld, Osiek mentions briefly the importance of race and class although she does not discuss these issues in detail.

Writing in Russell's *Feminist Interpretation of the Bible*, Sakenfeld offers a second categorization article in which she analyzes the ways that Christian feminists have used feminist approaches to biblical interpretation. Using theological language similar to that used by Trible, Sakenfeld defines *feminism* as "a contemporary prophetic movement that announces judgment on the patriarchy of contemporary culture and calls for repentance and change."[30] Sakenfeld argues that some questions may lead one to reject the authority of the Bible and to find engagement with biblical texts as not useful in overturning patriarchy. Yet she does not include rejection as an option as does Osiek.

Sakenfeld highlights three main types of engagement.

1. Looking to texts about women to counteract famous texts used "against" women
2. Looking to the Bible generally (not particularly to texts about women) for a theological perspective that offers a critique of patriarchy (some may call this a "liberation perspective")
3. Looking to texts about women to learn from the intersection of history and stories of ancient and modern women living in patriarchal cultures[31]

Sakenfeld notes that these three options are not mutually exclusive. These efforts at categorization demonstrate the variety of ways in which feminist biblical criticism was employed. Scholars such as Sakenfeld, Tolbert, Osiek, and Russell

29. Carolyn Osiek, "The Feminist and the Bible: Hermeneutical Alternatives," in Collins, ed., *Feminist Perspectives on Biblical Scholarship*, 93–105.

30. Katharine Doob Sakenfeld, "Feminist Uses of Biblical Materials," in Russell, ed., *Feminist Interpretation of the Bible*, 55.

31. Ibid., 56.

did not seek to delineate the contours of a feminist method but offered ways to classify current work.

In an effort to shape the contribution of feminist approaches to biblical scholarship, Trible revised a series of lectures and published them together as *Texts of Terror: Literary-Feminist Readings of Biblical Narratives*.[32] She regards this book as a companion to her previous book, *God and the Rhetoric of Sexuality*. In this second work, Trible outlines three types of feminist engagement:

1. Documenting the case against women in ancient Israel and the early church
2. Development of a remnant theology that challenges the sexism of Scripture
3. Incorporating 1 and 2 to recount tales of terror in memoriam to offer sympathetic readings of abused women[33]

Using the third form of engagement, Trible does not define "texts of terror" explicitly but sees her task as "to tell sad stories as I hear them."[34] Trible offers new interpretations of texts describing four women: Hagar (Gen. 16, 21); Tamar (2 Sam. 13:1–12); Jephthah's daughter (Judges 11); and the Levite's concubine (Judg. 19:1–30). This book popularized the notion of "texts of terror" and provides an example of the type of creative focus on female characters that characterized much of feminist scholarship at this time.

Elisabeth Schüssler Fiorenza's *Bread Not Stone: The Challenge of Feminist Biblical Interpretation* (1984) is a collection of previously published articles.[35] Like Trible, Schüssler Fiorenza does not seek to categorize previous work but offers her own model of feminist biblical interpretation that includes four elements: hermeneutics of suspicion, hermeneutics of proclamation, hermeneutics of remembrance, and hermeneutics of creative actualization. Drawing on the work of Paul Ricoeur, Schüssler Fiorenza contends that one must employ a hermeneutics of suspicion because biblical texts and their interpretations are androcentric and serve patriarchal functions. This hermeneutics of suspicion requires operating from a position of mistrust in interrogating that which is contradictory, counterintuitive, and concealed within the text. Within Christian worship, the hermeneutics of proclamation is used to insist that texts identified as sexist or patriarchal should be retained in the lectionary and be proclaimed in Christian worship. The hermeneutics of remembrance seeks to recover biblical traditions through a historical-critical reconstruction of biblical history, including the lives of biblical women. The hermeneutics of creative actualization reclaims imagination and creativity in retelling biblical stories. Out of these

32. Trible, *Texts of Terror*.
33. Ibid., 3.
34. Ibid., 1.
35. Elisabeth Schüssler Fiorenza, *Bread Not Stone: The Challenge of Feminist Biblical Interpretation* (Boston: Beacon Press, 1984).

four components of Schüssler Fiorenza's model, the notion of hermeneutics of suspicion gained significant popularity and became one of the recognized elements of feminist biblical interpretation.

Reassessment

In the 1980s, feminist approaches to biblical studies continued to proliferate. Some scholars made efforts to categorize this wide range of material. In doing so, they were identifying some reading strategies employed by various scholars. Still, no consensus developed regarding definitions of feminism or elements of feminist approaches apart from focused attention on gender issues and on female biblical characters. Given its great diversity, some biblical scholars questioned the purpose and aims of feminist biblical scholarship, and in the 1990s, some scholars began a significant reassessment of previous feminist work in biblical studies. This important development demonstrated that feminist biblical interpretation had produced a critical mass of scholarship such that its motivations and its effects could be interrogated.

As the use of feminist approaches in biblical studies expanded so did critiques of its usage, particularly from women who were not Christian, not Western, or not white. As discussed in the introduction, feminism and feminist activism have faced critiques due to their focus on gender without sufficiently acknowledging other categories of difference and for the attention to patriarchy to the exclusion of other forms of oppression. Within biblical studies, similar critiques have been lodged, including concerns regarding the focus on white, Christian women, particularly since the early 1990s.

Theologian Judith Plaskow's piece "Anti-Judaism in Feminist Christian Interpretation" (1993) exposes the ways in which anti-Judaism is rooted in Christian thought as well as in feminist Christian thought.[36] She surveys the anti-Judaism present in Stanton's *The Woman's Bible* and notes similar views in contemporary Christian feminist discourse (e.g., see chap. 2 of this book). Furthermore, Plaskow points out that the notion that "Jesus was a feminist" sets up a negative view of Judaism and positions Jesus as distinct from and opposed to traditional Jewish customs and beliefs, since Jesus is regarded positively against what are perceived as oppressive Jewish customs. Also, in "Racism and Ethnocentrism in Feminist Biblical Interpretation" (1993) theologian Kwok Pui-Lan provides ten theses regarding race and ethnicity in feminist biblical interpretation.[37] She critiques single-focus discussions and argues for the importance of addressing multiple oppressions in order to create a liberative biblical hermeneutic. Although

36. Judith Plaskow, "Anti-Judaism in Feminist Christian Interpretation," in *Searching the Scriptures*, vol. 1, *A Feminist Introduction*, ed. Elisabeth Schüssler Fiorenza (New York: Crossroad, 1993), 117–29.

37. Pui-Lan Kwok, "Racism and Ethnocentrism in Feminist Biblical Interpretation," in *Searching the Scriptures*, vol. 1, *A Feminist Introduction*, ed. Elisabeth Schüssler Fiorenza (New York: Crossroad, 1993), 101–16.

both Plaskow and Kwok are theologians, since their work appears in Schüssler Fiorenza's volume on biblical interpretation, their critiques were probably more widely read within biblical studies than they would have been otherwise.

Certainly, some feminist biblical criticism continues to focus primarily or even exclusively on issues of gender. Yet some interpreters have responded to critiques of feminist biblical scholarship as dominated by its focus on gender and on white, Christian women by identifying their own social location and specifying their particular definition of feminism and usage of a feminist approach. In doing so, they offer specific details such as religious and/or denominational affiliation, gender, or class and discuss the ways in which such factors influenced their work. These scholars provide such details in an effort to foreground their biases and presuppositions as well as their particular aims in conducting their research. Nevertheless, although some scholars self-identify in particular ways, some separate their identification from their work. That is, a scholar may acknowledge that she is a Roman Catholic, but she may separate her faith commitments from her scholarship.

Others scholars identify their social location as well as situate their readings from a particular ethnic group or geographic location and label their reading as such. For instance, some interpreters identify their reading as feminist and as an African American, South African, Caribbean, or Asian/Pacific Islander reading. For example, in 2001, New Testament scholar Gloria Kehilwe Plaatjie wrote "Toward a Post-apartheid Black Feminist Reading of the Bible: A Case of Luke 2:36–38." She interrogates the position of black South African women and reads the text with a group of South African women who are not professionally trained biblical interpreters in order to determine the types of feminist strategies that they employed in their interpretations.[38]

Despite the tendency of feminist biblical interpretation to focus primarily on gender, some feminist interpreters point out the importance of multiple oppressions and address issues of race, gender, class, and other categories of difference. For example, in 1993 Schüssler Fiorenza coined the term *kyriarchy*, which became an influential term within feminist discourse. She sought a "different understanding of patriarchy, one which does not limit it to the sex/gender system but conceptualizes it in terms of interlocking structures of domination [i.e., *kyriarchal*, elite male, relations of ruling (*Herr-shaft*)]".[39] Schüssler Fiorenza contrasted patriarchal systems ("rule of the father") and kyriarchal systems ("rule of the master or lord") in order to acknowledge the ways in which "elite propertied men have power over those subordinate to and dependent on them."[40] This

---

38. Gloria Kehilwe Plaatjie, "Toward a Post-Apartheid Black Feminist Reading of the Bible: A Case of Luke 2:36–38," in *Other Ways of Reading: African Women and the Bible*, ed. Musa W. Dube (Atlanta: Society of Biblical Literature, 2001), 114–42.

39. Schüssler Fiorenza, *But She Said: Feminist Practices of Biblical Interpretation* (Boston: Beacon Press, 1992), 8.

40. Ibid.

concept of kyriarchy signaled an explicit effort to move away from feminism's attention on gender.

Furthermore, the above-mentioned Plaskow and Kwok articles appear in the two-volume *Searching the Scriptures* project edited by Schüssler Fiorenza. This project interrogates the legacy of *The Woman's Bible* (discussed in chapter 2) near its 100th anniversary. Contributors included women scholars from various social and geographic locations. They were asked "to engage a 'feminist' hermeneutical perspective that does not focus simply on gender but also on class, race, ethnicity, and other structures of oppression."[41] Although not every contributor frames her work explicitly as a critique of previous feminist scholarship, the essays offer new perspectives on the approaches, methods, practices, and potential of feminist biblical scholarship. Thus this project with its diversity of contributors and methods demonstrated the continued growth and development of feminist approaches within biblical studies, including moving beyond a focus primarily on gender.

Hebrew Bible scholar Pamela Milne questions the efforts to label female biblical characters as positive or negative in her article "What Shall We Do with Judith? A Feminist Reassessment of a Biblical 'Heroine'" (1993).[42] Judith is a beautiful Israelite widow in the apocryphal/deuterocanonical book of Judith. She beheads Holofernes, one of Nebuchadnezzar's generals, with his own sword. Judith became an important female figure in the history of biblical interpretation, and many interpreters have understood her dramatic killing and display of Holofernes's severed head as heroic action on behalf of her people. Milne surveys a wide range of scholarship regarding Judith and details the various claims by interpreters, including those who maintained that Judith was a heroine. Milne argues that despite previous efforts to label Judith as positive, she was not a heroine. Milne questions the efforts of some feminist biblical scholars who not only focused attention on female biblical characters but who seemed intent on identifying those female characters as positive characters. Milne's work shows the growth of feminist biblical scholarship with her critique and questioning of its aims.

One well-known reconsideration of previous work is the study of Moses' deliverance as an infant by biblical scholar J. Cheryl Exum. In "You Shall Let Every Daughter Live: A Study of Exodus 1:8–2:10" (1983), Exum investigates the texts surrounding the birth of Moses.[43] She analyzes the role of women in two of Pharaoh's three unsuccessful attempts to limit the Israelite population growth and argues that the midwives, the mother of Moses, the sister of Moses, and the Egyptian princess worked together to foil Pharaoh's plans. Exum credits

41. Elisabeth Schüssler Fiorenza, ed., *Searching the Scriptures*, vol. 1, *A Feminist Introduction* (New York: Crossroad, 1993), x.

42. Pamela J. Milne, "What Shall We Do with Judith? A Feminist Reassessment of a Biblical 'Heroine,'" *Semeia* 62 (1993): 37–58.

43. J. Cheryl Exum, "You Shall Let Every Daughter Live: A Study of Exodus 1:8–2:10," *Semeia* 28 (1983): 63–82.

the future liberation of the Israelite slaves to the women's cooperation. Her reading emphasizes typically neglected female characters and attempts to uncover positive portrayals of female biblical characters. Yet in a later article titled "Second Thoughts about Secondary Characters" (1994), Exum offers a reconsideration of her 1983 article with greater attention to gender politics.[44] In this second reading of Exodus 1:8–2:10, Exum notes that many of the women are unnamed and that they save a male child while serving male interests. Exum claims that these characters are supporting patriarchy and that the deity, rather than the women, is the hero of the story. Like Milne, Exum questioned the desire of some earlier interpreters, including herself, to find positive or liberative images of female characters.

Similarly, Phyllis Trible reflects on her 1973 article on Genesis 2–3 in "Not a Jot, Not a Tittle: Gen 2–3 after Twenty Years" (2002).[45] Her earlier work, "Eve and Adam: Genesis 2–3 Reread" was one of the earliest examples of twentieth-century feminist biblical criticism.[46] Although she did not label her work as feminist, she was in conversation with feminists who find the biblical creation stories to be supportive of women's subordination. Trible claimed that in Genesis 2 the Hebrew word for "man or human being" is neither male nor female but androgynous until woman is created in Genesis 2:21–23. Contrary to mainstream interpretations, she argued that both male and female beings are created equal. In her 2002 article, Trible admits that her earlier argument for a sexually undifferentiated creature as the first human creation was not a sound textual argument. Nevertheless, in her reassessment, she is unapologetic for offering a provocative reading because it helped to spur the development of new approaches to biblical interpretation.

As part of the reassessment of feminist biblical interpretation, some scholars attempted to offer some definitions and requirements for a feminist approach in biblical studies, given the significant range of definitions and uses. Phyllis Bird and Pamela Thimmes provide examples of two different responses. In the edited volume *Escaping Eden: New Feminist Perspectives on the Bible*, published in 1998, Hebrew Bible scholar Phyllis Bird rejects the label "feminist" for her work in "What Makes a Feminist Reading Feminist: A Qualified Answer."[47] She defines *feminism* as a "critical and constructive stance that claims for women the full humanity accorded to men."[48] Bird identifies herself as a feminist

44. J. Cheryl Exum, "Second Thoughts about Secondary Characters: Women in Exodus 1.8:2.10," in *Feminist Companion to Exodus to Deuteronomy*, ed. A. Brenner (Sheffield: Sheffield Academic Press, 1994), 75–87.

45. Phyllis Trible, "Not a Jot, Not a Tittle: Genesis 2–3 after Twenty Years," in *Biblical Studies Alternatively: An Introductory Reader*, ed. S. Scholz (Upper Saddle River, NJ: Prentice Hall, 2002), 101–6.

46. Phyllis Trible, "Eve and Adam: Genesis 2–3 Reread," *Andover Newton Quarterly* 13 (1973b): 251–58.

47. Phyllis Bird, "What Makes a Feminist Reading Feminist? A Qualified Answer," in *Escaping Eden: New Feminist Perspectives on the Bible*, ed. Harold C. Washington, Susan Lochrie Graham, and Pamela Thimmes (Sheffield: Sheffield Academic Press, 1998), 124–31.

48. Ibid., 124.

biblical interpreter and as a Christian. She stresses the importance of historical-critical methods in her scholarship and emphasizes the primacy of the text in her reading. Bird classifies the two primary elements of feminist interpretation as "*systemic analysis* of gender relations and a *critique* of relationships, norms and expectations that limit or subordinate women's thought, action, and expression" (Bird's italics).[49] Thus, for Bird, analysis of issues of gender is not synonymous with feminist interpretation, although she admits that "feminist aims" may be served by readings that do not include a feminist critique.[50]

In the same *Escaping Eden* edited volume, Pamela Thimmes's "What Makes a Feminist Reading Feminist? Another Perspective," offers parameters for feminist engagement. She contends that there were four necessary elements for a feminist hermeneutics: feminism, experience, culture, and reading/interpretation (language.) She defines *feminism* as "a liberation movement that not only critiques the oppressive structures of society but, by its various voices and approaches, works for transformation."[51] For Thimmes, in determining what makes a feminist reading feminist, the gender of the reader is not as important as the "coherence the reading has with a feminist ideology."[52] These reassessments and efforts to define feminist approaches showed how feminist biblical scholarship had grown such that scholars could question and reassess their own work as well as the aims of feminist engagement.

As illustrated by Thimmes's argument, some scholars maintain that feminist biblical scholarship should involve advocacy as they regard scholarship as praxis and necessarily in service to some particular end. Thus, self-identification as a feminist and a self-conscious effort to advocate for an end to women's subordination and to create scholarship in the service of that commitment would be required elements of a feminist approach. Still, this is not acknowledged by all scholars as a prerequisite. For example, Schüssler Fiorenza writes, "While academic studies on 'women' or 'gender' in the Bible proliferate and sometimes explicitly claim to be feminist, one rarely can find in such academic works any reference to a wo/men's movement for change or any connection with the actual daily struggles of wo/men."[53] While Schüssler Fiorenza articulates a critique of the use of "feminist" here, others would not find this broad usage to be problematic.

Given the loose definition of feminist approaches, many different types of work could be identified as feminist. To compound the complexity regarding the use of the term *feminist*, some scholars do not use the term or identify themselves or their work as explicitly feminist. Yet their work may be regarded as

49. Ibid., 129.
50. Ibid., 127.
51. Pamela Thimmes, "What Makes a Feminist Reading Feminist? Another Perspective," in *Escaping Eden: New Feminist Perspectives on the Bible*, ed. H. C. Washington, S. L. Graham, and P. Thimmes (Sheffield: Sheffield Academic Press, 1998), 134–35.
52. Ibid., 138.
53. Elisabeth Schüssler Fiorenza, *Wisdom Ways: Introducing Feminist Biblical Interpretation* (Maryknoll, NY: Orbis Books, 2001), 10.

feminist or included in a volume that includes "feminist approaches" in the title. In our contemporary period, given the proliferation of feminist biblical criticism, some scholars find that their work on gender or on women is assumed to be feminist work, but they may not choose to label their work in that way. For example, in New Testament scholar Beverly Gaventa's *Mary: Glimpses of the Mother of Jesus*, Gaventa explains that while she was writing this project, she was asked numerous times if her project was a feminist one. For Gaventa, a feminist approach would involve "exposing the androcentric and patriarchal values of biblical texts."[54] But because this is not the aim of her work, she clarifies that, as she understands it, it is not feminist. Also, in Old Testament scholar Barbara Green's *What Profit for Us? Remembering the Story of Joseph*, Green specifies that she does not regard her work as feminist because "its aim is not to expose the androcentric bias of the text, its virtual ignoring of any woman except those whose main role is sexual."[55] It is unlikely that someone would assume that Gaventa or Green were source critics or form critics, since their work does not use those particular methodologies. Yet because they are women and because of the myriad definitions of feminist approaches, some assume that their work is feminist.

Gender and Intersectional Analyses

The diversity of approaches within feminist biblical scholarship has allowed a large body of scholarship to be subsumed under its umbrella. This scholarship includes gender-focused analysis as well as work with additional categories of difference. In addition, it includes work that may or may not have a feminist agenda. Given this variety of scholarly approaches, newer scholarship might draw on the legacy of feminist work but may or may not be identified as "feminist" for a variety of reasons. Yet the growth of feminist biblical scholarship may be inhibited if scholars use feminist insights without acknowledging the scholars and scholarship that pioneered its development.

Developments in feminism and in feminist biblical criticism do not occur in waves or in a neat, orderly, linear progression. There continues to be a great deal of diversity within feminist approaches. Such approaches include different types of methods, perspectives, and personal commitments. Since this diversity has been present since the early development of feminist biblical interpretation, there has not been a discernable third wave of feminist biblical interpretation. At least, there has not been a significant change or break with previous so-called second-wave scholarship. Yet there have been other developments that have been significantly influenced by the foundational work of feminist approaches

---

54. Beverly Roberts Gaventa, *Mary: Glimpses of the Mother of Jesus* (Columbia: University of South Carolina Press, 1995), x.

55. Barbara Green, *What Profit for Us? Remembering the Story of Joseph* (Lanham, MD: University Press of America, 1996), 4.

in biblical studies. Gender analysis and intersectional analysis are two examples of this type of work.

Some biblical scholars identify their work as gender analysis and focus on masculine and feminine behavior, constructions, and norms in biblical texts.[56] This type of analysis is regarded as a distinct enterprise that is separate from feminist analysis, particularly if one understands feminist analysis as requiring a particular type of ideological commitment as Bird's and Thimmes's definitions suggest. Given its focus on gender and due to the diversity of feminist approaches, this type of gender analysis may look very much like what could be called feminist analysis. For example, Timothy Beal discusses the interaction of gender and ethnicity in the book of Esther in *The Book of Hiding: Gender, Ethnicity, Annihilation, and Esther* (1997). If Beal had chosen to identify his work as feminist, the label would fit given the diversity of feminist approaches, but he does not do so. Instead, drawing on the work of a number of literary and feminist scholars, he attempts to move beyond the limitations of more traditional feminist biblical scholarship to focus on "how gender identities are formed, and how these formations become problematic, especially when put into play along with other codes of identity such as ethnicity."[57] Of course, like any scholar, Beal is free to label his work as he chooses. Still, his choice not to identify his work as feminist contributes to the continued questions regarding distinctions of gender and feminist analysis.

Just as gender analysis within biblical studies has developed in part from feminist approaches, some scholars are using the concept of intersectionality in their research. As discussed in chapter 1, intersectionality is an element of black feminist and womanist thought. It highlights the multiplicative forces of oppression, including race, gender, class, and other factors. In biblical studies, the edited volume *Prejudice and Christian Beginnings: Investigating Race, Gender, and Ethnicity in Early Christianity* (2012) is not labeled as feminist but includes questions raised by Schüssler Fiorenza's notion of kyriarchy as well as black feminist thought.[58] Focusing on notions of intersectionality, the volume addresses issues of identity construction in early Christian history by moving beyond binary categories and attending to the interactions of multiple categories of difference. Also, Marianne Bjelland Kartzow's *Destabilizing the Margins: An Intersectional Approach to Early Christian Memory* provides an early use of intersectionality in biblical studies.[59] Kartzow engages memory theory and intersectionality in order to address early Christian memory and complexities relating to power dynamics.

56. Beatrice Lawrence, "Gender Analysis: Gender and Method in Biblical Studies," in *Method Matters*, 333–48.

57. Timothy K. Beal, *The Book of Hiding: Gender, Ethnicity, Annihilation, and Esther* (New York: Routledge, 1997), x.

58. Laura Salah Nasrallah and Elisabeth Schüssler Fiorenza, eds., *Prejudice and Christian Beginnings: Investigating Race, Gender, and Ethnicity in Early Christian Studies* (Minneapolis: Fortress Press, 2009).

59. Marianne Bjelland Kartzow, *Destabilizing the Margins: An Intersectional Approach to Early Christian Memory* (Eugene, OR: Pickwick Publications, 2012).

In some ways, this type of intersectional approach may be an extension of feminist work as well as a response to critiques of feminist work in that it addresses issues of gender and power as well as other categories of difference.

Although scholars who do not use the term *feminist* or who choose to label their work as "gender analysis" or "intersectional" may have valid reasons for doing so, the nonuse of *feminist* and the use of gender analysis and intersectionality may contribute to the erasure of the contributions of feminist and womanist scholarship.[60] Each scholar may avoid or embrace particular methods and approaches as befitting his or her work. Yet drawing on feminist work and repackaging it without acknowledging those who have developed this work is concerning. Schüssler Fiorenza refers to this type of reworking as part of the potential for "co-optation and appropriation of feminist work."[61] If the work of those who have pioneered these approaches is not cited, quoted, engaged, and assigned in classrooms, then such work becomes further marginalized. In scholarship, citations are a form of currency. If there is no citation of the work of those who have done the heavy lifting of developing these approaches, one does not gain an appreciation for the significant legacy of earlier scholarship. This neglect strips away the history and development of an entire subfield.

IMPACT ON THE DISCIPLINE OF BIBLICAL STUDIES

Within the scholarly guild, feminist biblical criticism has moved from the margins of biblical scholarship. Two SBL program sections, Feminist Hermeneutics of the Bible and Women in the Biblical World, have been active since the 1980s. While these two sections were the predominant venues for feminist work in the past, currently many other program sections include and even welcome presentations that involve feminist or gender-focused scholarship.

Some of the key figures within the development of feminist biblical interpretation have been elected to the presidency of the SBL. While the executive director runs SBL operations, the presidency is an important symbolic position. Serving as SBL president indicates that one's scholarship and contributions have reached a level of prominence and respect by peers in the field. Women presidents have included Elisabeth Schüssler Fiorenza (1987), Phyllis Trible (1994), Adele Berlin (2000), Carolyn Osiek (2005), Katharine Sakenfeld (2007), and Carol Newsom (2011). All of these scholars have contributed to the growth of feminist approaches in the discipline although they may not all identify themselves or

---

60. Silma Bilge, "Intersectionality Undone: Saving Intersectionality from Feminist Intersectionality Studies," *Du Bois Review* 10, no. 2 (2013), 405–24; Flavia Dzodan, "My Feminism Will Be Intersectional or It Will Be Bullshit," Tiger Beatdown, http://tigerbeatdown.com/2011/10/10/my-feminism-will-be-intersectional-or-it-will-be-bullshit/.

61. Schüssler Fiorenza, *Wisdom Ways*, 11.

their work as feminist. Their service in leadership signals the recognition of their work and the recognition of the importance of feminist approaches.

Feminist biblical criticism has a significant track record of publications, including monographs, edited volumes, and peer-reviewed journal articles. Jewish New Testament scholar Amy-Jill Levine serves as the editor for the Feminist Companion to the Bible, which is now in its second series. This series is a recognized important resource within the field, and it has provided a consistent venue for feminist work within biblical studies for several decades. Major volumes that focus on women characters or feminist approaches are available, including *Searching the Scriptures (1997); A Feminist Companion to Reading the Bible: Approaches, Methods, and Strategies* (1997); *Women in Scripture: A Dictionary of Named and Unnamed Women in the Hebrew Bible, the Apocryphal/Deuterocanonical Books, and the New Testament* (2001); and *The Torah: A Women's Commentary (2007).* Also, there are many introductory volumes on feminist biblical scholarship for students and nonprofessionals. In addition, in reference volumes, feminist biblical interpretation is a major entry, and female characters and issues related to gender are covered in encyclopedias and other reference material.

While there is not a clear-cut third wave within feminist biblical studies, the publication of the twentieth-anniversary edition of *The Women's Bible Commentary* illustrates the importance and prominence of feminist approaches in biblical studies. With a title designed to evoke the nineteenth-century *The Woman's Bible*, the commentary was first published in 1992. It was revised and expanded in 1998 and revised again in 2012. It uses a broad definition of feminism as contributors use different approaches in highlighting women characters and in addressing issues of gender and power. It includes all women contributors and has become a standard reference work in biblical studies.[62]

In most mainstream seminaries, divinity schools, and religion departments it is not uncommon to find courses on feminist biblical interpretation. Even in places where there is some resistance to the term *feminist*, courses on women and the Bible or efforts to highlight female characters or to discuss the role of women in ancient societies demonstrate how feminist work has become part of conversation. Feminist biblical scholars serve as dissertation advisors and are training the next generation of scholars. Faculty position descriptions may list feminist approaches as one of several possible areas of specialization that would be viewed favorably in a candidate. In scholarship and teaching, feminist biblical interpretation has made a significant impact on the discipline of biblical studies. As discussed in chapter 6, feminist biblical interpretation is one of the major influences on the development of

---

62. Disclosure: I was one of the contributors to the *Women's Bible Commentary*. See Nyasha Junior, "Exodus," in *Women's Bible Commentary*, ed. Carol A. Newsom, Sharon H. Ringe, and Jacqueline E. Lapsley, rev. ed. (Louisville, KY: Westminster John Knox Press, 2012), 56–66.

womanist biblical interpretation, which has not had the same type of impact within biblical studies.

CONCLUSION

Despite links made with nineteenth-century efforts to interpret the Bible to support greater women's equality, feminist biblical interpretation in the twentieth century was developed by professionally trained biblical scholars and others in academia. In general, concern with gender and issues relating to women are elements of feminist approaches, but the definition of feminism and the use of feminist approaches remain without consensus. Used in conjunction with a variety of methods, feminist approaches have contributed to a wide range of scholarly output. The influence of such work has been felt even in work not labeled as feminist. Contemporary feminist biblical interpretation has been characterized by continued diversity, which has caused some scholars to question whether there are or should be some basic definitions, preconditions, or aims for feminist approaches to biblical texts. As with other feminist gains, it may be that we now take for granted the work of previous generations. Feminist biblical criticism remains important, influential, and divisive. Its connections to womanist biblical interpretation will be explored in chapter 6.

RESOURCE LIST

Brenner, Athalya, and Carol Fontaine, eds. *A Feminist Companion to Reading the Bible: Approaches, Methods and Strategies.* Sheffield: Sheffield Academic Press, 1997. This collection of essays provides helpful details on feminist approaches within biblical studies.

Newsom, Carol A., Sharon H. Ringe, and Jacqueline E. Lapsley, eds. *Women's Bible Commentary.* 3rd/twentieth anniversary ed. Louisville, KY: Westminster John Knox Press, 2012. This important commentary provides a brief and accessible essay on each book of the Bible.

Schüssler Fiorenza, Elisabeth. *Wisdom Ways: Introducing Feminist Biblical Interpretation.* Maryknoll, NY: Orbis Books, 2001. This volume provides an introduction to key issues within feminist biblical interpretation by one of its most well-known scholars.

Trible, Phyllis. *Texts of Terror: Literary-Feminist Readings of Biblical Narratives.* Philadelphia: Fortress Press, 1984. This classic work is an essential must-read for any student of feminist approaches to biblical texts.

Vander Stichele, C., and Todd Penner, eds. *Her Master's Tools? Feminist and Postcolonial Engagements of Historical-Critical Discourse.* Global Perspectives on Biblical Scholarship, no. 9, edited by Benjamin D. Sommer, and Sharon H. Ringe. Atlanta: Society of Biblical Literature, 2005. This edited volume offers a diverse range of feminist approaches in concert with other methodologies.

Chapter 6

Womanist Biblical Interpretation

When I begin a lecture in my Hebrew Bible classes, I try to provide clear definitions of key terms for my students. For example, I explain and define *Septuagint* or *Megillot*. I distinguish terms that could be easily confused like *Deuteronomic* and *Deuteronomistic*, and I attempt to clear up misperceptions, such as the notion that the Torah and the Pentateuch are synonymous. Before I launch into that day's course material, I want everyone to have a basic understanding of the terms that I will use. I wish that I could provide a definition of *womanist biblical interpretation*, but I confess that I cannot offer a clear definition because one does not exist.

The purpose of this chapter is to analyze what is labeled as womanist biblical interpretation within the larger discipline of biblical studies. This chapter describes the work of pioneering scholars Renita J. Weems and Clarice J. Martin and other womanist publications in biblical studies. It highlights the varied definitions of *womanist* and the diverse understandings of what constitutes a womanist approach within biblical studies. It ties together contemporary womanist biblical interpretation with influences from earlier womanist biblical interpreters, womanist scholarship in religious-studies-related fields, and feminist biblical interpretation. Also, it discusses the current impact of womanist work within the academic discipline of biblical studies. It illustrates that there is no clear consensus regarding a definition or distinctive elements of womanist approaches within biblical studies.[1]

I am limiting this discussion to the work of biblical scholars who identify their work as womanist in order to focus on the current uses of womanist approaches in biblical studies.[2] To be clear, although the term *womanist* is often regarded as synonymous with "African American woman," this discussion focuses on work that is labeled as womanist by its author. To reiterate, although some work that is not labeled as feminist is categorized as feminist biblical studies due to the very broad categories used for feminist biblical interpretation, such categorization refers to the scholar's work, not to the scholar herself or himself. Thus the work of women biblical scholars is not assumed to be feminist. Yet in biblical studies often the work of African American women biblical scholars is assumed to be womanist. This is a false assumption, as there are African American women scholars who do not identify themselves or their work as womanist.[3]

It may seem overly restrictive to focus on work labeled as womanist since chapter 5 notes the ways in which feminist biblical scholarship is sometimes not explicitly labeled as feminist. Yet feminist biblical interpretation is a large umbrella category that has developed broad parameters over the past forty years.

---

1. See my prior thoughts on womanist biblical interpretation in Nyasha Junior, "Womanist Biblical Interpretation," in *Engaging the Bible in a Gendered World: An Introduction to Feminist Biblical Interpretation in Honor of Katharine Doob Sakenfeld*, ed. Linda Day and Carolyn Pressler (Louisville, KY: Westminster John Knox Press, 2006), 37–46 and Nyasha Junior, "Womanist Biblical Interpretation," in *The Oxford Encyclopedia of Biblical Interpretation*, ed. Steven L. McKenzie (New York: Oxford University Press, 2013), 2:448–456.

2. It is beyond the scope of this volume to discuss non-U.S. biblical scholarship, whether using feminist approaches or not, but it is important to note that African women and women of the African diaspora have contributed to biblical scholarship, although they may not use the term *womanist*. For example, Madipoane (Ngwana' Mphahlele) Masenya has offered a *Bosadi* interpretation of Proverbs 31:10–31. See Mmadipoane Ngwana' Mphahlele Masenya, "A *Bosadi* (Womanhood) Reading of Proverbs 31:10–31," in *Other Ways of Reading: African Women and the Bible*, ed. Musa W. Dube (Atlanta: Society of Biblical Literature, 2001), 145–57. Masenya's *bosadi* reading stems from the Northern Sotho word *mosadi* for "woman." Masenya acknowledges the similarities of her reading with womanist approaches, but she does not use the term *womanist* due to her focus on an African/South African woman's Bible reading and notions of ideal womanhood from that context. Also, Musa Dube's edited collection offers postcolonial and feminist approaches to biblical interpretation. See Musa M. Dube, *Postcolonial Feminist Interpretation of the Bible* (St. Louis: Chalice Press, 2000).

3. Some, though certainly not all, African American women biblical scholars may identify their work more with contextual hermeneutics, minoritized hermeneutics, or specifically African American hermeneutics. See Randall C. Bailey and Jacquelyn Grant, eds., *The Recovery of Black Presence: An Interdisciplinary Exploration: Essays in Honor of Dr. Charles B. Copher* (Nashville: Abingdon Press, 1995); Randall C. Bailey, Tat-Siong Benny Liew, and Fernando F. Segovia, *They Were All Together in One Place: Toward Minority Biblical Criticism* (Atlanta: Society of Biblical Literature, 2009); Randall C. Bailey, *Yet with a Steady Beat: Contemporary U.S. Afrocentric Biblical Interpretation*, vol. 42 (Atlanta: Society of Biblical Literature, 2003); Brian K. Blount, *Cultural Interpretation: Reorienting New Testament Criticism* (Minneapolis: Fortress Press, 1995); Vincent L. Wimbush, "The Bible and African Americans: An Outline of an Interpretive History," in *Stony the Road We Trod: African American Biblical Interpretation*, ed. C. H. Felder (Minneapolis: Fortress Press, 1991), 81–97; and Michael Joseph Brown, *Blackening of the Bible: The Aims of African American Biblical Scholarship*, ed. Anthony B. Pinn and Victor Anderson (Harrisburg, PA.: Trinity Press International, 2004).

Scholars have published a significant body of feminist biblical scholarship such that it is possible to outline its basic contours and features and to offer examples culled from a large amount of published scholarship. In contrast, there is comparatively little womanist biblical scholarship. Therefore, it is important not to make generalizations by treating the small amount of available womanist biblical scholarship as representative of a much larger body of work. Since there is relatively little published womanist biblical scholarship, these scholars provide only some of the very few examples of womanist work within biblical studies. Thus this chapter focuses on the contributions of the very small number of biblical scholars who have published work that they have labeled as womanist biblical scholarship.[4]

PIONEERING SCHOLARS

Renita Weems and Clarice Martin are two biblical scholars who are considered to be the pioneers of womanist biblical scholarship. They are the authors of the first publications labeled as womanist within Hebrew Bible and New Testament scholarship, respectively. This section discusses selected examples of the work of Weems and Martin and analyzes their use of *womanist* and of womanist approaches.

Renita J. Weems

Renita Weems is the biblical scholar who is most often associated with womanist biblical interpretation. As a graduate of Princeton Theological Seminary, she was the first African American woman to earn a Ph.D. in Old Testament studies. Yet Weems's book *Just a Sister Away: A Womanist Vision of Women's Relationships in the Bible* was published in 1988 before she earned her doctoral degree.[5] The book focuses on the relationships between nine pairs of biblical women.[6] In the foreword, Weems describes her work as combining feminist biblical criticism and African American oral tradition. She identifies her perspective as womanist and mentions portions of Walker's definition, including "black feminist; a courageous woman who is committed to *whole* people, both men and

4. There are instances of male biblical scholars using some insights from black feminist and womanist thought. See the "neo-womanist" discussion in Brown, *Blackening of the Bible*. Also, see Randall C. Bailey, "'That's Why They Didn't Call the Book Hadassah!': The Interse(ct)/(x)Ionality of Race/Ethnicity, Gender, and Sexuality in the Book of Esther," in Bailey et al. eds., *They Were All Together in One Place*, 227–50.

5. Renita J. Weems, *Just a Sister Away: A Womanist Vision of Women's Relationships in the Bible* (San Diego, CA: LuraMedia, 1988).

6. The sets of women include Hagar and Sarah (Gen. 16:1–16 and 21:1–21); Naomi and Ruth (book of Ruth); Mary and Martha (Luke 10:38–42); Jephthah's daughter and the mourning women (Judg. 11:1–40); Miriam and her Cushite sister-in-law (Exod. 2:1–10; Num. 12:1–16); the women who followed Jesus (Matt. 27:55–28:10; Mark 15:40–41, 16:1–13; Luke 8:1–3; 24:1–11; John 20:1–18); Vashti and Esther (Esth. 1:1–2:4); Elizabeth and Mary (Luke 1:5–56); and Lot's wife and her daughters (Gen. 19).

women;" and understanding her work as "*audacious.*"[7] Although she mentions Walker, Weems does not engage Walker's full definition in any significant way.

Weems's work was revised and reissued as *Just a Sister Away: Understanding the Timeless Connection between Women of Today and Women in the Bible* (2005).[8] In the new introduction, she describes the first edition as having been written on a "dare" or invitation from a publisher who heard Weems lecture. Weems reasserts the influence of feminist biblical criticism as well as her experiences in the African American storytelling tradition as she did in the first edition, but she does not explain why the term *womanist* has been removed from the title of the second edition.

The first edition of *Just a Sister Away* was the first book labeled as womanist biblical interpretation, and in most discussions of feminist and womanist biblical studies, it is cited as the beginning of womanist biblical interpretation. Yet neither edition of the book was a scholarly monograph but what would be more appropriately called a popular trade book. Weems acknowledges her perspective and her intended audience and explains that she wrote *Just a Sister Away* for African American Christian women outside of the academy. Designed as a resource primarily for African American Christian women, this book provides creative interpretations of the relationships between biblical women and includes discussion questions following each chapter. Weems admits that her reconstructions of the conversations, emotions, and actions of biblical characters are not based on textual evidence, but she holds that they reflect commonalities in women's experiences.

Just a Sister Away is ground-breaking work in that it offers readings of biblical texts that address some of the experiences and concerns of African American Christian women. Since Weems is a biblical scholar and since there was no other womanist work in biblical studies when *Just a Sister Away* was published, it was regarded as the first womanist publication in biblical studies despite the lack of critical rigor that is typical of other scholarly monographs. This is not to deny the value of the work but to clarify that this volume is not in conversation with the critical work of feminist biblical scholars. As I discussed in chapter 1, distinguishing critical scholarship is not an elitist effort to disparage more accessible or popular publications or the work of those outside of the academy but a way to describe the genre of the material and its concomitant expectations. *Just a Sister Away* is important because it was one of the first books identified as womanist biblical interpretation. Nonetheless, it is misleading to cite it as if it represents the first scholarly monograph on womanist biblical interpretation.

Unlike most academics, Weems is a crossover writer in that she has written for popular media as well as academic publishers. Some of Weems's books are similar to *Just a Sister Away* in that they are intended for lay audiences. For

---

7. Weems, *Just a Sister Away*, ix.
8. Ibid. Weems revises her original chapters and adds new material on Mary Magdalene (Acts 1:12–26), the Queen of Sheba (1 Kgs. 10:1–10), Achsah and Caleb (Josh. 15:13–19; Judg. 1:11–15), and Zelophehad's daughters (Num. 27:1–11; 36).

instance, she has written *I Asked for Intimacy: Stories of Blessings, Betrayals, and Birthings* (1993);[9] *Showing Mary: How Women Can Share Prayers, Wisdom, and the Blessings of God* (2002);[10] *What Matters Most: Ten Passionate Lessons from the Song of Solomon* (2004).[11] Weems has also written a memoir, *Listening for God: A Minister's Journey through Silence and Doubt* (1999), in which she shares her personal faith crisis and describes her efforts to maintain her relationship to God.[12] These publications are not labeled as womanist and are not intended for scholarly audiences. In addition to her popular books, Weems has written for magazines such as *Essence* and *Ebony*. Also, she cowrote gospel singer CeCe Winans's autobiography, *On a Positive Note* (1999).[13]

Turning to her more academic publications, Weems's *Battered Love: Marriage, Sex, and Violence in the Hebrew Prophets* (1995) addresses the sexual imagery and violence in prophetic literature. Written for an academic audience, Weems states that she uses her experiences as an African American woman in her approach to prophetic literature, but she does not construct a womanist approach or identify this work as womanist.[14] Despite her reputation as a womanist biblical scholar, Weems's single scholarly monograph, *Battered Love*, does not mention womanism at all. Weems has not provided more technical discussions that illustrate the usefulness of womanist approaches for critical biblical scholarship.

In other scholarly publications, Weems uses womanist approaches irregularly. In a journal article "Gomer: Victim of Violence or Victim of Metaphor," Weems discusses the use of a marriage metaphor to characterize the relationship between Israel and Yahweh in Hosea 2:4–25.[15] She offers a literary approach that focuses on the use of this metaphorical language and its dependence on sexual violence. In expressing her attention to this language as well as the implications of the use of such language, Weems does not identify her approach as womanist, but in a footnote she identifies herself as both a feminist and womanist biblical scholar. She explains that as a "feminist biblical scholar," her attention is on the abuse of a "*woman*," but as a "black and womanist biblical scholar" her focus is on the exploitation of "*anyone*."[16] Her personal identification is that

9. Renita J. Weems, *I Asked for Intimacy: Stories of Blessings, Betrayals, and Birthings* (San Diego: LuraMedia, 1993a).

10. Renita J. Weems, *Showing Mary: How Women Can Share Prayers, Wisdom, and the Blessings of God* (West Bloomfield, MI: Walk Worthy Press, 2002).

11. Renita J. Weems, *What Matters Most: Ten Passionate Lessons from the Song of Solomon* (West Bloomfield, MI: Walk Worthy Press, 2004).

12. Renita J. Weems, *Listening for God: A Minister's Journey through Silence and Doubt* (New York: Touchstone, 1999).

13. CeCe Winans and Renita J. Weems, *On a Positive Note: Her Joyous Faith, Her Life in Music, and Her Everyday Blessings* (New York: Pocket Books, 1999).

14. Renita J. Weems, *Battered Love: Marriage, Sex, and Violence in the Hebrew Prophets* (Minneapolis: Fortress Press, 1995).

15. Renita J. Weems, "Gomer: Victim of Violence Or Victim of Metaphor?" *Semeia* 47 (1989): 87–104.

16. Ibid., 90n10.

of a feminist or womanist, but she does not label her work as womanist. Further-more, her research focus is not on African American women in particular but on "anyone." According to Weems, her feminist and womanist identity provide the impetus for her focused attention on exploitation in the text, but she does not characterize her exegesis as womanist.

In "Reading *Her* Way through the Struggle: African American Women and the Bible" (Weems's italics), Weems provides a historical survey of African American women's relationship to the Bible, but she does not describe her approach or perspective as womanist. Weems seeks to explain the enduring importance of the Bible for many African American women.[17] In this histori-cal overview, Weems addresses the use of the Bible in upholding gender, race/ethnicity, and class oppression. Also, she offers examples of reading strategies employed by some African American women in interpreting texts for those who are marginalized and in support of their liberation. She mentions Alice Walker and one portion of part 2 of her definition of *womanist* as "committed to survival and wholeness of entire people, male and female. Not a separatist, except periodically, for health."[18] Still, Weems does not address how womanist approaches can be employed in reading biblical texts.

In "Womanist Reflections on Biblical Hermeneutics" (1993) Weems offers some characteristics of womanist approaches in her efforts to distinguish wom-anist biblical criticism from both the historical-critical method and from femi-nist biblical criticism.[19] Arguing that feminist criticism focuses primarily on issues of gender, she writes, "Feminist scholarship, both within the theological field and outside the field, is largely an Anglo-American, bourgeois, matriarchal enterprise."[20] Weems mentions Alice Walker and refers to a segment of Walker's definition regarding survival and wholeness. Also, in a footnote, Weems observes that more African American women scholars have started to use the term *wom-anist* in an effort to distinguish themselves from feminists, and she contrasts the work of feminists with that of African American women. She contends that while white feminists focus on women, African American women, including nineteenth-century activists and twentieth-century scholars, have historically been concerned with the liberation of oppressed peoples.

Weems also contrasts feminist biblical hermeneutics with an African Ameri-can womanist perspective on biblical texts, which she regards as moving beyond concerns with gender oppression. Weems writes, "Victimized by multiple cat-egories of oppression (e.g., race, gender, class) and having experienced these victimizations oftentimes simultaneously, women of color bring to biblical

17. Renita J. Weems, "Reading Her Way through the Struggle: African American Women and the Bible," in *Stony the Road We Trod: African American Biblical Interpretation*, ed. Cain H. Felder (Minneapolis: Fortress Press, 1991), 57–77.

18. Ibid., 69–70n23.

19. Renita J. Weems, "Womanist Reflections on Biblical Hermeneutics," in *Black Theology: A Documentary History*, ed. James H. Cone and Gayraud S. Wilmore (Maryknoll, NY: Orbis Books, 1993b), 216–24.

20. Ibid., 217.

academic discourse a broader, and more subtle, understanding of systems of oppression."[21] For her, a womanist perspective stems from one's personal experience with oppression, which she claims creates a greater understanding of and sensitivity to the interconnected forms of oppression.

This emphasis on the lived experience of African American women continued in other work. For instance, in an essay that offers reflections following a symposium in Switzerland in 2000 on feminist exegesis and the hermeneutics of liberation, Weems discusses her personal identification in "Re-Reading for Liberation: African American Women and the Bible" (2003).[22] She regards herself personally as part of both "marginalized" and "privileged" reading communities as an "African American woman/womanist" and "Western/North American feminist," respectively.[23] Then she links this personal identification with her reading strategy. Weems explains that womanist biblical interpretation emerged from feminist biblical interpretation and liberation theology and argues that womanist biblical hermeneutics, like feminist biblical hermeneutics, does not begin with the Bible. Instead, she claims that womanist biblical hermeneutics comes from the perspective of African American women's experience, in particular as survivors of slavery and as survivors of various forms of oppression. Thus, for Weems, the central distinguishing factor of a womanist approach is the perspective of the African American woman writer offering this reading.

In "Re-Reading for Liberation," Weems parallels the development of feminist and womanist scholarship. She speaks of both feminist and womanist biblical scholarship in three waves or phases and claims that first-wave biblical feminist and womanist scholarship focused on recovering stories of overlooked and neglected women biblical characters. As well, she argues that second-wave feminist and womanist work in biblical studies involves recovering and reclaiming women characters. Weems identifies a third wave of scholarship that focuses on the construction of meaning and identity for flesh-and-blood readers. Weems claims that womanist biblical hermeneutics fits well within this third wave due to its concern with the ways in which African Americans read the Bible. She writes, "It is here in this third phase of biblical liberation criticism that womanist criticism situates itself best. Womanist biblical criticism is interested in the ways in which African Americans read the Bible, the strategies they use in negotiating meaning and identity from stories, and those they use when resisting the meaning(s) and identities attached to certain stories."[24] Weems claims that the primary work of womanist scholars is to empower African American women. She explains that a womanist biblical hermeneutics takes as its starting point

21. Ibid., 220.
22. Renita J. Weems, "Re-Reading for Liberation: African American Women and the Bible," in *Feminist Interpretation of the Bible and the Hermeneutics of Liberation*, ed. Silvia Schroer and Sophia Bietenhard (New York: Sheffield Academic Press, 2003), 19–32.
23. Ibid., 21.
24. Ibid., 29.

the notion that "people have power, not texts."[25] Weems claims that another element of the work of womanist scholars is to question the use of biblical texts about abuse of women such as Genesis 19 and Judges 19.

Weems makes sweeping statements about womanist biblical interpretation, but she does not make clear that her assertions are not backed as a body of work by biblical scholars. For example, in "Womanist Reflections on Biblical Hermeneutics" Weems describes an "African-American womanist" perspective and then expands this perspective to "women of color." Yet she does not engage the work of any African American women or women of color who use this approach in biblical studies. Instead, in a footnote she cites Latina theologian Ada Maria Isasí-Díaz and Asian theologian Kwok Pui-Lan. Weems does not clearly acknowledge the limited number of biblical scholars who have published womanist scholarship. She is unable to cite other African American biblical scholars who use this approach because their scholarship did not exist in 1993. Similarly, in "Re-Reading for Liberation" Weems does not identify any womanist biblical scholars who have produced the type of womanist work that she describes. Although this essay offers her personal reflections with limited footnotes, her broad generalizations are not offered as her hopes for the future or as her own views regarding womanist approaches.

When such a recognized scholar makes generalizations about womanist scholarship, it creates a strong impression. Despite the lack of footnotes to support her claims, many students and scholars would assume that Weems has several publications in mind. Weems's discussion of this perspective misleads the reader by describing womanist approaches in a way that suggests that there are a number of scholars who use this approach. Yet she does not cite one womanist biblical scholar who has offered a womanist perspective on these texts. Weems intimates that there is a body of womanist biblical scholarship from which she is offering representative examples, but she does not explain that she is not offering widely held views within a robust body of womanist biblical scholarship.

CLARICE J. MARTIN

Clarice Martin was the first African American woman to receive a Ph.D. in New Testament studies. She graduated from Duke University in 1985, and her dissertation was titled *The Function of Acts 8:26–40 within the Narrative Structure of the Book of Acts: The Significance of the Eunuch's Provenance for Acts 1:8c*. Although she has not published a scholarly monograph using womanist approaches, Martin is regarded as another pioneer in the development of womanist biblical interpretation because she was one of the first African American women to be formally trained in biblical studies.

25. Ibid., 26.

In one of her more well-known articles, "Womanist Interpretations of the New Testament: The Quest for Holistic and Inclusive Translation and Interpretation" (1990), Martin offers her understanding of womanist biblical criticism and addresses issues of biblical translation and interpretation from a womanist perspective.[26] Here she reviews the history of interpretation of *doulos* texts in light of the experiences of African Americans. She discusses the translation of Greek *doulos* as "servant" or "slave" and argues for the importance in translating the word as "slave" to avoid euphemistic language. Martin mentions Alice Walker and cites segments of Walker's definition in a cursory fashion. Martin claims, "Describing the courageous, audacious, and 'in charge' behavior of the black woman, the term *womanist* affirms black women's connection with both feminism and with the history, culture, and religion of the African-American community."[27] Later, Martin cites a portion of Walker's definition: "A womanist is 'committed to survival and wholeness of entire people, male and female."[28] Martin labels her approach as womanist and makes connections regarding African American women's experiences.

The article "The *Haustafeln* (Household Codes) in African American Biblical Interpretation: 'Free Slave' and 'Subordinate Women'" (1991) is perhaps one of Martin's most widely known publications because it appears in the popular edited volume *Stony the Road We Trod*.[29] Here Martin examines the household codes (Col. 3:18–41; Eph. 5:21–6:9; 1 Pet. 2:18–3:7), highlights selected African American approaches to these texts, and offers what she claims is a womanist perspective on the *Haustafeln*. She argues that a womanist perspective on the household codes would serve to foster greater gender equality between African American men and women. As in her 1990 article, Martin does not engage Walker's definition, although she mentions Walker in a footnote. Instead, Martin offers her own definition of a womanist as "a black feminist (or feminist of color) who claims her roots in black history, religion, and culture."[30]

As in previous work, Martin defines a womanist as relating to African American experiences in "Normative Biblical Motifs in African-American Women Leader's Moral Discourse" (1998).[31] Martin highlights the spiritual autobiography of nineteenth-century African American activist Maria Stewart as a source

26. Clarice J. Martin, "Womanist Interpretations of the New Testament: The Quest for Holistic and Inclusive Translation and Interpretation," *Journal of Feminist Studies in Religion* 6, no. 2 (Fall, 1990): 41–61.

27. Ibid., 41.

28. Ibid., 55.

29. Clarice J. Martin, "The *Haustafeln* (Household Codes) in African American Biblical Interpretation: 'Free Slave' and 'Subordinate Women,'" in *Stony the Road We Trod: African American Biblical Interpretation*, ed. Cain H. Felder (Minneapolis: Fortress Press, 1991), 206–31.

30. Ibid., 228.

31. Clarice J. Martin, "Normative Biblical Motifs in African-American Women Leaders' Moral Discourse: Maria Stewart's Autobiography as a Resource for Nurturing Leadership from the Black Church Tradition," in *The Stones That the Builders Rejected: The Development of Ethical Leadership from the Black Church Tradition*, ed. Walter Earl Fluker (Harrisburg, PA: Trinity Press, 1998), 47–72.

for moral wisdom for the black church. She mentions Alice Walker and segments of Walker's definition and defines *womanist* as a term that "affirms black women's connection with both feminism and with the history, culture, and religion of the African-American community."[32] Martin offers three elements of a working hypothesis regarding the potential sources of ethical leadership for African American women: womanist biblical and theological thought; use of biblical texts by African American women; and African American women's written work, especially as it evolves from private concerns to the public sphere and greater activism.

In her 1999 essay on womanist biblical interpretation for the *Dictionary of Biblical Interpretation* (*DBI*),[33] Martin argues that womanist biblical interpretation emerges from womanist theology, which developed out of black theology. She contends that the work of womanist theologians and the definition of *womanist* by Alice Walker have influenced womanist biblical interpretation in three aspects: a womanist self-identification, a focus on African American women's experiences, and the importance of family and community. Martin cites only one segment of Walker's definition without engaging Walker's statement regarding same-gender loving relationships, which has been a controversial element within womanist work as discussed in chapter 4.

In the *DBI* essay, Martin argues that womanist biblical interpretation is based on three assumptions: the authority of the Bible, the liberative power of the Bible, and multiple and interlocking forms of domination within biblical texts and interpretations of those texts. Martin claims that there are four primary tasks for womanist biblical interpreters: recovering texts and their worlds, reclaiming texts related to Africans and "blackness," challenging feminist theologians and biblical scholars regarding issues of race, and addressing the effects of biblical interpretation on African and African diasporic peoples.

In "Polishing the Unclouded Mirror: A Womanist Reading of Revelation 18:13" (2005),[34] Martin puts the critique of ancient slavery within the text of Revelation 18:13 into conversation with the experience of slavery by African Americans.[35] Her womanist method is based on four assumptions. First, "all interpretations are relative," and none are "value-neutral."[36] Second, she uses a womanist interpretive lens. Third, Martin situates herself within the African diaspora and within black feminist and womanist communities that include women activists within and outside of academic circles. Fourth, her womanist reading focuses on the critique of slavery by "John" or "the Seer" in the book of Revelation. In describing her womanist lens in this article, Martin mentions

32. Ibid., 56.

33. Clarice J. Martin, "Womanist Biblical Interpretation," in *Dictionary of Biblical Interpretation*, ed. John H. Hayes (Nashville: Abingdon Press, 1999), 2:655–58.

34. Clarice J. Martin, "Polishing the Unclouded Mirror: A Womanist Reading of Revelation 18:13," in *From Every People and Nation: The Book of Revelation in Intercultural Perspective*, ed. David M. Rhoads (Minneapolis: Fortress Press, 2005), 82–109.

35. Ibid.

36. Ibid., 84.

Alice Walker's definition of *womanist* but does not cite the definition. Martin highlights the influence of womanist theology and its growth from black theology of the 1960s and 1970s. She claims that womanist interpreters challenge "androcentrism and patriarchy" and address gender, race, and class oppression as well as the multiple ways in which these oppressions interact.[37] She writes, "Out of their identity and experience, womanist interpreters challenge the gender-exclusive hegemony of male-articulated understandings of the Christian faith. They affirm the significance of reading the Hebrew Bible and New Testament within the context of women's experience."[38] For Martin, a womanist perspective involves attention to the lived experiences of women and emerges out of the identity and experiences of African American women.

Similar to Weems, Martin makes generalizations regarding womanist biblical scholarship. In her *Haustafeln* article, she cites influential womanist scholars such as ethicist Katie Cannon and theologian Delores Williams in her footnotes but combines those in religion-related studies and in biblical studies as offering womanist theological reflection. Yet for biblical scholars Martin cites only herself and Weems's *Just a Sister Away*. Not specifying the academic discipline of these scholars gives the false impression that womanist biblical scholarship is more robust than it is in reality. To be fair, there were possibly only two African American women with doctoral degrees in biblical studies at the time this article was written. Nevertheless, Martin does not explain this fact to her readers.

In "Normative Biblical Motifs," Martin includes lengthy endnotes and highlights the work of African American women, but again she merges biblical and theological reflection and cites only herself and Weems as African American woman biblical scholars by citing Weems's *Just a Sister Away* and her own 1990 *Journal of Feminist Studies in Religion* article. In her *doulos* article Martin writes, "One discipline where womanist theological reflection is especially welcome is biblical studies,"[39] but she cites no scholarship to support this claim. In 1990, there were only a couple of African American women biblical scholars, including Martin herself. Still, she does not acknowledge the very limited numbers of scholars and the lack of womanist biblical scholarship. Also, in her discussion of womanist scholarship in various fields, she conflates theology and biblical studies, which are regarded as distinct disciplines. Furthermore, although she cites scholars in religious-studies-related fields who use womanist approaches, including Katie G. Canon and Delores Williams, Martin cites only one work by a biblical scholar, Weems's *Just a Sister Away*, which, as discussed above, is not a scholarly monograph.

Martin does not articulate the particular elements of her use of a womanist approach in "Womanist Interpretations." She writes, "In addition to importing gender, race, and class concerns to the task of biblical interpretation,

---

37. Ibid., 85.
38. Ibid.
39. Martin, "Womanist Interpretations of the New Testament," 41.

womanist theologians have addressed the issue of linguistic sexism with increasing urgency." Note that Martin refers to and cites womanist theologians, not biblical scholars. She goes on to claim that a particular concern of womanist biblical interpretation is the issue of translation of biblical texts into English and the impact of such translations. Yet she does not cite a single womanist biblical scholar whose work also expresses this concern. Also, Martin asserts that womanist biblical interpretation has a "quadruocentric" (four-fold) concern with "gender, race, class, and language."[40] She contrasts this approach with what she regards as the more typical concern with "gender, class, and language" in "white feminist biblical interpretation and translation."[41] Again Martin generalizes regarding womanist biblical scholars without clarifying that she is unable to cite biblical scholars who use this approach in work identified as womanist. Martin could describe these assumptions and tasks as her own proposals or suggestions, but by not doing so, her broad declarative statements suggest that she is offering consensus statements regarding womanist biblical interpretation based on a sizeable body of literature.

In her *DBI* article, Martin distinguishes womanist biblical studies from womanist theology by claiming that womanist biblical interpretation emerged from womanist theology. Martin cites only two articles by herself, Weems's *Just a Sister Away*, and two articles by Weems. Martin offers her opinions of womanist biblical interpretation without specifying that there has been little scholarly output from trained biblical scholars in this area. Again, this is a significant omission because Martin claims that womanist biblical interpretation emerges from womanist theology. As in other work, in "Polishing the Unclouded Mirror," published in 2005, fifteen years after her 1990 article, Martin continues to make generalizations regarding womanist approaches in biblical studies without acknowledging the very few number of biblical scholars who are using such approaches. Martin seems to require preconditions to offering a womanist approach, including Christian faith, lived experience as a woman, and self-identification as a womanist. Although she describes this approach in general terms, she does not cite other womanist biblical interpreters who share her understandings of this notion of a womanist approach. Martin misrepresents womanist biblical interpretation by failing to acknowledge that her personal views regarding womanist approaches are not reflective of a widely held consensus regarding characteristics of womanist approaches.

Martin attempts to distinguish the efforts of womanist biblical scholars from those of feminist biblical scholars. For example, in "Womanist Interpretations," Martin contends that feminist approaches focus on women and that they center on patriarchy as a primary form of oppression. Attempting to distinguish womanist approaches, she writes that womanist biblical interpreters are concerned with women as well as "all of those who by virtue of *race, class,* or other

40. Ibid., 42.
41. Ibid., 42–43.

anthropological referents, have been historically marginalized by the biblical traditions and/or writers themselves, and by interpreters of those traditions (Martin's
italics)."[42] Perhaps drawing on Schüssler Fiorenza, Martin claims that using "the
hermeneutics of suspicion, resistance, liberation, and hope" are key elements of
womanist biblical interpretation.[43] For Martin, womanist approaches are distinct from feminist approaches in that they focus more broadly on rediscovering
not only women's voices but also the voices of the marginalized.

Although Martin cites Schüssler Fiorenza, Trible, and others as representative
examples of feminist interpreters, she does not cite womanist biblical interpretations other than her own work, publications by scholars in religious-studies-
related fields (see chap. 5), and Weems's *Just a Sister Away*, which was written for
a lay audience. As a result, what she presents as a womanist approach to biblical
studies is merely her own opinion about womanist biblical interpretation. Her
citation of womanist scholars in religious-studies-related fields and her continued efforts to distinguish womanist biblical interpretation from feminist
biblical interpretation mislead the reader into believing that womanist biblical
scholars have produced a considerable body of work that is comparable to that
of womanist scholars in other disciplines and to feminist scholars in biblical
studies. By contrasting womanist approaches with feminist approaches, she
parallels two distinct entities that are not comparable in terms of their scholarly output.

As discussed in chapter 5, twenty years after Trible's initial work an entire
generation of biblical scholars were offering feminist approaches to biblical studies within scholarly monographs and journal articles in conversation with other
scholars. By the mid-1980s, survey articles on feminist biblical interpretation
could cite numerous studies. This is not the case for Weems and Martin, who
rely on generalizations. Their work has had great influence because there are
so few African American women biblical scholars. Since Weems and Martin
are so well-known, their work becomes accepted as the standard. The fact that
both Martin and Weems rely on work by womanist scholars in religious-studies-
related fields illustrates the lack of scholarly production in womanist biblical
studies. Twenty years after Weems's and Martin's initial womanist publications,
both are still citing only each other as biblical scholars in their discussions of
womanist biblical interpretation.

THE LEGACY OF WEEMS AND MARTIN

Weems and Martin contributed to the initial development of womanist work
in biblical studies by being the first African American, professionally trained,
women biblical scholars and by publishing the first biblical scholarship

42. Ibid., 51.
43. Ibid., 61.

self-identified as womanist. Since their pioneering work of the late 1980s and early 1990s, other biblical scholars have published work labeled as womanist, but there are no recognized distinguishing features of a womanist approach. The following brief discussion highlights the use of Walker's definition of *womanist* and the particular womanist approach of those who have identified their work as womanist biblical interpretation since Weems and Martin. Some womanist biblical scholars identify their approach as womanist but develop their own idiosyncratic understandings of what constitutes a womanist approach within biblical studies. Scholars may identify their work as they wish, but the use of the term *womanist* may lead some readers to assume that the approach described can be generalized to other womanist work in biblical studies. I must stress that these few examples do not provide representative examples of a large body of work. Rather, they are selected from among the relatively few examples of womanist biblical scholarship.[44]

Koala Jones-Warsaw

In one of the earliest works of womanist biblical interpretation not by Weems or Martin, Koala Jones-Warsaw's "Toward a Womanist Hermeneutic: A Reading of Judges 19–21" (1993) expresses concern with multiple oppressions. This article was written while Jones-Warsaw was a master's student. Relying on theologian Jacquelyn Grant's work, Jones-Warsaw contends that the purpose of womanist biblical hermeneutics is to "discover the significance and validity of the biblical text for black women who today experience the 'tridimensional reality' of racism, sexism, and classism."[45] For Jones-Warsaw, womanism provides a personal perspective from which contemporary African American women can reflect on the text and on their oppression.

44. Mitzi Smith regards Weems and Martin as first-generation womanist biblical scholars. She acknowledges, "The African American biblical scholars I name as womanist biblical scholars do not necessarily identify themselves solely using the adjective 'womanist.' For some African American biblical scholars 'womanist' refers more to a methodological or interpretive approach that they use from time to time, but it is not their only approach to biblical interpretation" (4n14). Smith includes me as a third-generation womanist biblical scholar (6), although she explains, "These categories (i.e., second, third, and fourth generation) are not fixed and may not accurately reflect how each womanist biblical scholar sees herself in relationship to others or the field. The categories are somewhat fluid. But they assist in talking about the development of womanist biblical scholarship in a cursory way." Mitzi J. Smith, ed., *I Found God in Me: A Womanist Biblical Hermeneutics Reader* (Eugene, OR: Wipf & Stock, 2015), 5.

45. Koala Jones-Warsaw, "Toward a Womanist Hermeneutic: A Reading of Judges 19–21," in *A Feminist Companion to Judges*, vol. 4, ed. Athalya Brenner (Sheffield: Sheffield Academic Press, 1993), 182.

Sarojini Nadar

Hebrew Bible scholar Sarojini Nadar uses the term *womanist* in her article "A South African Womanist Reading of the Character of Ruth."[46] She is not an African American woman, but Nadar claims that her use of the term is due to her engagement of multiple categories of oppression. Although Nadar identifies her methodology as postmodernist literary analysis, she writes, "I use the term *womanist* in the title as opposed to *feminist* because I am a South African Indian woman, and issues of color and class are a significant part of our lives. Furthermore, my ancestors, like ancestors of African women, stand in the history of discrimination. The term *womanist* takes these important issues into account."[47] Nadar embraces the term *womanist* and regards her reading as womanist due to its concern with multiple oppressions, which she connects with her lived experience as a South African woman.

Wil Gafney

Hebrew Bible scholar Wil (Wilda) Gafney creates her own unique womanist approach. In "A Black Feminist Approach to Biblical Studies" (2006) Gafney explains that she identifies herself as a feminist or as a womanist depending on the context.[48] Gafney mentions Walker's 1980 definition of *womanist* and provides a summary of Walker's four-part 1983 definition. Still, Gafney outlines her own version of a womanist approach by explaining what she contends are four key elements of womanist work: multidimensionality; a focus on women's experience, including the social location of the reader/interpreter; efforts toward the eradication of human oppression; and making scholarship accessible to a "wider nonspecialist worshipping community."[49] For Gafney, her role as a "black feminist biblical scholar" is to retell the story of the "silenced," "unknown," and "erased."[50] Gafney offers a unique understanding of a womanist approach within biblical studies, one that addresses multiple oppressions but does not focus exclusively on African American women's experiences.

Gafney combines queer readings with a womanist approach in "A Queer Womanist Midrashic Approach to Numbers 25:1–18."[51] Influenced by womanist ethicist Katie Geneva Cannon, Gafney constructs what she coins a

46. Sarojini Nadar, "A South African Indian Womanist Reading of the Character of Ruth," in *Other Ways of Reading: African Women and the Bible*, ed. Musa W. Dube (Atlanta: Society of Biblical Literature, 2001), 159–75.

47. Ibid., 159.

48. Wilda C. Gafney, *Daughters of Miriam: Women Prophets in Ancient Israel* (Minneapolis: Fortress Press, 2008).

49. Wilda C. M. Gafney, "A Black Feminist Approach to Biblical Studies," *Encounter* 67, no. 4 (2006): 392.

50. Ibid., 403.

51. Wil Gafney, "A Queer Womanist Midrashic Reading of Numbers 25:1–18," in *Leviticus and Numbers*, ed. Athalya Brenner and Archie Chi Chung Lee (Minneapolis: Augsburg Fortress, 2013), 189–98.

"womanist midrash," which involves "combining the deployment of the African American sanctified imagination as a womanist and feminist interpretive lens with the broader tradition of rabbinic and postrabbinic tradition of midrash."[52] With this unique combination of approaches, Gafney claims that her reading of Numbers 25 is both womanist and feminist and adds that it is womanist by being "womanish" in "talking back to the text," thereby invoking Walker.[53] Gafney declares, "Womanist interpretation *does not* privilege the embodiment and experiences of black women *at the expense of other members of the interpretive community*" (Gafney's italics).[54] She claims that womanist approaches are not focused on African American women but rather are inclusive of others, and she emphasizes the same-gender loving section of Walker's definition and its stress on the survival of an entire people. Gafney uses Walker to support her argument that both Israelite men and women could have been involved intimately (sexually and nonsexually) with Moabite women in "womanist community."[55] Her essay ends by questioning what are womanist and feminist approaches. Gafney's approach is unique, but she does not explain clearly how unique it is among womanist biblical interpreters. For instance, she could have indicated that she is expressing her opinion that womanist approaches should not privilege black women's experiences. Instead, she claims that they "do not," without citing sources.

Raquel A. St. Clair Lettsome

New Testament scholar Raquel A. St. Clair Lettsome provides one of the first published book-length treatments of a biblical text labeled as a womanist work in *Call and Consequences: A Womanist Reading of Mark* (2008), a revision of her 2005 Princeton Theological Seminary dissertation.[56] Lettsome identifies her methodology as following a cultural-interpretation model, which uses sociolinguistics in order to focus on language and the context of language. Nevertheless, she claims that she is reading the Gospel of Mark through a womanist lens because she uses this cultural-interpretation model in conjunction with what she calls a womanist hermeneutics of wholeness, which 1) is focused on the wholeness of African American women; 2) is grounded in the concrete reality of African American women's lives; 3) affirms that God supports African American women in their commitment to and struggle for wholeness; and 4) asserts that the significance of Jesus is his life and ministry.[57]

---

52. Ibid., 190.
53. Ibid., 197.
54. Ibid., 196.
55. Ibid., 194.
56. Raquel A. St. Clair, *Call and Consequences: A Womanist Reading of Mark* (Minneapolis: Fortress Press, 2008).
57. Ibid., 82–83. In a previous essay on womanist biblical interpretation, St. Clair offers the same four points regarding a womanist hermeneutics of wholeness. See Raquel A. St. Clair, "Womanist

Although she mentions Walker, Lettsome admits that the term *womanist* has no clear relation to Christian thought and acknowledges the concerns of ethicist Cheryl Sanders regarding the usefulness of the term for African American women's theological reflection. Yet Lettsome embraces the term as a way for African American women to distance themselves from the sexism of men and the racism of white men and women. Lettsome develops her own understanding of a uniquely and overtly Christian approach in using a womanist approach in biblical studies.

Shanell T. Smith

Based on her dissertation, Shanell Smith's *The Woman Babylon and the Marks of Empire: Reading Revelation with a Postcolonial Womanist Hermeneutics of Ambiveilence* is only the second monograph (following Lettsome) that uses a womanist approach in biblical studies.[58] Smith uses a womanist approach in concert with a postcolonial approach in her reading of the "whore" of Babylon (Revelation 17) as both an enslaved woman and as an empress or imperial city rather than as one or the other. Grounded in African American women's experiences, including her own, Smith analyzes issues of race, class, and gender while using W. E. B. Du Bois's concept of the "veil" and Homi Bhabha's notion of colonial ambivalence to create her own "hermeneutics of ambi*veil*ence (Smith's italics).[59]

Smith identifies several influences for her use of womanist thought. She draws on Wil Gafney's description of womanist biblical interpretation as "multidimensional," focused on "women's experience," seeking to "eradicate human oppression," and "accessible to a wider nonspecialist worshiping community."[60] In addition, she uses biblical scholar Clarice Martin's work on Revelation and cites Martin's description of womanist work that "foregrounds the hermeneutical lenses, epistemic assumptions, and cultural matrices of African American people in general and of African American women in particular."[61] Also, Smith claims that a womanist approach involves "choosing one's own labels" and cites Lorine Cummings on the African American woman's "self-determination and right to identify and name the parameters and character of [her] experience."[62] Due to her unique combination of approaches, Smith does not focus specifically on a singular notion of a womanist approach to biblical interpretation.

Biblical Interpretation," in *True to Our Native Land: An African American New Testament Commentary*, ed. Brian K. Blount et al. (Minneapolis: Fortress Press, 2007), 54–62.

58. Shanell T. Smith, *The Woman Babylon and the Marks of Empire: Reading Revelation with a Postcolonial Womanist Hermeneutics of Ambiveilence* (Minneapolis: Fortress Press, 2014).

59. Ibid., 11.

60. Ibid., 35–36, citing Gafney, *A Black Feminist Approach to Biblical Studies*, 391–92.

61. Smith, *The Woman Babylon*, 67, citing Martin, "Polishing the Unclouded Mirror," 84.

62. Smith, *The Woman Babylon*, 36, citing Lorine L. Cummings, "A Womanist Response to the Afrocentric Idea: Jarena Lee, Womanist Preacher," in *Living the Intersection: Womanism and Afrocentrism in Theology*, ed. Cheryl J. Sanders (Minneapolis: Fortress Press, 1995), 58.

Instead, she offers a lengthy description of her understanding of the development of womanist thought within various disciplines and discusses her unique concept of ambi*veil*ence in combination with both womanist and postcolonial approaches.

Mitzi J. Smith

There is currently only one edited volume on womanist biblical interpretation. Edited by New Testament scholar Mitzi J. Smith, *I Found God in Me: A Womanist Biblical Hermeneutics Reader* is a collection of sixteen essays, nine of which have been previously published, including four essays previously published by Mitzi Smith.[63] There are ten essays by biblical scholars, including five essays by Smith; three essays by graduate students in biblical studies; and three essays by scholars outside of biblical studies. The volume includes a range of uses of a womanist approach. Due to space limitations, this discussion focuses on the one new essay that Smith contributed to this volume, "'This Little Light of Mine': The Womanist Biblical Scholar as Prophetess, Iconoclast, and Activist,"[64] and one previously published article, "Give Them What You Have': A Womanist Reading of the Matthean Feeding Miracle (Matt 14:13–21)."

In "This Little Light of Mine," Smith offers her understanding of the role of womanist biblical scholars as prophetess, iconoclast, and activist. In a footnote, she claims that she does not regard black feminism and womanism as synonymous due to her view of womanism as a global phenomenon and as connected with other "critical theories and liberation movements," which she does not specify.[65] Smith's view of the work of womanist biblical scholars as prophetess reflects a Christian view of those scholars who address issues of oppression and injustice. She connects contemporary womanist work to what she terms "proto-womanist" such as that of Jarena Lee, Sojourner Truth, and other nineteenth-century African American women as well as women prophets in the Hebrew Bible. Emphasizing a confessional perspective, she asserts that "womanist biblical scholars understand the light of God and the goodness of God to be situated in black female bodies."[66] As iconoclast, Smith claims that womanist scholars challenge traditional interpretations. Also, as activist, she emphasizes the importance of the black church and African American women's activism. She combines within her discussion both claims about what womanist biblical scholars do and her hopes for the future of womanist biblical interpretation.

In her article "'Give Them What You Have': A Womanist Reading of the Matthean Feeding Miracle (Matt 14:13–21)," Smith constructs her own notion of a womanist approach by using what she terms as a "womanist legacy of

---

63. Smith, *I Found God in Me.*

64. Mitzi J. Smith, "'This Little Light of Mine': The Womanist Biblical Scholar as Prophetess, Iconoclast, and Activist," in Smith, *I Found God in Me*, 109–27.

65. Ibid., 111, n. 10.

66. Ibid., 113.

sharing."[67] She emphasizes the segment within section 2 of Walker's definition that focuses on the entire people and claims that her womanist approach allows a "focus on our theo-ethical responsibility to share what we have to help others, particularly when to do so would seem unreasonable in the context of our own sense of insufficient resources."[68] Her womanist approach involves sharing and community in what constitutes another individualized reading strategy.

Commonalities and Differences

As this brief survey of selected self-identified womanist biblical scholarship illustrates, there is a lack of consensus regarding understandings of womanist approaches within academic biblical studies. Beyond the scholar herself as an African American woman, some commonalities include the mention of Walker's definition of *womanist* or the use of selected elements of her definition. Also, some womanist biblical scholars may not engage Walker but use black feminist, womanist, or intersectional thought in addressing multiple oppressions. Yet in general, there is no clear consensus regarding the major features of a womanist approach in biblical studies. Such uses remain varied and broad such that a womanist perspective has as one of its most basic components the lived experience of the African American woman scholar producing the work.

The lack of consensus within womanist biblical interpretation is somewhat masked by the generalizations made by some womanist scholars in describing womanist biblical interpretation in terms that may give the mistaken impression that a consensus position exists. There is no consistency regarding the features of a womanist approach in biblical studies. Nearly all of the scholars surveyed above offer unique understandings of the term *womanist* within their work. Their loose usage of Walker means that the term becomes the primary element that these interpretations have in common. Scholars use womanist approaches in conjunction with other methods and read texts in a variety of ways. Of course, there is no requirement that these scholars must offer the same type of approach. Yet the utter lack of consistency means that the use of *womanist* does not signify any type of commonality in the ways in which scholars engage biblical texts. Womanist approaches are thus individualized and do not represent a scholarly consensus. There is nothing wrong with diversity among scholars, but this loose usage becomes problematic when these authors fail to acknowledge the considerable range of uses and allow the reader to assume that there is a consensus approach or a number of common features undergirding the scholar's reading of a text.

Furthermore, these authors make generalizations that are unsupported by the work of other womanist biblical scholars. When womanist biblical scholars

67. Mitzi J. Smith, "'Give Them What You Have': A Womanist Reading of the Matthean Feeding Miracle (Matt 14:13–21)," *Journal of Bible and Human Transformation* 3, no. 1 (2013): 6. Also reprinted in Smith, *I Found God in Me.*

68. Ibid.

make broad pronouncements about the concerns and perspectives of womanist biblical interpreters, they do not acknowledge the paucity of womanist biblical studies. It is not possible to offer the same types of generalizations regarding womanist biblical interpretation as in other womanist and feminist fields, because in womanist biblical scholarship one is not offering generalizations based on a large body of work. Womanist biblical interpretation, womanist religious-studies-related work, and feminist biblical interpretation are related but not easily paralleled, especially due to the limited amount of womanist biblical scholarship. These declarations contribute to the misconception that scholars have reached some consensus regarding the characteristics of womanist scholarship in biblical studies. As well, they create the impression of an inflated amount of published womanist scholarship.

Shared features would help scholars to continue to define and refine their use of womanist thought. A lack of shared features makes it less likely that any type of consensus will emerge. Furthermore, there is currently no debate regarding definitions or characteristics of a womanist approach in biblical studies. Within academia, a scholarly debate regarding an approach signifies that the approach has moved beyond its formative stages to a point of increased quantity and diversity of production. Thus, scholars have produced sufficient scholarship that it creates an opportunity for dialogue regarding that approach. A lack of debate inhibits the growth and development of a womanist approach as the approach remains unique to each scholar.

As discussed in chapter 3, nineteenth-century African American women dared to interpret biblical texts in ways that affirmed their humanity and their womanhood. Their personal testimonies and experiences of God as well as their own audacity in speaking on behalf of God as ministers and evangelists were elements of their activism. Their unique experiences as both African Americans and as women informed their biblical interpretations. The continued emphasis on the African American biblical scholar herself connects contemporary womanist biblical interpretation to this earlier period. The necessity of speaking for themselves as both African Americans and women was an important element of speaking for African American women's rights in earlier periods. For African American women to carve out their own particular space as African Americans and as women who interpret biblical texts within a white, male-dominated academic discipline connects the work of scholars with the work of earlier interpreters who likewise claimed their own voice within hostile spaces. For both earlier and contemporary African American women biblical interpreters, the perspective of the person who reads the text plays a significant role in the interpretation of that text, especially in light of the experiences of African American women.

Also, the emphasis on multiple oppressions and on the lived experience of African American women serves to link these two eras of African American biblical interpreters. Some womanist biblical scholars refer to their own experiences as helping them to be aware of the importance of addressing issues from an intersectional perspective or to deal with overlapping and multiple oppressions such as racism, classism, and sexism.

Womanist scholarship's emphasis on multiple oppressions is not merely a response to feminist biblical interpretation. Such an emphasis emerges from the lived experiences of African American women. Nevertheless, womanist biblical scholars have engaged the scholarship of feminist biblical scholars and their focus on gender and power. Thus, the concern with multiple oppressions dovetails with that of feminist biblical interpretation.

A womanist label does not provide any sense of cohesion among these disparate readings. Due to the emphasis on the lived experience of the scholar, the label becomes inextricably tied to both the person and her scholarship. An African American woman biblical scholar could self-identify as a womanist and produce a reading of a biblical text without labeling it as womanist. Identifying the reading itself as womanist requires greater clarity about what a womanist approach might be. As currently used in biblical studies, a womanist approach is not a tool that can be used by any scholar but a particular standpoint of some African American women scholars and other women-of-color scholars. Thus, the term *womanist* in biblical scholarship tends to refer to both the scholar and (some of) her scholarship. Yet even if a scholar chooses to identify herself as a womanist scholar, she may not use a womanist approach in all of her scholarly production. For instance, while Gafney has published articles using a womanist approach, her one scholarly monograph to date, *Daughters of Miriam: Women Prophets in Ancient Israel* (2008), does not utilize a womanist approach.[69] Despite her creative use of womanism, Gafney does not use a womanist approach in her most significant scholarly publication.

In scholarship, if *womanist* describes the scholar but not her work, then it is an element of one's social location. If it describes something other than the author, there is a need for some identifiable characteristics of this approach to be articulated. It does not contribute to the development of a womanist approach to biblical studies if each scholar is providing an individualized understanding of a womanist approach and then characterizing it as descriptive of a consensus position. This continues to support the notion that what is womanist about this approach is the scholar herself, as these approaches have little in common other than brief mentions of Walker's definition. In biblical studies, biblical texts and related literature and material culture are the focus of scholarly inquiry. One's experience is not a source in the same ways as in other disciplines.

At least currently, womanist approaches in biblical studies seem to require a personal identification as an African American women. This stands in contrast to other approaches that may have some links to a scholar's personal identity. Biblical scholars can and do explain their particular social location and their motivations for the work that they undertake, but a scholarly approach should not rely on a particular demographic for its continuation and growth. Within

69. Gafney, *Daughters of Miriam*.

biblical studies, some approaches that are associated with issues related to particular social locations do not restrict themselves to a particular demographic group. For example, disability studies and queer studies within biblical studies remain text-based approaches that are not dependent on the particular scholar's personal identification in order to contribute actively to that subfield.[70]

IMPACT ON THE DISCIPLINE OF BIBLICAL STUDIES

Currently, womanist biblical interpretation has not had a significant impact on the field of biblical studies in terms of its scholarly production or its presence within the Society of Biblical Literature (SBL). Database searches on the term *womanist* result in hundreds of publications in numerous fields. Within religion-related disciplines, many fields are covered, including ethics, theology, pastoral care, and homiletics. As discussed in chapter 4, some of this research includes engagement with biblical texts, but few of these publications are written by biblical scholars. Given the cross-disciplinary emphasis of many womanist works, it may seem unnecessary to separate work by field. Yet while many academic disciplines share commonalities, they are treated as separate and distinct by publishers and academic institutions as well as admissions committees, hiring committees, tenure and promotion committees, and scholars within each discipline. In addition, not separating by discipline could artificially inflate the amount of womanist biblical scholarship since nonbiblical scholars often write about biblical texts. Thus it is important to consider womanist scholarship within biblical studies as distinct from womanist work in other fields.[71]

Output

There is no current source of reliable information on the exact number of African American biblical scholars. According to SBL figures, in 2013 there were 8,254 members. Of those, 1981 (24 percent) were women, and 6,273 (76 percent) were men.[72] No membership data are available by U.S.-based race/ethnicity or race/ethnicity and gender. A 2001 unofficial count of African Americans with doctoral degrees in biblical studies (e.g., ancient Christianity, Christian origins,

70. Nyasha Junior and Jeremy Schipper, "Disability Studies and the Bible," in *New Meanings for Ancient Texts: Recent Approaches to Biblical Criticisms and their Applications*, ed. Steven L. McKenzie and John Kaltner (Louisville, KY: Westminster John Knox Press, 2013), 21–37.

71. I am arguing contra Shanell Smith, who contends, "It is necessary that I include the work of womanist theologians and ethicists in my discussion of womanist *biblical* hermeneutics because womanist work is not categorized according to academic disciplines. What is important to note is that the ways in which these women discuss the implications of their work in the lives of African American women in church and society correspond to the aims of womanist biblical scholarship" (Smith's italics). Smith, *The Woman Babylon*, 19n1.

72. Society of Biblical Literature, "SBL Dashboard: Facts and Figures," https://www.sbl-site.org/SBLDashboard.aspx.

early Christianity, Hebrew Bible, Near Eastern languages and civilizations, New Testament, religions of late antiquity, and Semitics)[73] and a 2007 unofficial supplement of New Testament scholars[74] combine to include 61 persons. Of those 61 scholars, 21 are in Hebrew Bible, and 40 are in New Testament. Also, 17 of the 61 are women. Of those 17 women, 8 are in Hebrew Bible, and 9 are in New Testament. Other biblical scholars, including myself, have earned their doctoral degrees since these numbers were published, but it is clear that there are very few African American women biblical scholars.

Womanist biblical interpretation has not had a significant impact on the field of biblical studies in terms of the production of material for scholarly discourse. Furthermore, womanist and nonwomanist scholars cite womanist work in the broader field of religious studies (theology, ethics, homiletics, etc.) or Weems's popular trade book *Just a Sister Away* as a representative example of womanist biblical interpretation and do not acknowledge the limited amount of womanist biblical scholarship produced by biblical scholars. Among biblical-studies scholarly publications, to date there are only two published monographs that are self-identified as a work of womanist biblical interpretation: Raquel (St. Clair) Lettsome's *Call and Consequences* and Shanell Smith's *The Woman Babylon and the Marks of Empire*. Currently, there is one edited volume in biblical studies using womanist approaches: *I Found God in Me: A Womanist Biblical Hermeneutics Reader*. This is important to acknowledge because in general monographs carry more weight than do journal articles in terms of scholarly prestige, influence, and, in most cases, tenure and promotion. In addition, there is no scholarly journal dedicated to womanist biblical studies. Of the few womanist biblical interpretation articles, most appear in edited volumes rather than peer-reviewed journals. Active since 1880, the *Journal of Biblical Literature*, the primary publication of SBL, has not published one journal article to date using a self-identified womanist approach. In contrast, as discussed in chapter 5, feminist biblical interpretation has had numerous scholarly monographs, edited volumes, and journal articles. This comparison is in no way intended to dismiss the accomplishments of womanist scholars but to distinguish the impact of these two approaches despite their being consistently linked together as if they are parallel in their output and development.

Unlike the significant impact of feminist approaches, the impact of womanist biblical interpretation has also been minimal within the scholarly guild. At the annual meetings of the SBL, the largest professional scholarly organization for biblical studies, there is little engagement with womanist approaches. While individual papers may use womanist thought in their paper presentations, there is no program unit (an SBL section focused on particular texts, issues, or approaches) or even consultation (an exploratory stage before approval as a

73. Randall C. Bailey, "Academic Biblical Interpretation among African Americans in the United States," in *African Americans and the Bible: Sacred Texts and Social Textures*, ed. Vincent L. Wimbush (New York: Continuum, 2001), 707.

74. "Appendix: African American New Testament Scholars Holding Doctorates." *True to Our Native Land*, 559–60.

program unit) that is devoted to womanist approaches to biblical studies. Feminist approaches are represented at SBL sessions both within program units that are dedicated to feminist approaches, such as the Feminist Hermeneutics of the Bible section, and within those that are not.

Unlike womanist biblical scholarship, critical-disability studies within biblical studies does not require a scholar engaging in work with disability to be a person with a disability. Also, while emerging from the disability rights movement, critical-disability studies scholars are not positioning themselves as disability rights advocates, but they investigate constructions of notions of disability and nondisability.[75] Within biblical scholarship, there are books, edited volumes, and journal articles that focus on disability, and an SBL program unit, Healthcare and Disability in the Ancient World, which began under a different title in 2004. In contrast to womanist biblical scholarship, critical-disability scholarship allows greater inclusion, which has contributed to its growth and development within biblical studies.[76]

Use of Terminology

Within biblical scholarship, there is a little acknowledgment of womanist thought in nonwomanist work. When the term *womanist* is mentioned in biblical scholarship, it is often paralleled with feminist biblical interpretation without clarification of the differences. When the term is occasionally mentioned in biblical studies publications it is often linked with *feminist* and appears frequently as *feminist/womanist*. Yet even when mentioned, in combination with *feminist* or on its own, there is relatively little actual engagement with womanist thought. Often the use of the term appears to be a weak attempt at inclusion of women of color without careful engagement of the complexities underlying the term as used and developed by Walker and others. Using *feminist* and *womanist* together, particularly within biblical studies, makes them seem as if they are parallel in their history, development, and production. This usage downplays the fact that there are significant differences in the amount of scholarship produced and the impact on the discipline.

Carolyn Pressler's article on Deuteronomy in the third edition of the *Women's Bible Commentary* provides an example of the type of imprecise use of *womanist* within biblical studies. Pressler uses *womanist* in conjunction with *feminist* or in conjunction with both *mujerista* and *feminist* eight times in a fifteen-page article. For example, in discussing the family laws of Deuteronomy 21–26 she writes, "Not surprisingly, they [these laws] have garnered much attention from womanist and feminist Deuteronomic scholars."[77] Linking *womanist* and *feminist*

---

75. Junior and Schipper, "Disability Studies and the Bible," 21–37.

76. Junior, "Womanist Biblical Interpretation."

77. Carolyn Pressler, "Deuteronomy," in *Women's Bible Commentary*, ed. Jacqueline E. Lapsley, Carol A. Newsom, and Sharon H. Ringe, 3rd ed. (Louisville, KY: Westminster John Knox Press, 2012), 93.

in this way might suggest that there are a comparable number of womanist and feminist biblical scholars whose research includes work on Deuteronomy. Without much effort, I can find biblical scholars who have published feminist work on Deuteronomy. Immediately, I think of Pressler's own work as well as *A Feminist Companion to Exodus to Deuteronomy*, which includes several articles on Deuteronomy.[78] Also, Pressler's bibliography includes the work of biblical scholars Tikva Frymer-Kensky and Carol L. Meyers, who have published on Deuteronomy.

But who are these womanist Deuteronomic scholars? Database queries on "Deuteronomy and womanist" yields zero results. One work that Pressler may have in mind is Cheryl Anderson's book *Women, Ideology, and Violence*, which is included in Pressler's bibliography.[79] Anderson is an African American woman who identifies herself as a "Christian (Protestant) and feminist/womanist" in *Women, Ideology, and Violence*.[80] Yet in identifying her method, she describes it as eclectic with borrowings from "hermeneutics, critical theory, and poststructuralism."[81] Furthermore, she mentions several types of theory that have influenced her work, including deconstruction, postmodern legal theory, gender theory, and feminist theory, and she highlights disciplines outside of biblical studies that have influenced her work, including anthropology, theology, and pastoral care.[82] At no point does Anderson name her approach as womanist; she names only herself as womanist.

The conflation of the scholar as womanist and her approach as womanist is not usually made in regard to feminist biblical interpretation. In feminist biblical interpretation, the scholar using a feminist approach may self-identify as a feminist, but the description of the work refers to the approach used in the work, not the scholar herself. Her personal experiences as a woman are not, in the main, regarded as mandatory for the use of the approach, especially as both men and women use feminist approaches within biblical studies. The term *feminist* refers to the work, not to the scholar. Despite the variations in definitions of approaches to feminist biblical studies, it is not the scholar herself that is paramount. Although some feminist biblical scholars regard feminism as part of their identity, in general feminist approaches are a tool that can be used by anyone. A minority opinion would hold that advocacy and other efforts in the service of ending women's subordination are necessary elements of a feminist approach. Yet for womanist biblical scholarship, *womanist* is often used to identify the scholar and her work. I assume that authors such as Pressler who use this

---

78. Athalya Brenner, ed., *A Feminist Companion to Exodus to Deuteronomy*, vol. 6 (Sheffield: Sheffield Academic Press, 1994). The second series, *Exodus to Deuteronomy: A Feminist Companion to the Bible*, was published in 2000, but it focuses on Exodus.

79. Cheryl B. Anderson, *Women, Ideology, and Violence: Critical Theory and the Construction of Gender in the Book of the Covenant and the Deuteronomic Law*, ed. David J. A. Clines, Philip R. Davies, and David M. Gunn (New York: T. & T. Clark International, 2004).

80. Ibid., 19–20.

81. Ibid.

82. Ibid., 17.

conjoined term are making a well-intentioned effort at inclusivity, but without clarifying the definitions and distinctiveness of both terms, their imprecise use terms suggests that womanist biblical interpretation is feminist biblical interpretation done by women of color.

To be fair to Pressler, in a brief article writers are instructed not to use footnotes or endnotes and to offer only a few bibliographic citations.[83] Nonetheless, if Pressler is using Anderson's work as an example of womanist scholarship on Deuteronomy, it is inaccurate because Anderson does not identify the work in that manner. Furthermore, Pressler's usage is misleading as it suggests that there is a body of womanist Deuteronomic scholarship that is comparable to that of feminist Deuteronomic scholarship when there is no published womanist Deuteronomic scholarship.

This linking of *feminist* and *womanist* without critical scrutiny appears in other biblical scholarship. For example, in the edited volume *The Postmodern Bible*, the essay "Feminist and Womanist Criticism" makes generalizations about feminist and womanist criticism but does not clarify that womanist biblical criticism has much less scholarly production.[84] It proceeds to analyze the work of Renita Weems, Tikva Frymer-Kensky, and Mary Joan Winn Leith as if they offer representative examples of womanist and feminist work, but it does not acknowledge how rare womanist readings like Weems's are in biblical studies. Although other womanist scholars in other fields are mentioned, the only biblical scholars cited in the essay are Weems and Martin, with citations of only Weems's and Martin's articles in *Stony the Road We Trod*, a landmark volume on African American biblical interpretation.

CONCLUSION

Womanist biblical interpretation within the discipline of biblical studies is often linked with womanist religious-studies-related fields and feminist biblical interpretation, but it is separate and distinct from both of these areas. Womanist biblical scholars define womanist and use womanist approaches in diverse ways. Womanist biblical interpretation does not have any clearly identifiable common features, other than some mention of Walker's definition and the personal identification of the scholar herself. Yet often, the work of womanist biblical scholars involves generalizations that do not acknowledge the paucity of womanist scholarship in biblical studies. Womanist biblical interpretation does not have a clear definition or a consensus regarding key characteristics. Furthermore, currently, it does not involve any debate regarding a definition or characteristics. Based on scholarly output and activity within the scholarly guild, womanist biblical

83. Disclosure: I am one of the contributors to the third edition of the *Women's Bible Commentary*. See Junior, "Exodus," 56–66.

84. Bible and Culture Collective, "Feminist and Womanist Criticism," in *The Postmodern Bible* (New Haven, CT: Yale University Press, 1995), 225–71.

interpretation has had minimal impact on the discipline of biblical studies so far. I hope that my contribution in this book helps to stimulate further conversation about womanist biblical interpretation and potential areas for growth and development.

RESOURCE LIST

Byron, Gay L. *Symbolic Blackness and Ethnic Difference in Early Christian Literature.* New York: Routledge, 2002. Provides an example of biblical scholarship by an African American woman that is not labeled as a womanist work.

St. Clair, Raquel Annette. *Call and Consequences: A Womanist Reading of Mark.* Minneapolis: Fortress Press, 2008. This is the first scholarly monograph using a self-identified womanist approach in biblical studies.

Smith, Mitzi J. *I Found God in Me: A Womanist Biblical Hermeneutics Reader.* Eugene, OR: Wipf & Stock, 2015. This is the first edited volume including biblical scholars and others using womanist approaches in reading biblical texts.

Smith, Shanell T. *The Woman Babylon and the Marks of Empire: Reading Revelation with a Postcolonial Womanist Hermeneutics of Ambiveilence.* Minneapolis: Fortress Press, 2014. This monograph uses a womanist perspective in combination with a postcolonial approach in reading Revelation.

Weems, Renita J. *Just a Sister Away: A Womanist Vision of Women's Relationships in the Bible.* San Diego: LuraMedia, 1988. This is the classic volume that is often identified as the first self-identified womanist work in biblical studies.

Conclusion

When I was on the job market as a graduate student, I was a finalist for a position in Hebrew Bible at a seminary. During an interview with the search committee, I was asked a question about being a womanist. I explained that I did not identify myself as a womanist, but I offered a few general characteristics of a womanist approach in biblical studies. Sensing that I was already on the wrong track with this committee, I decided to go for broke and went on to explain that one should not assume that a scholar uses a particular approach based on his or her gender or race. We quickly moved on to other topics. One committee member had arrived late to the meeting and at a pause in the conversation asked me, "Aren't you a womanist?" This incident crystallized for the committee and for me how entrenched is the notion that a womanist is synonymous with an African American woman, especially in the academy.

My aim in this book has been to introduce womanist biblical interpretation that centers on its history and development rather than treating it as merely ancillary to feminist biblical interpretation. The presence of African American women biblical scholars is a recent development within the academic discipline of biblical studies, but their contributions are part of a tradition of African American women's engagement with biblical texts. Some of these scholars identify themselves and their work as womanist biblical interpretation. Understanding womanist biblical interpretation from a historical perspective contributes to African American women's intellectual history and to the history of biblical interpretation.

Part 1 of this book highlights historical issues relating to feminism and womanism. Chapter 1 provides an overview of key terminology, including the "wave" concept of feminism. Also, it addresses the importance of both race and gender in women's early activism in the United States. Chapter 2 focuses on nineteenth-century women's rights activists and their efforts to use biblical texts to support women's rights. Such efforts link to the development of twentieth-century feminist biblical interpretation with its attention to issues of gender and power within biblical texts and biblical interpretation. Chapter 3 highlights how African American women activists emphasize their lived experience as African American women to address issues of both race and gender. Their use of biblical interpretation to support their public activism connects with the importance of lived experience for womanist work within academic religious-studies-related disciplines and in academic biblical studies in the twentieth and twenty-first centuries.

Part 2 focuses on contemporary scholarship. In chapter 4, I discuss womanist work in religious-studies-related academic fields apart from biblical studies with attention to its use of Walker's definition of *womanist*, its emphasis on lived experience, and its engagement with biblical texts. Since womanist work in biblical studies is often linked with womanist work in religious-studies-related fields, this chapter illustrates the limited engagement with biblical texts and biblical scholarship in much of the womanist religious studies scholarship. Despite these limitations, this womanist scholarship is often grouped together with scholarship by biblical scholars. Chapter 5 details the growth and development of contemporary feminist biblical scholarship, which highlights the importance of gender and power. Such scholarship links back to the nineteenth-century use of biblical interpretation by women activists, but it is conducted by biblical scholars. In chapter 6, I outline the growth and development of womanist biblical interpretation. It connects to nineteenth-century African American women's activism with its emphasis on the lived experience of African American women. As well, it uses contemporary womanist scholarship in religious-studies-related fields as scholarly conversation partners and reflects a continued focus on the lived experience of African American women. Furthermore, womanist biblical interpretation and its attention to race, class, gender, and multiple oppressions connects it to feminist biblical interpretation. I have shown that womanist biblical interpretation is related to the work of other biblical interpreters, to scholars outside of biblical studies, and to nonprofessionally trained biblical interpreters in order to offer a longer range view of African American women's engagement with biblical texts and to illustrate the various influence on the development of womanist biblical interpretation. In this conclusion, I identify some issues for the future of womanist biblical interpretation and offer my reflections on writing this book.

ISSUES FOR THE FUTURE

Marginalization

African American women will continue to interpret biblical texts, but for professional interpreters, if one's personal experience as an African American woman serves as the primary requirement for using womanist approaches in biblical studies, womanist approaches will remain marginalized in the field. By marginalized, I mean that this work will not be engaged seriously by other scholars, taught in classrooms, or regarded as making significant contributions to the field. Several elements contribute to this continued marginalization. First, if one must be an African American woman or woman of color in order to do womanist work, there will continue to be little of it published. As discussed in chapter 6, there are few African American women in biblical studies, and not all of them choose to identify as womanists or to use womanist approaches. As well, if the personal experience of being an African American woman or woman of color is required, it is highly unlikely that scholars who are not African American women or women of color will use the term. Granted, some might argue that white women should not use the term, given its significance for African American women. Yet restricting the approach to African American women reinforces the notion that womanism is a statement of personal identity rather than a scholarly approach. Thus womanist biblical scholarship will remain marginalized as there will not be enough scholarly production for it to become a recognized element within mainstream biblical studies.

Another potential result of the marginalization of womanist approaches may be the pigeon-holing of African American women biblical scholars. Graduate advisors, other faculty, or editors may pressure some graduate students and early career scholars into identifying as womanists or labeling their work as womanist. These advisors may regard such advice as a strategic move so that their students or colleagues stand out in a crowded job market or publication market. Yet it may limit those students and scholars by discouraging them from exploring other forms of scholarship, including more "traditional" scholarship.

Also, African American women scholars who do not use womanist approaches may continue to be questioned about their choice of methods. If a womanist is an African American woman, then womanist scholarship will often be understood as simply work conducted by any African American woman biblical scholar. Even when a womanist scholar specifies the elements of her particular womanist approach, the term *womanist* is so consistently identified with African American women that it may overshadow attempts to specify one's usage of this approach. Thus, if a self-identified womanist scholar uses source criticism alongside of a womanist perspective, her work may not be received as making a contribution within source-critical scholarship because it may be perceived unfairly as primarily a womanist work.

Another possible result of the emphasis on personal identity is the lack of engagement with womanist work by nonwomanist scholars. In speaking about this project with one of my white colleagues, I was asked if I had read a particular work by an African American woman biblical scholar. I said that I thought that the author had a very weak thesis and that the work was long on speculation and short on evidence. My colleague said, "Oh, I'm so glad that you said that!" When I asked her to clarify she explained that she had the same response that I had. She went on to say that she would never have said anything negative without hearing from me first. Furthermore, she said that she would absolutely never say anything negative in public or write a negative review. She feared being labeled as a racist. Perhaps my colleague's view is an extreme one, but I doubt it. Due to the current exclusivity of womanist biblical studies, it may receive a "free pass" from other scholars. That is, it may not be scrutinized in a fashion that is typical of academic engagement because nonwomanist scholars may fear being accused of racism or of being a race traitor. Thus, even when womanist work is published, it may not be reviewed or critiqued as other work would be. This type of "free pass" is not a benefit but a form of neglect or scholarly ostracism that results in less press or publicity than other similarly placed publications. In order for approaches and methods to advance, scholars must create a critical mass of work that is in dialogue with other scholarship. Critical discourse, including substantive critique, is required if womanist biblical scholarship is to flourish, but due to concerns of being labeled negatively, some scholars may choose to neglect this work altogether. A negative review is favorable to no review at all. A citation that offers a substantive critique of a particular scholarly argument is preferable to not being cited at all. Without scholarly dialogue and debate, scholarship does not develop as quickly or as solidly as might otherwise be the case.

Niche

Despite the negative aspects of marginalization, there are some potentially positive benefits that may accrue to womanist biblical scholars as a result of the exclusivity of womanist approaches. Womanist biblical scholarship can benefit from its limited supply and significant barriers to entry by operating as a niche within biblical studies. As discussed in chapter 5, this niche is part of what theologian Monica Coleman refers to as the "commercialization and commodification" of womanist work.[1] For example, instead of treating womanist work as marginal, some publishers and editors may be more interested in work labeled as womanist. Some conference conveners may be more likely to invite a self-identified womanist scholar to serve as a speaker than another African American woman. If a job description mentions womanist approaches in a list of possible areas of specialization, it may be advantageous for an African American woman scholar to identify as a womanist in her cover letter. Certainly, nonwomanists manage to secure publishing contracts, speaking engagements, and employment offers. Yet womanism is an important piece of real estate. Although such possible advantages may support the individual scholar, these benefits do not support the overall advancement and development of womanist approaches in biblical studies as they rely on the scholar herself as an individual and not her scholarship.

Some womanist biblical scholars may desire to maintain the exclusivity of womanist circles as there are some positive elements to operating from a

1. Monica A. Coleman, "Must I Be a Womanist?," *Journal of Feminist Studies in Religion* 22, no. 1 (2006): 93.

marginalized position. Womanist exclusivity and self-imposed isolation were demonstrated clearly at the womanist consultation meeting at the 2010 annual meeting of the Society of Biblical Literature (SBL) if my recollection is correct. Although the consultation was posted in the SBL program book, this meeting was by invitation only. A message was sent through the womanist listserv inviting listserv members to the meeting. One of the senior women at the meeting explained that the invitation-only notice was posted in the program book to ensure that it was for "just us" or only African American women. I attended and enjoyed the fellowship with other women in the field. Nevertheless, I left feeling disturbed. That year there was no panel discussion devoted to womanist biblical studies or review panel for a book on womanist biblical studies because no such book had been published that year.

Gatherings of affinity groups take place in formal and informal ways at SBL. Friends, classmates, contributors to a volume, scholars who work in the same narrow specialization, or other groups may gather for cocktails, meals, and numerous evening receptions, but the program sessions provide an opportunity for the formal presentation of scholarly work. While I understand the need for private spaces in which to share joys and concerns or to offer encouragement and mentoring, in order for womanist work to thrive, those private spaces should supplement the public spaces in which one works and engages with others as is the case with more established subdisciplines and approaches within biblical studies. The private womanist consultation was the only designated space for womanist biblical scholarship at SBL.

A private meeting with invitations extended only to African American women is a form of community gathering within an environment that has a majority of white men. According to the 2014 SBL membership profile, based on self-reported information, 86.4 percent of the respondents identify as Caucasian or of European descent.[2] Yet this type of private gathering also contributes to the notion that womanist is synonymous with African American woman scholar. Again, I admit that I went to the gathering and appreciated the opportunity to share with other scholars. It is possible that such a private meeting of scholars could serve a networking function and provide opportunities for scholars to not only offer personal support but also discuss matters pertaining to their scholarship. Still, such gatherings do not have as their primary function the publication and dissemination of biblical scholarship as other formal program units do.

For example, in contrast to the womanist consultation, the SBL Committee on the Status of Women in the Profession, of which I was a member, sponsors a breakfast for women members every year. This gathering is a place for celebrating the accomplishments of women SBL members and for offering a space for socialization and networking opportunities. Occasionally a man attends, but the meeting is planned for and by women members. Yet this networking breakfast

2. Society of Biblical Literature, *Membership Profile 2014*, http://www.sbl-site.org/assets/pdfs/memberProfileReport2014.pdf.

is completely separate and distinct from program sessions in which male and female SBL members present and participate, some of which include feminist biblical scholarship. Unlike the womanist private gathering, the networking breakfast is not the only opportunity for women scholars to gather. Official program units such as Feminist Hermeneutics of the Bible and Women in the Biblical World provide spaces for scholars to offer presentations that engage feminist approaches.[3]

FUTURE

I believe that womanist biblical scholarship will continue in the future in some form. Yet, especially given the relatively few numbers of African American women biblical scholars, womanist biblical scholarship by biblical scholars will have a limited impact in the field of biblical studies as long as *womanist* refers to the individual scholar instead of to her work.

One of the key issues within womanist biblical interpretation involves terminology. As discussed in chapters 4 and 6, some African American women and other women of color have chosen to use Alice Walker's term *womanist*, while others have not. Those who do use the term will continue to find it necessary to clarify their particular usage given its diversity. Those who use feminist approaches and other approaches may feel it necessary to clarify their particular usage of those approaches and how they use them in combination with other methodologies. Yet I imagine that there will continue to be an additional burden on African American women as the popularity of the term *womanist* combined with the limited number of African American women biblical scholar may lead many scholars to assume that African American women biblical scholars self-identify as womanists. Given the ongoing issues regarding terminology, it will remain important for African American women biblical scholars to identify themselves clearly and to label their work and their methodology clearly as their work may be grouped with that of other scholars, including those outside of biblical scholarship with whom their work has little in common. Again, there may be some small advantage to the womanist niche, but scholars will still need to explain their use or nonuse of the term.

For those who are not African American women, it will remain crucial that they not make assumptions about African American women scholars or their work. Although including *womanist* next to *feminist* is often a well-intentioned effort at inclusivity, it is necessary to be more careful with language. If the discussion focuses on women scholars, one should use precise language rather than assuming that white women are feminists and that African American women or women of color are womanists.

---

3. Disclosure: I served as a member and co-chair of Feminist Hermeneutics of the Bible.

The influence of black feminist and womanist thought will be felt in biblical studies in the sense of greater attention to multiple categories of difference, multiplicative forces of oppression, and power dynamics. I anticipate that this influence will emerge in three ways in biblical studies. First, feminist biblical scholarship will continue to expand to be more inclusive of issues of race, gender, class, ability, and other forms of difference within its analysis. I anticipate that greater awareness and interaction with intersectional approaches will be increasingly influential within feminist biblical scholarship. Such scholarship may be identified as feminist, but unlike previous generations of feminist biblical scholarship, it will not be focused only on women or on issues related to gender.

Second, although it may look very similar to feminist approaches, an increasing number of biblical scholars will use intersectional approaches and label their work as intersectional perhaps in greater dialogue with black feminist and womanist thought. Such scholarship may be labeled as feminist, intersectional, or intersectional feminist. Also, biblical scholars may use insights from black feminist, womanist, or intersectional theory without labeling it as such but identifying their work by its primary methodology.

Third, some biblical scholars will draw on the insights of womanist thought without referring to their work specifically as womanist. Some African American women may reject the term womanist, especially if it is associated with Weems and Martin to such an extent that it becomes linked with a particular generation of scholarship. Therefore, some scholars may find the term to be old-fashioned. Others may choose to identify themselves as third- or fourth-wave womanists in order to distance themselves from previous generations. Also, non–African American women biblical scholars may feel that the term is not available to them. They and other scholars may develop alternate terms to describe their concerns and approaches. All three of these options will owe a debt to black feminist and womanist thought, but the extent to which this influence is acknowledged or termed *womanist* may vary.

These three options can happen with or without African American women biblical scholars. Scholars may arrive at the same areas of study from different entry points. For example, one scholar may engage gender and ethnicity through feminist approaches in biblical studies, and another may address gender and disability through disability studies in biblical studies. Although both are trained as biblical scholars, their engagement with secondary literature on gender may differ as they arrive at their questions in different ways. Their graduate training, comprehensive exams, and conversation partners may differ despite their shared interest in issues of gender within biblical texts.

Through publication and presentations, scholars may find potential common points of interest and may begin to engage the work of scholars in other disciplines or subfields that may be useful. Greater inclusivity and more inclusive terminology could still involve the use and citation of black feminist and womanist thought, but it could also provide new conversation partners and greater cross-pollination for those interested in black feminist and womanist thought. Not joining the conversation may result in missed opportunities and continued isolation. If womanist biblical scholarship remains "of black women, by black women, and for black women,"[4] it will remain on the margins of biblical scholarship. If it becomes a broader feminist, intersectional, or unnamed eclectic project, it has the potential to become more influential within biblical studies.

Across the academy, African American women and others have had to fight admissions committees, dissertation committees, curriculum committees, tenure and promotion committees, and hiring committees in order to have the voices and experiences of African Americans included within the academy's notions of acceptable scholarship. Giving up *womanist*, the one term that signifies race and gender, may seem as if it will result in giving up hard-fought gains. Yet one can use the insights of black feminist and womanist thought without referring to the work as womanist. I recognize that using a term other than *womanist* or not using the term, despite its influence, could contribute to the erasure of African American women's significant contributions to biblical studies. This is a very serious concern, but it need not be the case. Discussing and citing black feminist and womanist work would provide opportunities for engagement with that scholarship without the need to identify the approach as womanist. To do that responsibly involves careful reading of the literature and proper citation and clarification of one's use or nonuse of particular terms. For example, a scholar using feminist approaches could still cite the work of scholars whose work has been influential in the development of the concept of intersectionality. The acknowledgment of the importance of womanist scholarship may be the central way that biblical studies engages womanist work even if it is not labeled womanist or offered by an African American woman scholar.

REFLECTIONS

To some, it may seem strange that I should write a book about womanist biblical interpretation since I do not identify myself as a womanist. As I explained in chapter 1, I found that there was little material available on womanist biblical studies, and I wanted to write a book that would be helpful for those who were interested in womanist biblical interpretation. In addition, I wanted to provide some historical background and clarity regarding African American women's engagement with biblical texts. I attempted to reframe womanist biblical interpretation. Instead of regarding womanist biblical interpretation as a corrective to feminist biblical interpretation, I have offered a longer-range view that includes African American biblical interpreters inside and outside of the academy and inside and outside of biblical studies.

4. Coleman, "Must I Be a Womanist?," 93.

Some might argue that I am contributing to the commodification of womanist work by labeling this work as an introduction to womanist biblical interpretation. Certainly, this book makes use of this marketing niche through its labeling. As an author, I am aware that the term *womanist* is attention grabbing and would be of interest to my publisher and to potential readers. I would argue that my intention is to contribute to the conversation regarding womanist work, not to exploit it. The book is properly labeled as it is about womanist biblical interpretation regardless of my self-identification, although the book is not perhaps what some readers would have anticipated. In my mind, this is not an appropriation of the term *womanist* but scholarly engagement with womanist work.

Is this a womanist book? Like Gaventa, whose work I discuss in chapter 5, I have had to explain to various curious people that I am not writing a womanist book. Unlike Gaventa's work and its assumed connection to feminism, since this book is about womanist biblical interpretation, there is a clear connection to womanism due to my use of the term in the title and the subject matter regardless of the fact that it was written by an African American woman and centers on the work of African American activists and scholars. Given the limited amount of womanist scholarship within biblical studies, some may want to identify it as a womanist book.

Whatever my intention, I still recognize that for some, anything less than glowing praise and approval of womanist biblical scholarship will be regarded as airing dirty laundry or being disrespectful to womanist pioneers in the field. This view is reflected in the firestorm of controversy surrounding writer Wanda Coleman's 2002 negative review[5] of award-winning poet and author Maya Angelou.[6] Angelou is an African American literary icon, and Coleman's negative review was regarded as "out of bounds" in some regards. Some African Americans believe that any disagreement or negative views regarding the work of other African Americans should not be made public. They contend that African Americans should offer praise or silence in a show of solidarity with other African Americans, because those writers could expect to receive more than their fair share of overly critical, negative, and possibly racially biased reviews or feedback from non–African Americans.

My aim in writing this book is not to air dirty laundry in any sense but to trace the history of womanist biblical interpretation. I do not regard this book as an indictment of womanist biblical scholarship but an effort to understand its development and current uses as something more than a by-product of feminist biblical interpretation. African American women have been interpreting biblical texts for centuries and will continue to do so in unique and exciting ways.

---

5. Wanda Coleman, "Coulda, Woulda, Shoulda: Review of *A Song Flung Up to Heaven* by Maya Angelou," *Los Angeles Times*, April 14, 2002, http://articles.latimes.com/2002/apr/14/books/bk-coleman14.

6. Tim Rutten, "'Flung' into Controversy by Negative Book Review," *Los Angeles Times*, May 24, 2002, http://articles.latimes.com/2002/may/24/news/lv-media24.

My hope is that I have been successful in my primary task, which was to explain the history and development of womanist biblical interpretation and to provide resources for students and others. As well, I hope that my work succeeds in making the issue of womanist biblical interpretation more prominent and more complex within biblical studies. I hope that scholars will not relegate the work of African American women biblical scholars to the last week of class or the supplemental bibliography but will be encouraged to seek out the work of more African American women. I hope that scholars will read, review, engage, cite, and assign the publications of African American women biblical scholars. Furthermore, I hope that fewer African American women will be assumed to be womanists.

Consistently, African American women have said, "We are here," and they have read biblical texts in ways that acknowledge the experiences of African American women and their experiences as both African Americans and as women. The interpretation of biblical texts by African American women constitutes an important and neglected element of African American women's intellectual and activist history. African American women have been reading biblical texts for much longer than they have been professional biblical scholars. Yet biblical scholarship, when it does acknowledge womanist biblical interpretation, tends to treat it merely as an offshoot of feminist biblical interpretation. In contrast, this volume traces the antecedents of womanist biblical interpretation not strictly from the academy but from the rich history of African American women's engagement with biblical texts. It illustrates how womanist biblical interpretation is related to feminist biblical interpretation but also deeply rooted in the work of previous generations of African American women interpreters of the Bible.

Bibliography

Abbott, Lyman. "Why Women Do Not Wish the Suffrage." *The Atlantic* 92, no. 551 (September 1903): 289–96.

American Equal Rights Association, Henry M. Parkhurst, Carrie Chapman Catt, National American Woman Suffrage Association Collection, and Susan B. Anthony Collection. *Proceedings of the First Anniversary of the American Equal Rights Association.* Held at the Church of the Puritans, New York, May 9–10, 1867. Phonographic Report by H. M. Parkhurst. New York: R. J. Johnston, printer, 1867.

Anderson, Cheryl B. *Women, Ideology, and Violence: Critical Theory and the Construction of Gender in the Book of the Covenant and the Deuteronomic Law.* Edited by David J. A. Clines, Philip R. Davies, and David M. Gunn. New York: T. & T. Clark, 2004.

Austin, Allan D. *African Muslims in Antebellum America: Transatlantic Stories and Spiritual Struggles.* Rev. ed. New York: Routledge, 1997.

Awkward, Michael. *Negotiating Difference: Race, Gender, and the Politics of Positionality.* Chicago: University of Chicago, 1995.

Baden, Joel S. *The Composition of the Pentateuch: Renewing the Documentary Hypothesis.* Anchor Yale Bible Reference Library. New Haven, CT: Yale University Press, 2012.

Bailey, Randall C. "Academic Biblical Interpretation among African Americans in the United States." In *African Americans and the Bible: Sacred Texts and Social Textures.* Edited by Vincent L. Wimbush, 696–711. New York: Continuum, 2001.

———. "'That's Why They Didn't Call the Book Hadassah!': The Interse(ct)/(x)ionality of Race/Ethnicity, Gender, and Sexuality in the Book of Esther." In *They Were All Together in One Place: Toward Minority Biblical Criticism.* Society of Biblical Literature *Semeia* Studies 57. Edited by Randall C. Bailey, Tat-Siong Benny Liew, and Fernando F. Segovia, 227–50. Atlanta: Society of Biblical Literature, 2009.

———. *Yet with a Steady Beat: Contemporary U.S. Afrocentric Biblical Interpretation.* Society of Biblical Literature *Semeia* Studies, Vol. 42. Atlanta: Society of Biblical Literature, 2003.

Bailey, Randall C., and Jacquelyn Grant, eds. *The Recovery of Black Presence: An Interdisciplinary Exploration: Essays in Honor of Dr. Charles B. Copher.* Nashville: Abingdon Press, 1995.

Bailey, Randall C., Tat-Siong Benny Liew, and Fernando F. Segovia. *They Were All Together in One Place: Toward Minority Biblical Criticism*. Society of Biblical Literature *Semeia* Studies. Vol. 57. Atlanta: Society of Biblical Literature, 2009.

Bal, Mieke. *Anti-Covenant: Counter-Reading Women's Lives in the Hebrew Bible*. Bible and Literature 81. Sheffield, England: Almond Press, 1989.

———. *Death & Dissymmetry: The Politics of Coherence in the Book of Judges*. Chicago Studies in the History of Judaism. Chicago: University of Chicago Press, 1988.

———. *Lethal Love: Feminist Literary Readings of Biblical Love Stories*. Indiana Studies in Biblical Literature. Bloomington: Indiana University Press, 1987.

———. *Murder and Difference: Gender, Genre, and Scholarship on Sisera's Death*. Indiana Studies in Biblical Literature. Bloomington: Indiana University Press, 1988.

Bartlow, R. Dianne. "'No Throw-Away Woman': Maria W. Stewart as a Forerunner of Black Feminist Thought." In *Black Women's Intellectual Traditions: Speaking Their Minds*, edited by Kristin Waters and Carol B. Conaway, 72–88. Lebanon, NH: University Press of New England, 2007.

Barton, John. *Reading the Old Testament: Method in Biblical Study*. Rev. ed. Louisville, KY: Westminster John Knox Press, 1996.

Bassard, Katherine Clay. *Transforming Scriptures: African American Women Writers and the Bible*. Athens: University of Georgia Press, 2010.

Baumgardner, Jennifer, and Amy Richards. *Manifesta: Young Women, Feminism, and the Future*. New York: Farrar, Straus & Giroux, 2000.

Beal, Timothy K. *The Book of Hiding: Gender, Ethnicity, Annihilation, and Esther*. New York: Routledge, 1997.

Beale, Frances. "Double Jeopardy: To Be Black and Female." In *Words of Fire: An Anthology of African-American Feminist Thought*, edited by Beverly Guy-Sheftall, 146–55. New York: New Press, 1995. Reprinted from *The Black Woman: An Anthology*, edited by Toni Cade Bambara (New York: Signet, 1970).

Beecher, Catharine Esther. *An Essay on Slavery and Abolitionism with Reference to the Duty of American Females*. Philadelphia: Henry Perkins, 1837.

Bible and Culture Collective. "Feminist and Womanist Criticism." In *The Postmodern Bible*, 225–71. New Haven, CT: Yale University Press, 1995.

Bilge, Silma. "Intersectionality Undone: Saving Intersectionality from Feminist Intersectionality Studies." *Du Bois Review* 10, no. 2 (2013): 405–24.

Bird, Phyllis. "What Makes a Feminist Reading Feminist? A Qualified Answer." In *Escaping Eden: New Feminist Perspectives on the Bible*, edited by Harold C. Washington, Susan Lochrie Graham, and Pamela Thimmes, 124–31. Sheffield: Sheffield Academic Press, 1998.

Blount, Brian K. *Cultural Interpretation: Reorienting New Testament Criticism*. Minneapolis: Fortress Press, 1995.

Blount, Brian K., et al., eds. *True to Our Native Land: An African American New Testament Commentary*. Minneapolis: Fortress Press, 2007.

Bradley, David. "Novelist Alice Walker: Telling the Black Woman's Story." *New York Times*, January 8, 1984.

Breines, Wini. *The Trouble between Us: An Uneasy History of White and Black Women in the Feminist Movement*. New York: Oxford University Press, 2006.

Brenner, Athalya, ed. *A Feminist Companion to Exodus to Deuteronomy*. Feminist Companion to the Bible 6. Sheffield: Sheffield Academic Press, 1994.

Brooten, Bernadette J. "Early Christian Women and their Cultural Context: Issues of Method in Historical Reconstruction." In *Feminist Perspectives on Biblical Scholarship*, edited by Adela Yarbro Collins, 65–91. Chico, CA: Scholars Press, 1985.

Brown, Michael Joseph. *Blackening of the Bible: The Aims of African American Biblical Scholarship*. African American Religious Thought and Life. Edited by Anthony

B. Pinn and Victor Anderson. Harrisburg, PA: Trinity Press International, 2004.

Burnap, George Washington. *The Sphere and Duties of Woman: A Course of Lectures.* Baltimore: J. Murphy, 1848.

Byrd, James P. *Sacred Scripture, Sacred War: The Bible and the American Revolution.* New York: Oxford University Press, 2013.

Byrd, Rudolph P., and Beverly Guy-Sheftall, eds. *Traps: African American Men on Gender and Sexuality.* Bloomington: Indiana University Press, 2001.

Byron, Gay L. *Symbolic Blackness and Ethnic Difference in Early Christian Literature.* New York: Routledge, 2002.

Calvert-Koyzis, Nancy, and Heather E. Weir. *Strangely Familiar: Protofeminist Interpretations of Patriarchal Biblical Texts.* Boston: Brill, 2009.

Cannon, Katie G. *Black Womanist Ethics.* American Academy of Religion Academy 60. Atlanta: Scholars Press, 1988.

———. "The Emergence of Black Feminist Consciousness." In *Feminist Interpretation of the Bible,* edited by Letty M. Russell, 30–40. Louisville, KY: Westminster John Knox Press, 1985.

Chisholm, Shirley. "Equal Rights for Women." Duke University Special Collections Library Digital Scriptorium, http://scriptorium.lib.duke.edu/wlm/equal/.

Christ, Carol P. "The New Feminist Theology: A Review of the Literature." *Religious Studies Review* 3 (1977): 203–12.

Coleman, Monica A. *Ain't I a Womanist, Too? Third-Wave Womanist Religious Thought.* Minneapolis: Fortress Press, 2013.

———. *Making a Way Out of No Way: A Womanist Theology.* Innovations: African American Religious Thought. Minneapolis: Fortress Press, 2008.

———. "Must I Be a Womanist?" *Journal of Feminist Studies in Religion* 22, no. 1 (2006): 85–96.

———. "'Must I Be a Womanist?': Roundtable Discussion and Responses." *Journal of Feminist Studies in Religion* 22, no. 1 (2006): 85–134.

Coleman, Wanda. "Coulda, Woulda, Shoulda: Review of *A Song Flung Up to Heaven* by Maya Angelou." *Los Angeles Times,* April 14, 2002.

Collier-Thomas, Bettye. *Jesus, Jobs, and Justice: African American Women and Religion.* Philadelphia: Temple University Press, 2014.

Collins, Adela Yarbro. "New Testament Perspectives: The Gospel of John." *Journal for the Study of the Old Testament* 7 (1982): 47–53.

———, ed. *Feminist Perspectives on Biblical Scholarship.* Chico, CA: Scholars Press, 1985.

Collins, Patricia Hill. *Black Feminist Thought: Knowledge, Consciousness, and the Politics of Empowerment.* New York: Routledge, 2000.

———. "Distinguishing Features of Black Feminist Thought." In *Black Feminist Thought: Knowledge, Consciousness, and the Politics of Empowerment.* 2nd ed., 21–43. New York: Routledge, 2000.

———. "The Social Construction of Black Feminist Thought." *Signs* 14, no. 4 (Summer, 1989): 745–73.

———. "What's in a Name? Womanist, Black Feminism, and Beyond." *The Black Scholar* 26, no. 1 (1996): 9–17.

Combahee River Collective, "A Black Feminist Statement." In *All the Women Are White, All the Blacks Are Men, but Some of Us Are Brave: Black Women's Studies,* edited by Gloria T. Hull, Patricia Bell Scott, and Barbara Smith. Old Westbury, NY: Feminist Press, 1982.

Cooper, Valerie C. *Word, Like Fire: Maria Stewart, the Bible, and the Rights of African Americans.* Carter G. Woodson Institute. Charlottesville: University of Virginia Press, 2011.

Crenshaw, Kimberlé W. "Demarginalizing the Intersection of Race and Sex: A Black Feminist Critique of Antidiscrimination Doctrine, Feminist Theory and Antiracist Politics." *University of Chicago Legal Forum* 140 (1989): 139–67.

———. "Mapping the Margins: Intersectionality, Identity Politics, and Violence against Women of Color." *Stanford Law Review* 43, no. 6 (1991): 1241–99.

Cummings, Lorine L. "A Womanist Response to the Afrocentric Idea: Jarena Lee, Womanist Preacher." In *Living the Intersection: Womanism and Afrocentrism in Theology*, edited by Cheryl J. Sanders, 57–64. Minneapolis: Fortress Press, 1995.

de Groot, Christiana, and Marion Ann Taylor. *Recovering Nineteenth-Century Women Interpreters of the Bible*. Symposium 38. Atlanta: Society of Biblical Literature, 2007.

Diouf, Sylviane A. *Servants of Allah: African Muslims Enslaved in the Americas*. 15th anniversary ed. New York: New York University Press, 2013.

Douglas, Kelly Brown. *Sexuality and the Black Church: A Womanist Perspective*. Maryknoll, NY: Orbis Books, 1999.

Dube, Musa W. *Postcolonial Feminist Interpretation of the Bible*. St. Louis: Chalice Press, 2000.

Dzodan, Flavia. "My Feminism Will Be Intersectional or It Will Be Bullshit." Tiger Beatdown. http://tigerbeatdown.com/2011/10/10/my-feminism-will-be -intersectional-or-it-will-be-bullshit/.

Elizabeth. *Elizabeth, A Colored Minister of the Gospel*. Philadelphia, 1889. Reprinted in *Black Women in Nineteenth-Century American Life: Their Words, Their Thoughts, Their Feelings*, edited by Bert James Loewenberg and Ruth Bogin University Park: Pennsylvania State University Press, 1976, 127–34.

Exum, J. Cheryl. "Second Thoughts about Secondary Characters: Women in Exodus 1.8:2.10." In *Feminist Companion to Exodus to Deuteronomy*, edited by Athalya Brenner, 75–87. Sheffield: Sheffield Academic Press, 1994.

———. "You Shall Let Every Daughter Live: A Study of Exodus 1:8–2:10." *Semeia* 28, (1983): 63–82.

Fiorenza, Elisabeth Schüssler. *Bread Not Stone: The Challenge of Feminist Biblical Interpretation*. Boston: Beacon Press, 1984.

Floyd-Thomas, Stacey M., ed. *Deeper Shades of Purple: Womanism in Religion and Society*. Religion, Race, and Ethnicity. New York: New York University Press, 2006.

———. *Mining the Motherlode: Methods in Womanist Ethics*. Cleveland: Pilgrim Press, 2006.

Friedan, Betty. *The Feminine Mystique*. New York: W.W. Norton, 1997.

Fuchs, Esther. "Who Is Hiding the Truth? Deceptive Women and Biblical Androcentrism." In *Feminist Perspectives on Biblical Scholarship*, edited by Adela Yarbro Collins, 137–44. Chico, CA: Scholars Press, 1985.

Fulop, Timothy Earl, and Albert J. Raboteau. *African-American Religion: Interpretive Essays in History and Culture*. New York: Routledge, 1997.

Gafney, Wilda C. M. "A Black Feminist Approach to Biblical Studies." *Encounter* 67, no. 4 (2006): 391–403.

———. *Daughters of Miriam: Women Prophets in Ancient Israel*. Minneapolis: Fortress Press, 2008.

———. "A Queer Womanist Midrashic Reading of Numbers 25:1–18." In *Leviticus and Numbers*, edited by Athalya Brenner and Archie Chi Chung Lee, 189–98. Minneapolis: Augsburg Fortress, 2013.

Gates, Henry Louis. *The Signifying Monkey: A Theory of Afro-American Literary Criticism*. New York: Oxford University Press, 1988.

Gaventa, Beverly Roberts. *Mary: Glimpses of the Mother of Jesus*. Studies on Personalities of the New Testament. Columbia: University of South Carolina Press, 1995.

General Association of the Congregational Churches of Massachusetts. "Pastoral Letter, June 28, 1837." In *Minutes of the General Association of Massachusetts*. Boston: Crocker & Brewster, 1831–1840.

Giddings, Paula. *When and Where I Enter: The Impact of Black Women on Race and Sex in America*. 2nd Quill ed. New York: W. Morrow, 2001.

Gilbert, Olive, Sojourner Truth, and Nell Irvin Painter. 1884. *Narrative of Sojourner Truth: A Bondswoman of Olden Time, with a History of Her Labors and Correspondence Drawn from Her Book of Life; also, A Memorial Chapter*. Penguin Classics. New York: Penguin Books, 1998.

Gilkes, Cheryl Townsend. "'Mother to the Motherless, Father to the Fatherless': Power, Gender, and Community in an Afrocentric Biblical Tradition." *Semeia* 47 (1989): 57–85.

———. *If It Wasn't for the Women…: Black Women's Experience and Womanist Culture in Church and Community*. Maryknoll, NY: Orbis Books, 2001.

Grant, Jacquelyn. *White Women's Christ and Black Women's Jesus: Feminist Christology and Womanist Response*. American Academy of Religion Academy 64. Atlanta: Scholars Press, 1989.

Green, Barbara. *What Profit for Us? Remembering the Story of Joseph*. Lanham, MD: University Press of America, 1996.

Grimké, Sarah Moore. *Letters on the Equality of the Sexes and the Condition of Women, Addressed to Mary S. Parker*. Edited and with an introduction by Elizabeth Ann Bartlett. New Haven, CT: Yale University Press, 1988.

Grimké, Angelina Emily. *Letters to Catherine E. Beecher, in Reply to an Essay on Slavery and Abolitionism, Addressed to A. E. Grimke*. Anti-Slavery Crusade in America. Boston: Isaac Knapp, 1838. Reprint, New York: Arno Press, 1969.

Guest, Deryn. *When Deborah Met Jael: Lesbian Biblical Hermeneutics*. London: SCM Press, 2005.

Guy-Sheftall, Beverly, ed. *Words of Fire: An Anthology of African-American Feminist Thought*. New York: New Press, 1995.

Harper, Ida Husted, ed. *History of Woman Suffrage*, Vol. 5, New York: National American Woman Suffrage Association, 1922. Reprint New York: Arno & The New York Times, 1969.

Harper, Frances Ellen Watkins, and Frances Smith Foster. *A Brighter Coming Day: A Frances Ellen Watkins Harper Reader*. New York: Feminist Press at the City University of New York, 1990.

Harris-Perry, Melissa V. *Sister Citizen: Shame, Stereotypes, and Black Women in America*. New Haven, CT: Yale University Press, 2011.

Hatch, Nathan O., and Mark A. Noll. *The Bible in America: Essays in Cultural History*. New York: Oxford University Press, 1982.

Haynes, Stephen R. *Noah's Curse: The Biblical Justification of American Slavery*. Religion in America. New York: Oxford University Press, 2007.

Hill, Anita. *Speaking Truth to Power*. New York: Doubleday, 1997.

hooks, bell. *Ain't I a Woman: Black Women and Feminism*. Boston: South End Press, 1981.

———. *Talking Back: Thinking Feminist, Thinking Black*. Boston: South End Press, 1989.

Houchins, Sue E. *Spiritual Narratives*. Schomburg Library of Nineteenth-Century Black Women Writers. New York: Oxford University Press, 1988.

Huddy, Leonie, Francis K. Neely, and Marilyn R. Lafay. "Support for the Women's Movement." *Public Opinion Quarterly* 64, no. 3 (2000): 309–50.

Hudson-Weems, Clenora. *Africana Womanism: Reclaiming Ourselves*. Troy, MI: Bedford, 1993.

Hull, Gloria T., Patricia Bell Scott, and Barbara Smith, eds. *All the Women Are White, All the Blacks Are Men, but Some of Us Are Brave: Black Women's Studies*. Old Westbury, NY: Feminist Press, 1982.

James, Stanlie M., and Abena P. A. Busia. *Theorizing Black Feminisms: The Visionary Pragmatism of Black Women*. New York: Routledge, 1993.

Johnson, Helen Kendrick. *Woman and the Republic: A Survey of the Woman-Suffrage Movement in the United States and a Discussion of the Claims and Arguments of Its Foremost Advocates*. New York: D. Appleton & Co., 1897.

Junior, Nyasha. "Exodus." In *Women's Bible Commentary*, edited by Carol A. Newsom, Sharon H. Ringe, and Jacqueline E. Lapsley. Rev. ed., 56–66. Louisville, KY: Westminster John Knox Press, 2012.

———. "Womanist Biblical Interpretation." In *Engaging the Bible in a Gendered World: An Introduction to Feminist Biblical Interpretation in Honor of Katharine Doob Sakenfeld*, edited by Linda Day and Carolyn Pressler, 37–46. Louisville, KY: Westminster John Knox Press, 2006.

———. "Womanist Biblical Interpretation." In *The Oxford Encyclopedia of Biblical Interpretation*, edited by Steven L. McKenzie, 2:448-56. New York: Oxford University Press, 2013.

Junior, Nyasha, and Jeremy Schipper. "Disability Studies and the Bible." In *New Meanings for Ancient Texts: Recent Approaches to Biblical Criticisms and Their Applications*, edited by Steven L. McKenzie and John Kaltner, 21–37. Louisville, KY: Westminster John Knox Press, 2013.

Kartzow, Marianne Bjelland. *Destabilizing the Margins: An Intersectional Approach to Early Christian Memory*. Eugene, OR: Pickwick Publications, 2012.

Kern, Kathi. *Mrs. Stanton's Bible*. Ithaca, NY: Cornell University Press, 2001.

King, Deborah. "Multiple Jeopardy: The Context of a Black Feminist Ideology." In *Feminist Frameworks: Alternative Theoretical Accounts of the Relations between Women and Men*, edited by Alison M. Jaggar and Paula S. Rothenberg, 220–36. New York: McGraw-Hill, 1993.

Kirk-Duggan, Cheryl A. *Exorcizing Evil: A Womanist Perspective on the Spirituals*. Bishop Henry McNeal Turner/Sojourner Truth Series in Black Religion 14. Maryknoll, NY: Orbis Books, 1997.

Kwok, Pui-Lan. "Racism and Ethnocentrism in Feminist Biblical Interpretation." In *Searching the Scriptures*. Vol. 1. *A Feminist Introduction*, edited by Elisabeth Schüssler Fiorenza, 101–16. New York: Crossroad, 1993.

LaRue, Linda. "The Black Movement and Women's Liberation." In *Words of Fire: An Anthology of African-American Feminist Thought*, edited by Beverly Guy-Sheftall, 164–73. New York: New Press, 1995. Reprinted from *Black Scholar* 1 (May 1970): 36–42.

Lawrence, Beatrice. "Gender Analysis: Gender and Method in Biblical Studies." In *Method Matters: Essays on the Interpretation of the Hebrew Bible in Honor of David L. Petersen*, edited by David L. Petersen, Joel M. LeMon, and Kent Harold Richards, 333–48. Atlanta: Society of Biblical Literature, 2009.

Lear, Marsha. "The Second Feminist Wave." *New York Times Magazine*. March 10, 1968. 24–25, 50–62.

Lemert, Charles, and Esme Bhan, eds. *The Voice of Anna Julia Cooper, including a Voice from the South and Other Important Essays, Papers, and Letters*. Legacies of Social Thought, edited by Charles Lemert. Lanham, MD: Rowan & Littlefield, 1998.

Lemons, Gary L. *Black Male Outsider: Teaching as a Pro-Feminist Man: A Memoir*. Albany, NY: State University of New York Press, 2008.

Levin, Christopher. "Source Criticism: The Miracle at the Sea." In *Method Matters: Essays on the Interpretation of the Hebrew Bible in Honor of David L. Petersen*, edited by

David L. Petersen, Joel M. LeMon, and Kent Harold Richards. Society of Biblical Literature Resources for Biblical Study 56, 39–61. Atlanta: Society of Biblical Literature, 2009.

Livermore, Harriet. *Scriptural Evidence in Favor of Female Testimony in Meetings for Christian Worship in Letters to a Friend.* Portsmouth, NH: R. Foster, 1825.

Loewenberg, Bert James, and Ruth Bogin. *Black Women in Nineteenth-Century American Life: Their Words, Their Thoughts, Their Feelings.* University Park, PA: Pennsylvania State University Press, 1976.

Mandziuk, Roseann M., and Suzanne Pullon Fitch. "The Rhetorical Construction of Sojourner Truth." *Southern Communication Journal* 66, no. 2 (2001): 120–38.

Mann, Susan A. "Slavery, Sharecropping, and Sexual Inequality." *Signs* 14, no. 4 (1989): 774–98.

Maparyan, Layli. "Womanist Origins: Reading Alice Walker, Chikwenye Okonjo Ogunyemi, and Clenora Hudson-Weems." In *The Womanist Idea*, 15–32. New York: Routledge, 2012.

Martin, Clarice J. "The *Haustafeln* (Household Codes) in African American Biblical Interpretation: 'Free Slave' and 'Subordinate Women.'" In *Stony the Road We Trod: African American Biblical Interpretation*, edited by Cain H. Felder, 206–31. Minneapolis: Fortress Press, 1991.

———. "Normative Biblical Motifs in African-American Women Leaders' Moral Discourse: Maria Stewart's Autobiography as a Resource for Nurturing Leadership from the Black Church Tradition." In *The Stones That the Builders Rejected: The Development of Ethical Leadership from the Black Church Tradition*, edited by Walter Earl Fluker, 47–72. Harrisburg, PA: Trinity Press, 1998.

———. "Polishing the Unclouded Mirror: A Womanist Reading of Revelation 18:13." In *From Every People and Nation: The Book of Revelation in Intercultural Perspective*, edited by David M. Rhoads, 82–109. Minneapolis: Fortress Press, 2005.

———. "Womanist Biblical Interpretation." In *Dictionary of Biblical Interpretation.* Vol. 2, edited by John H. Hayes, 655–58. Nashville: Abingdon Press, 1999.

———. "Womanist Interpretations of the New Testament: The Quest for Holistic and Inclusive Translation and Interpretation." *Journal of Feminist Studies in Religion* 6, no. 2 (Fall, 1990): 41–61.

Masenya, Mmadipoane Ngwana 'Mphahlele. "A *Bosadi* (Womanhood) Reading of Proverbs 31:10–31." In *Other Ways of Reading: African Women and the Bible*, edited by Musa W. Dube, 145–57. Atlanta: Society of Biblical Literature, 2001.

McCabe, Janice. "What's in a Label? The Relationship between Feminist Self-Identification and 'Feminist' Attitudes among U.S. Women and Men." *Gender and Society* 19, no. 4 (2005): 480–505.

McDougald, Elise Johnson. "The Double Task: The Struggle of Negro Women for Sex and Race Emancipation." In *Words of Fire: An Anthology of African-American Feminist Thought*, edited by Beverly Guy-Sheftall, 80–83. New York: New Press, 1995.

McGuire, Danielle L. *At the Dark End of the Street: Black Women, Rape, and Resistance: A New History of the Civil Rights Movement from Rosa Parks to the Rise of Black Power.* New York: Alfred A. Knopf, 2010.

Milne, Pamela J. "What Shall We Do with Judith?: A Feminist Reassessment of a Biblical 'Heroine.'" *Semeia* 62 (1993): 37–58.

Milton, John. *Paradise Lost: A Poem in Twelve Books.* Edited by Merritt Y. Hughes. Indianapolis: Hackett Publishing Co., 2003.

Mitchem, Stephanie Y. *Introducing Womanist Theology.* Maryknoll, NY: Orbis Books, 2002.

Morgan, Joan. *When Chickenheads Come Home to Roost: My Life as a Hip-Hop Feminist.* New York: Simon & Schuster, 1999.

Nadar, Sarojini. "A South African Indian Womanist Reading of the Character of Ruth." In *Other Ways of Reading: African Women and the Bible*, edited by Musa W. Dube, 159–75. Atlanta: Society of Biblical Literature, 2001.

Nasrallah, Laura Salah, and Elisabeth Schüssler Fiorenza, eds. *Prejudice and Christian Beginnings: Investigating Race, Gender, and Ethnicity in Early Christian Studies.* Minneapolis: Fortress Press, 2009.

New York State Association Opposed to Woman Suffrage. *New York State Association Opposed to Woman Suffrage Thirteenth Annual Report,* 1908, http://hdl.loc.gov/loc.rbc/rbcmil.scrp5011203.

Noll, Mark A. *The Civil War as a Theological Crisis.* Steven and Janice Brose Lectures in the Civil War Era. Chapel Hill: University of North Carolina Press, 2006.

Ogunyemi, Chikwenye Okonjo. *African Wo/Man Palava: The Nigerian Novel by Women.* Chicago: University of Chicago, 1996.

———. "Womanism: The Dynamics of the Contemporary Black Female Novel in English." *Signs* 11, no. 1 (1985): 63–85.

Oshatz, Molly. *Slavery and Sin: The Fight against Slavery and the Rise of Liberal Protestantism.* New York: Oxford University Press, 2012.

Osiek, Carolyn. "The Feminist and the Bible: Hermeneutical Alternatives." In *Feminist Perspectives on Biblical Scholarship*, edited by Adela Yarbro Collins, 93–105. Chico, CA: Scholars Press, 1985.

Painter, Nell Irvin. *Sojourner Truth: A Life, a Symbol.* New York: W.W. Norton, 1996.

Patmore, Coventry. *The Angel in the House,* 5th ed. (London: George Bell and Sons, [n.d.]).

Petersen, David L., Joel M. LeMon, and Kent Harold Richards. *Method Matters: Essays on the Interpretation of the Hebrew Bible in Honor of David L. Petersen.* Society of Biblical Literature Resources for Biblical Study 56. Atlanta: Society of Biblical Literature, 2009.

Phillips, Layli. "Womanism: On Its Own." In *The Womanist Reader*, xix–lv. New York: Routledge, 2006.

———. "A Womanist Bibliography (including Internet Resources)." In *The Womanist Reader*, 405–13. New York: Routledge, 2006.

———. *The Womanist Reader.* New York: Routledge, 2006.

Plaatjie, Gloria Kehilwe. "Toward a Post-Apartheid Black Feminist Reading of the Bible: A Case of Luke 2:36–38" In *Other Ways of Reading: African Women and the Bible*, edited by Musa W. Dube, 114–42. Atlanta: Society of Biblical Literature, 2001.

Plaskow, Judith. "Anti-Judaism in Feminist Christian Interpretation." In *Searching the Scriptures.* Vol. 1. *A Feminist Introduction*, edited by Elisabeth Schüssler Fiorenza, 117–29. New York: Crossroad, 1993.

Pressler, Carolyn. "Deuteronomy." In *Women's Bible Commentary*, edited by Jacqueline E. Lapsley, Carol A. Newsom, and Sharon H. Ringe. 3rd ed., 88–102. Louisville, KY: Westminster John Knox Press, 2012.

Raboteau, Albert J. *Slave Religion: The "Invisible Institution" in the Antebellum South.* New York: Oxford University Press, 2004.

Reinhartz, Adele. "Feminist Criticism and Biblical Studies on the Verge of the Twenty-First Century." In *A Feminist Companion to Reading the Bible: Approaches, Methods and Strategies*, edited by Athalya Brenner and Carole Fontaine, 30–38. Sheffield: Sheffield Academic Press, 1997.

Ringe, Sharon H. "A Gentile Woman's Story." In *Feminist Interpretation of the Bible*, edited by Letty M. Russell, 65–72. Philadelphia: Westminster Press, 1985.

Ruether, Rosemary Radford, ed. *Religion and Sexism: Images of Woman in the Jewish and Christian Traditions.* New York: Simon & Schuster, 1974.

Russell, Letty M. *Feminist Interpretation of the Bible*. Louisville, KY: Westminster John Knox Press, 1985.

Rutten, Tim. "'Flung' into Controversy by Negative Book Review." *Los Angeles Times*. May 24, 2002.

Sakenfeld, Katharine Doob. "Old Testament Perspectives: Methodological Considerations." *Journal for the Study of the Old Testament* 22 (1982): 13–20.

Sakenfeld, Katharine Doob. "Feminist Uses of Biblical Materials." In *Feminist Interpretation of the Bible*, edited by Letty M. Russell, 55–64. Philadelphia: Westminster Press, 1985.

Sanders, Cheryl. "Roundtable Discussion: Christian Ethics and Theology in Womanist Perspective." *Journal of Feminist Studies in Religion* 5 no. 2 (Fall 1989): 83–91.

Schüssler Fiorenza, Elisabeth. *But She Said: Feminist Practices of Biblical Interpretation*. Boston: Beacon Press, 1992.

———. *Searching the Scriptures*. Vol. 1. *A Feminist Introduction*. New York: Crossroad, 1993.

———. *Wisdom Ways: Introducing Feminist Biblical Interpretation*. Maryknoll, NY: Orbis Books, 2001.

Sernett, Milton C. *African American Religious History: A Documentary Witness*. C. Eric Lincoln Series on the Black Experience. 2nd ed. Durham, NC: Duke University Press, 1999.

Setel, T. Drorah. "Prophets and Pornography: Female Sexual Imagery in Hosea." In *Feminist Interpretation of the Bible*, edited by Letty M. Russell, 86–95. Philadelphia: Westminster Press, 1985.

Smith, Mitzi J. " 'Give Them What You Have': A Womanist Reading of the Matthean Feeding Miracle (Matt 14: 13–21)." *Journal of Bible and Human Transformation* 3, no. 1 (2013): 1–22. Also reprinted in *I Found God in Me: A Womanist Biblical Hermeneutics Reader*, edited by Mitzi J. Smith (Eugene, OR: Wipf & Stock, 2015).

———. "'This Little Light of Mine': The Womanist Biblical Scholar as Prophetess, Iconoclast, and Activist." In *I Found God in Me: A Womanist Biblical Hermeneutics Reader*, edited by Mitzi J. Smith, 109–27. Eugene, OR: Wipf & Stock, 2015.

———, ed. *I Found God in Me: A Womanist Biblical Hermeneutics Reader*. Eugene, OR: Wipf & Stock, 2015.

Smith, Shanell T. *The Woman Babylon and the Marks of Empire: Reading Revelation with a Postcolonial Womanist Hermeneutics of Ambiveilence*. Minneapolis: Fortress Press, 2014.

Smith, Barbara, ed. *Home Girls: A Black Feminist Anthology*. New York: Kitchen Table: Women of Color Press, 1983.

Society of Biblical Literature. *SBL Dashboard: Facts and Figures*. https://www.sbl-site.org/SBLDashboard.aspx.

Soulen, Richard N., and R. Kendall Soulen. *Handbook of Biblical Criticism*. 4th ed. Louisville, KY: Westminster John Knox Press, 2011.

St. Clair, Raquel A. *Call and Consequences: A Womanist Reading of Mark*. Minneapolis: Fortress Press, 2008.

———. "Womanist Biblical Interpretation." In *True to Our Native Land: An African American New Testament Commentary*, edited by Brian K. Blount, Cain Hope Felder, Clarice Jannette Martin, and Emerson B. Powery, 54–62. Minneapolis: Fortress Press, 2007.

Stanton, Elizabeth Cady. *The Woman's Bible*. New York: European Publishing Co., 1895–1898. Reprinted with foreword by Maureen Fitzgerald. Boston: Northeastern University Press, 1993.

Stanton, Elizabeth Cady, Susan B. Anthony, and Matilda Joslyn Gage. *History of Woman Suffrage.* Vol. 1–2, New York: Fowler & Wells, 1881–1882. Reprint, New York: Arno Press, 1969.

Terborg-Penn, Rosalyn. *African American Women in the Struggle for the Vote, 1850–1920.* Blacks in the Diaspora. Bloomington: Indiana University Press, 1998.

Tetrault, Lisa. *The Myth of Seneca Falls: Memory and the Women's Suffrage Movement, 1848–1898.* Gender and American Culture. Chapel Hill: University of North Carolina Press, 2014.

Thimmes, Pamela. "What Makes a Feminist Reading Feminist? Another Perspective." In *Escaping Eden: New Feminist Perspectives on the Bible*, edited by H. C. Washington, S. L. Graham, and P. Thimmes, 132–40. Sheffield: Sheffield Academic Press, 1998.

Thomas, Linda E. "Womanist Theology, Epistemology, and a New Anthropological Paradigm." *Cross Currents* 48, no. 4 (1998).

Thurman, Howard. *Jesus and the Disinherited.* New York: Abingdon-Cokesbury Press, 1949.

Tolbert, Mary Ann, ed. *The Bible and Feminist Hermeneutics.* Vol. 28. Atlanta: Scholars Press, 1983.

———. "Defining the Problem: The Bible and Feminist Hermeneutics." *Semeia* 28, (1983b): 113–26.

———. "Introduction." *Semeia* 28, (1983) [n.p.].

Townes, Emilie M. *Womanist Justice, Womanist Hope.* Vol. 79. American Academy of Religion Academy. Atlanta: Scholars Press, 1993.

Trible, Phyllis. "Depatriarchalizing in Biblical Interpretation." *Journal of the American Academy of Religion* 41 (1973): 30–48.

———. "The Effects of Women's Studies on Biblical Studies." *Journal for the Study of the Old Testament* 22 (1982): 3–5.

———. "Eve and Adam: Genesis 2–3 Reread." *Andover Newton Quarterly* 13 (1973b): 251–58.

———. *God and the Rhetoric of Sexuality.* Philadelphia: Fortress Press, 1978.

———. "Not a Jot, Not a Tittle: Genesis 2–3 after Twenty Years." In *Biblical Studies Alternatively: An Introductory Reader*, edited by S. Scholz, 101–06. Upper Saddle River, NJ: Prentice Hall, 2002.

———. *Texts of Terror: Literary-Feminist Readings of Biblical Narratives.* Philadelphia: Fortress Press, 1984.

Tsui, Bonnie. *She Went to the Field: Women Soldiers of the Civil War.* Guilford, CT: TwoDot, 2003.

Viviano, Pauline A. "Source Criticism." In *To Each Its Own Meaning*, Rev. ed., edited by Steven L. McKenzie and Stephen R. Hayes, 35–57. Louisville, KY: Westminster John Knox Press, 1999.

Wakeman, Mary K. "Sacred Marriage." *Journal for the Study of the Old Testament* 7 (1982): 21–31.

Walker, Alice. "Coming Apart: By Way of Introduction to Lorde, Teish and Gardner." In *You Can't Keep a Good Woman Down*, 41–53. Orlando, FL: Harcourt, 1981.

———. "Saving the Life That Is Your Own: The Importance of Models in the Artist's Life." In *In Search of Our Mothers' Gardens: Womanist Prose*, 3–14. Orlando, FL: Harcourt, Inc., 1983.

———. "When Women Confront Porn at Home." *Ms. Magazine* 8, no. 8 (1980): 67, 69–70, 75–76.

———. "Coming Apart." In *Take Back the Night: Women on Pornography*, edited by Laura Lederer, 95–104. New York: W. Morrow, 1980.

————. "Gifts of Power: The Writings of Rebecca Jackson." In *In Search of Our Mothers' Gardens: Womanist Prose*, 71–82. Orlando, FL: Harcourt, Inc., 1983.

————. *In Search of Our Mothers' Gardens: Womanist Prose*. Orlando, FL: Harcourt, Inc., 1983.

Walker, Rebecca. "Becoming the Third Wave." *Ms. Magazine* 39 (1992): 39–41.

Wallace, Michelle. "A Black Feminist's Search for Sisterhood." In *All the Women Are White, All the Blacks Are Men, but Some of Us Are Brave: Black Women's Studies*, edited by Gloria T. Hull, Patricia Bell Scott, and Barbara Smith, 5–12. Old Westbury, NY: Feminist Press, 1982.

Warsaw-Jones, Koala. "Toward a Womanist Hermeneutic: A Reading of Judges 19–21." In *A Feminist Companion to Judges*. Vol. 4, edited by Athalaya Brenner, 172–86. Sheffield: Sheffield Academic Press, 1993.

Waters, Kristin, and Carol B. Conaway. *Black Women's Intellectual Traditions: Speaking their Minds*. Lebanon, NH: University Press of New England, 2007.

Weems, Renita J. *Battered Love: Marriage, Sex, and Violence in the Hebrew Prophets*. Minneapolis: Fortress Press, 1995.

————. "Gomer: Victim of Violence Or Victim of Metaphor?" *Semeia* 47 (1989): 87–104.

————. *I Asked for Intimacy: Stories of Blessings, Betrayals, and Birthings*. San Diego: LuraMedia, 1993.

————. *Just a Sister Away: A Womanist Vision of Women's Relationships in the Bible*. San Diego: LuraMedia, 1988.

————. *Just a Sister Away: Understanding the Timeless Connection between Women of Today and Women in the Bible*. New York: Warner Books, 2005.

————. *Listening for God: A Minister's Journey through Silence and Doubt*. New York: Touchstone, 1999.

————. "Reading Her Way through the Struggle: African American Women and the Bible." In *Stony the Road We Trod: African American Biblical Interpretation*, edited by Cain H. Felder, 57–77. Minneapolis: Fortress Press, 1991.

————. "Re-Reading for Liberation: African American Women and the Bible." In *Feminist Interpretation of the Bible and the Hermeneutics of Liberation*, edited by Silvia Schroer and Sophia Bietenhard, 19–32. New York: Sheffield Academic Press, 2003.

————. *Showing Mary: How Women Can Share Prayers, Wisdom, and the Blessings of God*. West Bloomfield, MI: Walk Worthy Press, 2002.

————. *What Matters Most: Ten Passionate Lessons from the Song of Solomon*. West Bloomfield, MI: Walk Worthy Press, 2004.

————. "Womanist Reflections on Biblical Hermeneutics." In *Black Theology: A Documentary History*, edited by James H. Cone and Gayraud S. Wilmore, 216–24. Maryknoll, NY: Orbis Books, 1993.

Welter, Barbara. "The Cult of True Womanhood: 1820–1860." *American Quarterly* 18, no. 2, pt. 1 (Summer, 1966): 151–74.

West, Traci C. "Is a Womanist a Black Feminist? Marking the Distinctions and Defying Term." In *Deeper Shades of Purple: Womanism in Religion and Society*, edited by Stacey M. Floyd-Thomas, 291–95. New York: New York University Press, 2006.

White, Deborah Gray. *Ar'n't I a Woman? Female Slaves in the Plantation South*. Rev. ed. New York: W.W. Norton, 1999.

————. *Too Heavy a Load: Black Women in Defense of Themselves, 1894–1994*. New York: W.W. Norton, 1999.

Williams, Delores S. *Sisters in the Wilderness: The Challenge of Womanist God-Talk*. Maryknoll, NY: Orbis Books, 1993.

Wimbush, Vincent L. *The Bible and African Americans: A Brief History*. Facets. Minneapolis: Fortress Press, 2003.

———. "The Bible and African Americans: An Outline of an Interpretive History." In *Stony the Road We Trod: African American Biblical Interpretation*, edited by C. H. Felder, 81–97. Minneapolis: Fortress Press, 1991.

———. "Interpreters—Enslaved/Enslaving/Runagate." *Journal of Biblical Literature* 130, no. 1 (2011): 5–24

Winans, CeCe, and Renita J. Weems. *On a Positive Note: Her Joyous Faith, Her Life in Music, and Her Everyday Blessings*. New York: Pocket Books, 1999.

"The Women of Philadelphia." Philadelphia *Public Ledger* and *Daily Transcript.*, ca. 1848. Elizabeth Cady Stanton, Susan B. Anthony, and Matilda Joslyn Gage, eds. *History of Woman Suffrage*. Vol 1. Reprint New York: Fowler & Wells, 1881.

Index

Livermore, Harriet
  Scriptural Evidence in Favor of Female Testimony, 28–30

Martin, Clarice, 102–8, 108n44, 111
  Function of Acts 8:26-40, The, 102
  "The *Haustafeln* (Household Codes) in African American Biblical Interpretation," 103, 105
  legacy of, 107–8
  "Normative Biblical Motifs in African-American Women Leaders' Moral Discourse," 103–4, 105
  "Polishing the Unclouded Mirror," 104–5, 106
  "Womanist Biblical Interpretation," 104, 106
  womanist interpretation defined by, 104–7
  "Womanist Interpretations of the New Testament," 103, 105–7
Mary (mother of Jesus), 36, 49
masculinization of African American women, 42–43, 51
Masenya, Madipoane, 96n2
matrix of domination, xix
McDougald, Elise Johnson
  "The Double Task," xx
men
  as intellectually superior, 34
  as pro-feminist, xvn12
metaphysics, 73
midrash, 109–10
Milne, Pamela
  "What Shall We Do with Judith?," 87
Milton, John
  Paradise Lost, 31–32
Miriam, 37
Mitchem, Stephanie
  Introducing Womanist Theology, 59
monographs *vs.* journal articles, 117
Moses narrative, 87–88
Mott, Lucretia, 4
  as abolitionist, 8
multiple jeopardy, xix, xx
music, 70–71

Nadar, Sarojini
  "A South African Feminist Reading of the Character of Ruth," 109
narrative theology, 70
National American Woman Suffrage Association (NAWSA), 11, 13, 37

National Association of Colored Women (NACW), 15
National Black Feminist Organization, 17
National Organization for Women (NOW), 5, 16
National Woman Suffrage Association (NWSA), 13
National Women's Rights Convention, 12
nativism, 11
natural law, 21, 25, 34
"negro" as referring only to men, 13
New York State Association Opposed to Woman Suffrage, 25
Nineteenth Amendment, 8
nineteenth-century women's biblical interpretation, 28–37

obedience, 22
Ogunyemi, Chikwenye Okonjo, xvii–xviii
oppression
  "common," xiv
  multiple forms of, xix, xx, 86, 100–101, 109, 114–15
oral traditions, 40, 69, 97, 98
Osiek, Carolyn
  "The Feminist and the Bible," 83

Paradise Lost (Milton), 31–32
Parks, Rosa, 16
"Pastoral Letter of the General Association of Massachusetts," 22–23, 32
Patmore, Coventry
  The Angel in the House, 27
patriarchy
  Bible as tool of, 19, 21, 27–28
  feminism as judgment on, 83
  normative, 20, 28, 42
Paul, Alice, 5
Pauline writings, 29, 32, 36–37, 43, 47
Phillips, Layli, 74n64
Plaatjie, Gloria Kehilwe
  "Toward a Post-Apartheid Black Feminist Reading of the Bible," 86
Plaskow, Judith
  "Anti-Judaism in Feminist Christian Interpretation," 85, 87
pluralism, 62, 72–73
postcolonialism, 111–12
postfeminism, 6, 6n10
preaching of women, 28–29, 41–42, 44–45, 48–50
Prejudice and Christian Beginnings (ed. Nasrallah and Schüssler Fiorenza), 91

Pressler, Carolyn, 118–20
public roles of women, 22–24, 28–29, 44–45,
        48, 52
    opposition to, 45–47, 48–49

racism
    feminism and, xix–xx, 9, 10–17, 62, 65, 85
    sexism and, xix, xx, 3, 10–18, 111
    voting rights and, 11–12, 13
Reconstruction, 10
"reformist," 82, 82n27
Religion and Sexism (ed. Reuther), 79
*Religious Experience and Journal of Mrs. Jarena
        Lee*, 48–50
Richards, Amy, 9–10
Ricoeur, Paul, 68n37
Ringe, Sharon, 81
Russell, Letty
    Feminist Interpretation of the Bible, 64–65,
        80, 81, 83

Sakenfeld, Katherine Doob, 82, 83
Sanders, Cheryl, 61–62, 111
Schüssler Fiorenza, Elizabeth, 89
    Bread Not Stone, 84–85
    "kyriarchy" coined by, 86–87
    Searching the Scriptures, 87
segregation, 15
Seneca Falls Convention, 4, 8–9, 10, 33
    Declaration of Sentiments, 9, 33–35
separate spheres ideology, 21–27, 34
    definition of, 22
    used in arguments for equality, 52
Setel, T. Drorah, 81
sexuality, xiii, 61, 62, 69–70, 109–10
slavery
    abolition of, 10
    ancient, 104–5
    in the ancient Near East, 67
    biblical texts used to justify, 39, 43
    and dehumanization of enslaved women,
        42–43
    doulos and, 103
    personal experience of, 30, 41, 104–5
    rhetoric of, 10
Smith, Mitzi, 112–13
    "'Give Them What You Have,'" 112–13
    I Found God in Me, 108n44, 112, 117
    "This Little Light of Mine," 112
Smith, Shanell, 116n71
    *The Woman Babylon and the Marks of
        Empire*, 111–12, 117

social hierarchy, 41–42
social location, 86, 115–16
Society of Biblical Literature (SBL), xxiii
    Committee on the Status of Women in the
        Profession, 126–27
    feminist critique of, 80–81
    feminist program sections of, 92, 118
    womanism and, 116, 117–18, 126–27
    women presidents of, 92
Song of Songs, 79
spiritual autobiography, 43–45, 46–47, 48–50
spirituals, 70–71
Stanton, Elizabeth Cady, 4, 13
    as abolitionist, 8
    "The Bible and the Church Degrade
        Women," 26
    racism of, 11
    The Woman's Bible and, 35–37, 85
Stewart, Maria W., xx, 103–4
    "Farewell address to her friends in the city
        of Boston," 45–48
subordination of women, 4, 20
    seen as natural, 20
suffrage. *See* voting rights
"Surely God Is Able," 72
survival, womanist focus on, 66, 70, 71
suspicion, hermeneutic of, 68, 68n37, 69,
        84, 85

terminology controversies, 60–63
Terrell, Mary Church, 15
theological education, 35, 50
Thimmes, Pamela
    "What Makes a Feminist Reading
        Feminist? Another Perspective," 89
Thirteenth Amendment, 10
Thomas, Clarence, 6
Thomas, Linda, 59
Thurman, Howard
    Jesus and the Disinherited, 39, 65
Title IX of the Education Amendment, 5
Tolbert, Mary Ann
    The Bible and Feminist Hermeneutics, 80,
        81, 82
    "Defining the Problem: The Bible and
        Feminist Hermeneutics," 82, 82n27
Townes, Emilie
    Womanist Justice, Womanist Hope, 68–69
translation, 30–31, 103, 106
Trible, Phyllis, 80–81
    "Depatriarchalizing in Biblical
        Interpretation," 79

womanist biblical interpretation: feminist
        interpretation and *(continued)*
    inclusivity of, 110
    language analysis and, 99, 103, 110
    liberation focus of, 17, 67, 68,
        100–102
    male scholars using, 97n4
    by nonprofessional readers, xxiii–xxiv
    origins of, xxiii–xxiv, 104, 105, 122–23
    popular books on, 98
    queer perspectives combined with, 109–10
    in religious-studies-related fields, 57–74
Woman's Bible, The, 35–37, 85, 87
women
    credibility of, 6
    as dependent, 22–23
    dissatisfaction of, 5
    employment issues of, 7
    as morally superior, 34
    as "persuasive," 22, 23

    in public, 22–24, 28–29, 44–46
    relationship status of, 24, 27, 51–52
    as religious leaders, 29, 32–33, 35, 43–52,
        103–4
    roles of, 8, 21–27
    subordination of, 4, 20, 23, 31
    traditional views of, xviii, 22, 25–28
Women in the Biblical World (SBL program
        section), 92
"The Women of Philadelphia," 23–24
Women's Bible Commentary, 37, 93
Women's Club Movement, 15
women's rights
    Bible and arguments for, 28–37, 41, 44–52
    to education, 33, 34–35
    in Seneca Falls Declaration of Sentiments
        and Resolutions, 33–35
women's studies, 80, 82
World Anti-Slavery Convention, 8
worship, 72, 84

CPSIA information can be obtained
at www.ICGtesting.com
Printed in the USA
BVHW082030240122
627021BV00003B/44